CHINESE WHISPERS

THINKING LITERATURE
A series edited by Nan Z. Da and Anahid Nersessian

Chinese Whispers

TOWARD A TRANSPACIFIC POETICS

Yunte Huang

The University of Chicago Press
Chicago and London

The University of Chicago Press, Chicago 60637
The University of Chicago Press, Ltd., London

Published 2022
Printed in the United States of America

31 30 29 28 27 26 25 24 23 22   1 2 3 4 5

ISBN-13: 978-0-226-82264-8 (cloth)
ISBN-13: 978-0-226-82265-5 (paper)
ISBN-13: 978-0-226-82266-2 (e-book)
DOI: https://doi.org/10.7208/chicago/9780226822662.001.0001

Library of Congress Cataloging-in-Publication Data

Names: Huang, Yunte, author.
Title: Chinese whispers : toward a transpacific poetics / Yunte Huang.
Other titles: Thinking literature.
Description: Chicago : University of Chicago Press, 2022. | Series: Thinking literature | Includes bibliographical references and index.
Identifiers: LCCN 2022009701 | ISBN 9780226822648 (cloth) | ISBN 9780226822655 (paperback) | ISBN 9780226822662 (ebook)
Subjects: LCSH: American poetry—Chinese influences. | American poetry—20th century—History and criticism. | American poetry—21st century—History and criticism. | Chinese poetry—Appreciation—United States. | LCGFT: Literary criticism.
Classification: LCC PS159.C5 H83 2022 | DDC 811/.5098951—dc23/eng/20220420
LC record available at https://lccn.loc.gov/2022009701

♾ This paper meets the requirements of ANSI/NISO Z39.48-1992 (Permanence of Paper).

TO CHARLES BERNSTEIN AND MARJORIE PERLOFF,
WHO HAVE TAUGHT ME
HOW TO READ POETRY

Finally the rumors grew more fabulous than the real thing.

JOHN ASHBERY, "Chinese Whispers"

Placement between l *and* r.

MYUNG MI KIM, *Dura*

Contents

Figures

Serve the People, Read Them Verse

[INTRODUCTION]

A Transpacific Journey in Poetics and Politics

In fall 2003, resuming my peripatetic travels that had brought me from China to Tuscaloosa, Alabama, then to Buffalo, New York, and then Cambridge, Massachusetts, I relocated from New England to California to join the English faculty at the University of California, Santa Barbara. Upon arrival, I went to school to set up my new office. Like a country doctor getting ready for practice in a new town, I put up a sign (fig. 1) on the door that read:

SERVE THE PEOPLE
READ THEM VERSE

1. Office door sign, late 2003.

Soon, a colleague in the English department ran into me in the hallway. A silver-haired man in his sixties, copper-skinned like a surfer after years under the California sun, he pointed at the sign and asked, "Do you really believe in that?" I wish I were glibber, for then I would have been able to quip, quoting Woody Guthrie, "I ain't necessarily a pink commie, but I been in the red all my life." Instead, I explained to my colleague in earnest that the word *serve* in the Maoist shibboleth was actually an anagram of *verse*. And that's the reason, I added, in case he did not notice, for the special alignment of the two anagrammatic words in the middle of the sign:

SERVE
VERSE

I thought that clarifying the embedded wordplay, as well as the fact that I'm a sucker for puns, would satisfy my colleague's curiosity. But I was wrong. He asked again, "Still, do you actually believe in that?" I could almost hear Freud turning in his grave, for I was at a loss explaining what I had meant to be a joke. Maybe by repurposing the slogan "Serve the people" and adding my own twist, "Read them verse," I unconsciously did, to paraphrase Stanley Cavell, "mean what I say." After all, I had been hired to teach poetry, and my colleague knew that. And coming from China, I had at least a penchant for believing in serving the people by reading them verse, whether biblical or Satanic, proletarian or bourgeois. Nothing, as Freud said, is more dead serious than a joke. My reply to my colleague's follow-up query was a halfhearted, noncommittal "Maybe." That brief encounter stayed with me, making me constantly look back on my own intellectual journey in poetry, my wandering itinerary across the Pacific and between English and Chinese, trying to figure out what purpose, pardon my pun again, does verse serve?

In summer 1991, fresh out of college, I left China, swearing never to return to a country ruled by a government that had so brutally crushed a student protest in which I, like millions of others, had participated. I landed, of all places, in Tuscaloosa, Alabama. Not knowing a thing about the Deep South, I had thought I could see Times Square from there, sort of like Tina Fey's impersonation of Sarah Palin hallucinating that she could see Russia from her bedroom window in Alaska. I was one disoriented Oriental.

The proverbial culture shock came in other forms as well. At the University of Alabama, I took a Directed Reading course with my mentor, Hank Lazer. One of the books I had to read was *Tender Buttons* by Gertrude Stein, a modernist text full of puns, polyentendre, and labyrinthine sentences. With a BA in English, I knew most of the words in that neat little volume, but I was clueless about how to make sense of such sentences as "Carafe, that is a blind glass," "Roast potatoes for," or "Dining is west." I was insomniac the night before my meeting with Hank to discuss Stein, inconsolably depressed thinking it must be the deficiency of my English that had made the book so incomprehensible. The next day, at the meeting, Hank assured me that it's not me, or my English, but almost everyone, every native speaker of English, would find Stein baffling or challenging, at least initially. Sure enough, over the years, Stein grew on me, and I now regularly teach *Tender Buttons* in my courses, in part to torture my students a little as the book had once tormented me.

Compared to Stein, the other book on the syllabus was a harder nut to crack and induced a real shock in me. It was *Repression and Recovery: Modern American Poetry and the Politics of Cultural Memory, 1910–1945* by Cary Nelson, a well-known left-wing, pro-Marxist intellectual from the University of Illinois. Nelson's book, as its title indicates, intends to recover a repressed cultural memory of the modern era, a period in which a tradition of political poetry flourished in important subcultures and in moments of national crisis before it came to full fruition in the Harlem Renaissance and in the widely politicized 1930s. Nelson goes beyond the dominant story of modern poetry, revises our notion of the social function of poetry, and reexamines the work of marginalized or forgotten poets—particularly women, Blacks, and writers on the Left. He argues that what we now worship as the great modernist canon, consisting of a handful of literary giants (some of whom I study in the current volume), was really a cultural construction of post–World War II America. "By the 1950s a limited canon of primary authors and texts was already in place," Nelson writes. "The names in the canon continued to change, but a substantial majority of interesting poems from 1910–1945 had already been forgotten. Academic critics had come to concentrate on close readings of a limited number of texts by 'major' authors. University course requirements were increasingly influential in shaping the market for new anthologies. And the professoriate, largely white and male and rarely challenged from within its own ranks, found it easy to reinforce the culture's existing racism and sexism by ignoring poetry by minorities and women."[1] Nelson's line of argument may sound convincing, but for a twenty-something me, fresh off the boat, the kind of poetry he tried to recover and promote as "interesting" was almost exactly the kind of literature I was running away from. Let me explain.

Leaving aside Nelson's argument for a moment, the illustrations in his book assaulted my senses. Many of the images, magazine covers, billboards, and pamphlets, looked eerily familiar. Growing up in the waning days of Mao's China, I had seen these politicized images everywhere every day. Even after Mao's death and as China opened up in the Reform Era under Deng Xiaoping, socialist iconography, glorifying the power of the proletariat and propagating the centrality of class struggle, remained ubiquitous in China.

Besides imagery, the kind of poetry Nelson reexamines, or "recovers," was also familiar to me. One of the poets he touts, H. H. Lewis, also known as the "Plowboy Poet" of Missouri, published a poetry pamphlet called "Thinking of Russia" in 1932. Lewis's title poem goes like this:

> I'm always thinking of Russia,
> I can't keep her out of my head,
> I don't give a damn for Uncle Sam,
> I'm a left-wing radical Red.

Or, the following famous poem, "The Preacher and the Slave," by Joe Hill, a Swedish-born labor activist, songwriter, and member of the Industrial

Workers of the World (or Wobblies), who was executed in 1915 after a controversial murder trial:

> Long-haired preachers come out every night,
> Try to tell you what's wrong and what's right;
> But when asked how 'bout something to eat
> They will answer with voices so sweet:
>   You will eat, bye and bye,
>   In that glorious land above the sky;
>   Work and pray, live on hay,
>   You'll get pie in the sky when you die.

The English phrase "pie in the sky" was coined by Joe Hill in this poem. I remembered listening to the popular song "I Dreamed I Saw Joe Hill Last Night" when I had first started learning English, a song that had been performed by singers ranging from Paul Robeson to, most recently, Bruce Springsteen. As interesting as these poems were, they were all highly politicized, used as propaganda to raise social consciousness, generate class solidarity, and advance a political cause. Or, to adopt the Maoist parlance, these are examples of literature serving the people. Or, as often happened in socialist China when I was growing up, literature was part of the government-controlled propaganda machine designed for the purpose of social engineering. Given my intellectual orientations upon my arrival in the United States, that kind of literature was anathema to me.

Up to that point, my journey in literature was somewhat typical of what my generation of Chinese had experienced. Growing up in the wake of the Cultural Revolution, we were offered at school an ideologically cleansed curriculum. But many of us, by happenstance or by choice, found nutrition and inspiration elsewhere, outside of the classrooms. As I describe in chapter 1, I was hooked on the Special English programs of the Voice of America. Totally oblivious to the fact that the VOA was a Cold War propaganda arm of the US State Department, I had not only learned a great deal of English from the daily programs but also gathered plenty of knowledge about American culture and literature. Besides listening to the VOA, I had also read a lot of Western literature in translation, anything from Goethe to Leo Tolstoy, Ivan Turgenev, Mark Twain, Jack London, Pablo Neruda, Lord Byron, Percy Shelley, Victor Hugo, and Gustave Flaubert. In high school, I was addicted to the poetry of Alexander Pushkin. In college, I encountered a group of Chinese poets called the Misty School, including Bei Dao, Gu Cheng, Shu Ting, Yang Lian, and Jiang He. A radical departure from the formulaic language of Mao's era, the work of the Misty poets was dense with symbolism, rebellious in emotions, and unconventional in technique. As we know, they acquired the trademark "misty" for their poetry's semantic opacity, a quality dreaded by a regime that favors literature with clear messages. Eschewing overt political agendas, then, became a rebellious political gesture. Or, as said in what has now become almost a cliché, being apolitical was paradoxically the most political in 1980s China, a sentiment aptly expressed by Bei Dao in a poem, "The Answer":

> I came into this world
> Bringing only paper, rope, a shadow
> To proclaim before the judgement
> The voices that have been judged[2]

Influenced by the Misty poets, I studied twentieth-century American poetry in college and immersed myself in the work of Ezra Pound, T. S. Eliot, Wallace Stevens, Robert Lowell, Sylvia Plath, Adrienne Rich, and so on. My senior thesis was on Lowell's "Skunk Hour," and my familiarity with that poem enabled me to pass a quixotic interview when I applied for my visa at the American consulate in Beijing, a story better left for another occasion. At any rate, poetry, or a particular kind of conception of poetry, intentionally apolitical, dwelling on the personal and interior, spurning overt ideological agendas, was my ticket to America. Until, that is, I came across the book by Nelson and was exposed once again to the use of literature as propaganda, albeit in an entirely different cultural milieu.

I was also surprised to find that many of the American intellectuals, especially baby boomers who came of age during the tumultuous sixties, were well versed in the complicated relations between literature and politics and were not averse at all to the idea of literature as propaganda. In fact, the more sophisticated and radical among them taught me to understand how mainstream American poetry, or what Charles Bernstein has dubbed the Official Verse Culture, is ideologically problematic in its endless pursuit of lyrical interiority, a narrow concept of craft, and a consumptive mode of close reading. I began to understand that, for instance, Pound's work is not limited to his short imagistic poems and that his poetry and politics, including his half-baked economic theory and noisome racial attitude, are inseparable.

More important, it was in this period following my arrival in the United States and then my subsequent graduate study at SUNY Buffalo's Poetics Program that I began to look anew at contemporary Chinese poetry as it had been translated and received in the United States. As I looked at the English translations from contemporary China, most of which were still limited to selections of the Misty poets and their associates, I identified a dominant theme, a preference of political rhetoric to aesthetic values.

Indeed, when treated thematically, much of what had been available in English translation of contemporary Chinese poetry often yielded the expected content, familiar in political science and in self-serving US narratives of what it is like to suffer under nondemocratic regimes. Typically, the poems that were introduced told the story of fighting for democracy, yearning for freedom, awakening to self-consciousness, and rediscovering subjectivity. In other words, these were poems that might easily be contextualized with respect to an image of contemporary China familiar to US readers. In my subsequent PhD dissertation, later turned into a book, I called this approach "ethnographic," because poetry in this case was used to describe a culture.[3]

Such an ethnographic approach, as I later discovered, was not a far cry from an earlier period when American modernism was secretly but actively used as a weapon in what has become known as the "cultural Cold War." According to scholars of Cold War history, in the 1950s and 1960s, the US State Department and the CIA refashioned and weaponized modernist art and literature, using them in the "struggle for cultural prestige and influence between the Communist Soviet Union and its Eastern Bloc satellites on one side and the United States and the nations of Western Europe on the other."[4] As the journalist and author Frances Stonor Saunders shows in her groundbreaking *The Cultural Cold War: The CIA and the World of Arts and Letters*, "During the height of the Cold War, the U.S. government committed vast resources to a secret program of cultural propaganda in Western Europe.... Its mission was to nudge the intelligentsia of Western Europe away from its lingering fascination with Marxism and Communism towards a view more accommodating of 'the American way.'"[5] Under the leadership of the poet and assistant secretary of state Archibald MacLeish, a cohort of poets, writers, critics, editors, and scholars, including Charles Olson, Malcolm Cowley, James Laughlin, Robert Lowell, and Norman Pearson, were recruited by the government to promote modernism at home and abroad.

As Nelson points out, the 1950s were a crucial period when what we now know as the modernist canon came into being. But what he does not say, or what we did not know for a long while, was that Cold War propaganda played an important role in fashioning the image of modernism. In the immediate postwar period, most Americans still disliked or even despised modernist art. As Greg Barnhisel shows in *Cold War Modernists*, the CIA, founded in 1947 and staffed mainly by Yale and Harvard graduates, sought to promote, inter alia, American Abstract painters such as Jackson Pollack, Robert Motherwell, Willem de Kooning, and Mark Rothko as proof of the creativity, the intellectual freedom, and the cultural power of the United States. The same strategy was used to repurpose modernist literature and poetry, first by advocating the notion that art and literature should be "autonomous from the practice of daily life, not subject to evaluation by social or political criteria." It then "dispensed with the more revolutionary or reactionary political associations that had marked modernism in the public mind in the first part of the century, replacing them with a celebration of the virtues of freedom and the assertion that the individual is sovereign."[6]

As we know, such an interpretation of modernism promoted during the Cold War was an abrupt departure from the often subversive poetics of Pound, Stein, and their fellow travelers. But it has been the canonical reading since the heyday of New Criticism, an intentionally depoliticized, decontextualized approach to literature. Ironically, it was an approach I had learned in China as a gesture of political rebellion, a mark of resistance to ideological control. It seemed that my transpacific journey in poetry had come to a full circle. If I had started out by running away from politics, I would only later realize that in pursuing depoliticized reading, as I did in college or as a teenager listening to the VOA, I had unwittingly internalized some of the cultural logic of Cold War propaganda. It seemed that I needed to, as Nietzsche terms it, *verlernen* (unlearn).[7]

Remarkably, my unlearning in transpacific poetics and politics was provided, albeit indirectly, by the person who had taught me to read and write: my father. It was also a lesson the full weight and meaning of which I was able to appreciate only years later, partly because, to quote Nietzsche again, such unlearning requires "something for which one has almost to be a cow and in any sense not a 'modern man': rumination."[8]

About the same time as I chanced upon the VOA radio programs and thus began my bildungsroman in the English language, I also stumbled upon one of my father's secrets: his red notebook. One day, my father showed me a notebook he had kept since he was young. It had a red plastic cover, making it look like *Mao's Little Red Book*. Inside he had pasted clippings, all poems and essays he had published under various pseudonyms in newspapers and magazines. His grandfather (my great-grandfather) was a landlord, from an "exploitative and parasitic class," a factor that doomed my father's future. Attending college, a privilege reserved only for working-class children, was a dream beyond his reach, and he became instead a "barefoot doctor," carrying a medicine kit, roaming the countryside to cure sick peasants. A literary aficionado, he did not stop writing, a secret he had long kept from everyone, including his family. I found the notebook by accident one day when I, a curious kid, was rummaging through his things. Shocked a little, he got me to promise not to tell anyone, and then he let me read a few short poems. From what I can remember, those tofu-shaped poems were mostly about the virtues of the proletarian revolution, the joys of agricultural harvesting, and other topics common to Communist literature. Despite the formulaic quality of the writing, even my prepubescent eye could see that my father's love for literature and desire for creativity were as real as the heartbeats pulsing under his bare skin.

In October 2016, my father suddenly passed away after a fall. I was devastated not only by his death but also by the fact that I did not get there in time to say goodbye. The sheer distance from California to China made it impossible for my speedy return. After I finally got back to my hometown and laid him to rest, I had to clean up his bedroom. Once again, I was rummaging through his things, only this time I knew exactly what I was looking for: his red notebook (fig. 2). After much effort, I successfully located the object. It had already lost its red plastic cover, the pages coming loose at the binding. But those clippings of poems and essays were still there. My attention was especially drawn by those tofu-sized poems, which I had once read as a teenager unschooled in the art of poetry. Reading them now, almost four decades later, I felt the poems jumping out at me with their crude freshness and bittersweet innocence.

His debut poem, titled "Going to Work," was written when my father was eighteen years old. Apparently, it is a decent enough poem, for after its initial publication in our small county newspaper, it was reprinted a month later by our district newspaper, with a much larger distribution. It reads in my translation:

> Rise before dawn,
> Return after sundown.
> More sweat now
> Greater harvest in autumn.

And the companion piece was titled "Adding":

> If day is not enough, add night
> If men are not enough, add women
> If the young are not enough, add the old
> Passion not enough, we must add perseverance

These two poems were first published on June 11, 1958, in the depths of the "Great Leap Forward." The infamous movement was a dystopian social campaign, lasting for three years, aiming to boost China's economy but in fact ending in disaster, with millions of people starved to death.[9]

Read against such a historical fact, my father's poems, especially like

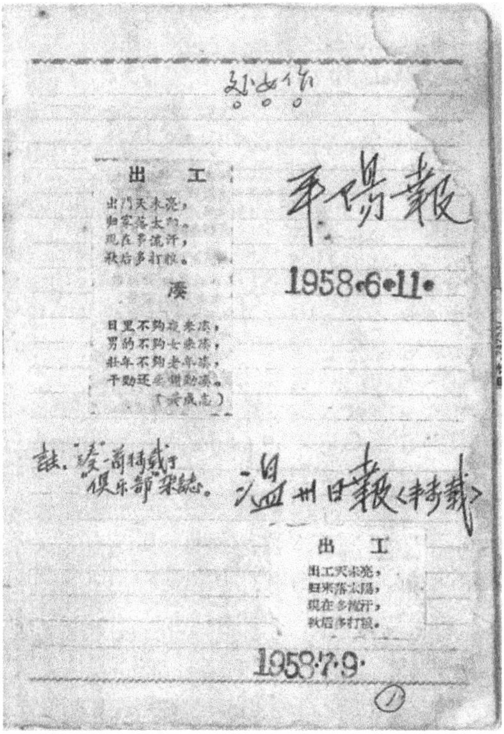

2. A page from my father's notebook, mid-twentieth century. Private collection.

the following one, titled "Harvest Celebration," may rightly be regarded as propaganda.

> When grain fills up the barn
> Joy overflows the hearts of the people
> Heavens shaken by the gong and drum
> We are celebrating a year of cornucopia

Indeed, the entire period of Chinese revolutionary literature, from 1949 to 1976, has often been interpreted as producing formulaic potboilers that rarely deviate from Party lines and only serve politics. Interpreted through the prism of the West, which regards individual free expression as the golden rule for aesthetic production, revolutionary literature may indeed lack aesthetic value.

Case in point, in 2016, the year my father passed away, I edited and published *The Big Red Book of Modern Chinese Literature*, a Norton anthology that includes writings by about fifty Chinese authors. I chose the colorful title in part to pun on *Mao's Little Red Book*, in part to pay tribute to my father's notebook.[10] The anthology, to my surprise and delight, was reviewed by the *New York Times*, the *New York Review of Books*, the *Times Literary Supplement*, the *Los Angeles Review of Books*, and others. Among these reviews, there was one that struck a chord, or rather, a discord, with me, because it made me, once again, reflect upon my own peregrinations on the transpacific route of poetics and politics, the lessons I have repeatedly had to learn and unlearn.

In his review article, "If Mao Had Been a Hermit," in the *New York Review of Books*, Perry Link, a professor emeritus of Princeton University, took issues with some of my selections. Link was, in his own word, "stunned" by my decision to include Mao Zedong in the anthology. Although he acknowledged that Mao's actions as a political leader "had fateful effects on more human lives than arguably anyone else in history," Link asked how good Mao's poems "actually are ... on strictly aesthetic grounds." In fact, the eminent scholar of Chinese history and literature had an answer ready, as he asserted that "Mao's poems are competent but not brilliant." Therefore, he doubted that "we would be talking about them today if Mao had been a hermit."[11]

What Link failed to understand was that aesthetics was not the only criterion by which I had made my selections for the anthology in the first place. As I stated in the introduction, the book is above all "a search for the soul of modern China." I wanted to choose literary works that, independent of their aesthetic values, have made a large impact on the spiritual, cultural life of twentieth-century China. In other words, I was interested in what Philip Fisher calls "the cultural work of literature." In his study of nineteenth-century American popular novels, Fisher argues that the most important cultural work was often done by those genres or representative works that, from a later perspective, say, that of twentieth-century modernism, have seemed weak or lacking in aesthetic values.[12] In terms of cultural work, it might be hard to find any literary work that has left a larger footprint in modern China than Mao's poems and his analect-style quotations that make up his *Little Red Book*. Therefore, regardless of what one thinks of how good Mao's poems really are aesthetically, they occupy a unique place in modern Chinese literature.

Link's blind spot is the notion that literature must be the expression of a free individual, an assumption that dates back to William Wordsworth's definition of poetry as "the spontaneous overflow of powerful feelings." Anything short of that would be deemed bad literature or just propaganda. But as I have learned through my experience shuttling between China and America, East and West, the belief in literature as an expression of a free individual is as ideologically suspect as Mao's revolutionary shibboleths. Just like those proletarian poems recovered by Nelson in his book, which once baffled me, Mao's writings, my father's tofu-shaped poems, and many more like them are not relics from a bygone era. Most of them are records of creative souls struggling, negotiating, and coping with a national dream gone bad. They are testimonials, not to the corrosion of literature by politics, but to the power of writing as politics. In a twisted way, we should admit that Communism may have done much damage to literature, but at least it takes literature seriously, in fact so seriously that it wants to control all forms of artistic expression, weeding out the "one hundred flowers" that dare to blossom. Or, in an equally perverted manner, I am reminded of what transpired with the CIA and its cultural Cold War. As Saunders tells us, "The CIA took art very seriously.... There may be a really perverse argument that says the CIA were the best art critics in America in the Fifties ... [because] they saw the potential power in that kind of art and ran with it."[13]

Somewhere Mark Twain said, "History doesn't repeat; it rhymes."

As the foregoing pages indicate, the current volume, pardon the oxymoron, is a deeply personal book of literary studies. If one of the hallmarks of good academic scholarship is disinterestedness, I must admit to the guilt of having infused perhaps too much subjectivity, in the form of anecdotes, memories, and sentiments, into what is supposed to be an objective study of literature. However, as I hope the book will bear out, I have not done so out of solipsism or self-indulgence. Instead, I see myself as a tiny speck in the global, transpacific flows of cultural capital. My personal experience, including my bildungsroman in the English language, my subsequent training in Anglo-American literature, and my work as a literary translator, is part and parcel of what I hereby call a transpacific poetics. It is a geopoetics whose multiple nodes, crisscrossing routes, and palimpsestic inscriptions have, in the past two decades or so, remained as the fount of my imagination, as well as the focus of my research.

Beginning with my earlier book, *Transpacific Displacement* (2002), I have devoted attention to a scholarly topic intimately tied to my own experience as an intellectual migrant. In that book, derived from my PhD dissertation, I take an ethnographic approach to well-known American literary texts and trace the transpacific migration of cultural meanings through twentieth-century America's imaging of Asia. It opens with a radically new reading of Imagism, goes on to describe the countermockery of literary Orientalism by Asian American writers, and concludes with a study of transpacific geopolitics embedded in the English translations and interpretations of contemporary Chinese poetry.

Subsequently, in my second academic book, *Transpacific Imaginations*

(2008),[14] I track a genealogy of counterpoetics in the literary and historical imaginations across the Pacific. Arguing against Emersonian geometrics of expansive circularity, the book traces the subversive poetics of the transpacific lines of flight from Herman Melville's *Moby-Dick* to Theresa Cha's *DICTEE*, from Mark Twain's *Letters from Hawaii* to the Angel Island poems by Chinese immigrants. It ends with a call for locating an ethical ground between the modernist fallacy of poetic appropriation and the postmodernist denial of historical knowledge, a ground where knowledge is replaced by acknowledgment, cognition by recognition.

The current volume follows the path paved by the earlier two books but focuses more on the genre of poetry. Continuing my interest in the transpacific crossover, in the cultural and linguistic transactions between the Anglo-American and Chinese worlds, this work explores the dynamics of poetry and poetics in the age of globalization, particularly the questions of translatability, universality, and risk in the transpacific context. I examine multiple contact zones between the Anglophone and the Sinophone, those almost inscrutable moments of "Chinese whispers" when poetry imbricates with national language, intangible economy, translation, risk management, digital technology, and political propaganda. I try, for instance, to connect dots between hexagrams in the *I Ching* and the actuarial tables on the mind of an American insurance agent who also happened to be a major poet; or, between sound symbolism of the Chinese language and the multilingual cantos by a poet condemned to a mental hospital in Washington, DC, while the digital revolution—a major cultural transformation in which a Chinese book would be seen as merely an English book that happens to be coded in Chinese—quietly took place against the backdrop of Sinophobia and Cold War propaganda. Tracking these crisscrossed routes and multiple nodes, I argue for a transpacific, materialist, embodied poetics in which poetry actively engages in the making and unmaking of the world, and I thereby warn against the risks in the search for universal intelligibility and global translatability.

Chapter 1, "Through the Looking Glass: Basic English, Chinglish, and Translocal Dialect," examines the efforts of I. A. Richards, arguably the founder of Anglo-American academic literary criticism, to promote Basic English in China in the early twentieth century. Like his trademark New Criticism, Richards's initiative of globalizing English shares some of the underlying principles of modernist poetry: a global ambition built on translocal cultural sampling and a desire for control in a poetic Babel. These features and self-contradictions of Anglo-American modernism buttressed but also doomed the campaign for Basic English in China. Richards's linguistic enterprise ran up against Chinese nationalism as well as the more sophisticated positions held by some Chinese writers, such as

Lin Yutang, who offered "Chinglish," a sort of pidgin, as an alternative to Basic English. As my later chapters show, Basic English is no simple linguistic experiment, a solution to the confusion of tongues; it actually foreshadows the rise of digital technology, a dry run of the search for universal intelligibility.

Chapter 2, "Listening to Marco Polo: Sound, Money, and Vernacular Imagination," ponders the increasingly acoustic, intangible quality of value, truth, and reality in the twenty-first century. Ranging from the first mention of paper money in Marco Polo's travel narrative to the imperial dreams of conquest through sound in Italo Calvino's *Invisible Cities*, from the use of imagination in Samuel Taylor Coleridge's "Kubla Khan" to cryptocurrency in the age of financial capitalism, I describe the poetics of intangible economy, which constantly eludes the grasp of our logic-based, vision-biased rationality. I propose vernacular imagination as a poetic mode of being in a world built on sound. In this acoustic space, where center is everywhere but boundaries nowhere, we hear the sound bites of reality as echoes of poetic dreams, transcendental truth uttered in local currencies, and a clash of empires set off by a few mistranslated, misheard words.

Chapter 3, "Words Made in China: Ezra Pound as a Translational Poet," studies the translational poetics of Ezra Pound. Following the previous chapters, I argue that translational poetics, as exemplified by Pound's *Cantos*, represents the greatest achievement of Anglo-American poetic modernism. Having learned the ideogrammic method from the Chinese, Pound becomes a translational poet, one who uses over twenty languages in his work and creates a relationship between languages that Walter Benjamin prescribes in his famous essay on translation. Indeed, what Benjamin articulates in theory has been realized in poetic practice by Pound, who, jailed for a decade at the mental asylum of St. Elizabeths, digs deep into the echo chamber of sound symbolism and explores the treacherous frontiers of language. Pound's "madhouse" method is not such a far cry from what once haunted Ferdinand de Saussure, who, as I discuss in chapter 5, pored over linguistic enigmas he disparaged as "Chinese puzzles."

Chapter 4, "Thirteen Ways of Looking at a Blackbird Too Big to Fail: Wallace Stevens, John Cage, and the Poetics of Risk," studies poetry as an exercise and experiment in risk management. It tracks the double career of Wallace Stevens as a poet and an insurance man and reveals the intersection between poetic imagination and statistical imagination. Reinterpreting a host of poems, essays, and lectures by Stevens, I argue that his penchant for abstraction represents both the aesthetics of avant-garde poetry and the logic of the insurance industry. Moreover, steeped in American pragmatism, which readily accepts the waywardness of the human experience, Stevens was also profoundly influenced by Zen Buddhism, which endows his poetry with a quality of meditative detachment and a profound understanding of a world becoming increasingly risky, a universe where chance and uncertainty cannot be tamed. Against the backdrop of what Ulrich Beck has termed "risk society," I not only suggest that Stevens conceives poetry essentially as a form of risk management but also explore the triangulation of poetry, risk discourse, and his imaginative engagement with the East. It is worth noting that the East Asian philosophical understanding of risk and its unique brand of risk management have largely remained absent in contemporary Western thought on the subject, except in the field of poetry and poetics, where Zen Buddhism, Daoism, and the *I Ching* have exerted a profound impact. Via Stevens and other American poets, such as John Cage, who embodies genuine influence by Asian thoughts, I hope to open up a new path toward worlding in a risky world.

Chapter 5, "Chinese Whispers: The Future of Meaning in the Age of Information," investigates the poetics of the Chinese language against the background of digital technology. After a brief visit to the history of the cybernetic movement in which information was defined as a disembodied entity that is devoid of meaning, I revisit Ernest Fenollosa's definitive essay "The Chinese Written Character as a Medium for Poetry" to tease out, in a somewhat tongue-in-cheek, ersatz techno-Orientalist fashion, the poetics of paragram or transcoding at work not just in Chinese, but across languages. The stark contrast between disembodied information and materialist poetics sets the stage for my study of Lin Yutang's Chinese typewriter as an instance of breaking down the false dichotomy between alphabetic and nonalphabetic languages, conceptualizing the mechanized word as a technology of embodiment, and reclaiming the function of worldmaking for art and aesthetics.

Completing a book on Chinese whispers at a time of rampant disinformation by means of bots, viral videos, trending tweets, memes, and deep fakes is certainly not to celebrate a culture of deception, or to give credence to the denial of facts. If anything, the dark forces unleashed in the Trumpian era and aided by digital technology reveal exactly the pitfall and risk of the search for universal intelligibility and global translatability. By tracking these transpacific routes, I am in some sense writing a prehistory of the age of (dis)information. Rather than a world of transparency, accountability, and certainty—all qualities desired by many of the poets and cultural workers I study in this volume—we are living in a world characterized by global surveillance, trolling, and risk. Inspired by a line from an eponymous poem by John Ashbery, "Finally the rumors grew more fabulous than the real thing," and informed by a transpacific poetics encapsulated in a phrase of Myung Mi Kim, "Placement between *l* and *r*,"[15] my book seeks alternative routes, the poetic maybes, by recovering those muffled or buried moments of transpacific encounter: not Basic English's impulse for control, but Chinglish's embodied openness; not financial capitalism's exploitation of the intangible, but the moneyed utterance of local dialects; not the doomsday nuclear mushroom, but John Cage's mycological diet; not the Cold War tactics of the Russian Telephone, but the poetics of Chinese whispers, the click-clacks of Lin Yutang's Chinese typewriter, and the babbles of an improbable Chinese poem performed at one of those historical Macy conferences.

"To err is human," Chao Yuen Ren once said about our use of language, "to correct is worse."[16] Behind such a counterintuitive statement by a globetrotting linguist there lies, as I try to articulate in this book, a recognition of the disruptive force of linguistic slippage, the kinetic excess of language, and the errancy of words from their semantic destiny by virtue of their irreducible materiality.

Through the Looking Glass

[CHAPTER ONE]

Basic English, Chinglish, and Translocal Dialect

"The radio listener," says Walter Benjamin, "welcomes the human voice into his house like a visitor."[1] The human voice I used to welcome into my house at night when I was a teenager was certainly no ordinary visitor to a small town in southern China. It was the Voice of America.

I was eleven, and like many Chinese kids my age, I had just started learning English in school. One night, I was fiddling with an old battered transistor radio that had belonged to my grandfather but was now left to lie around in our house. I pulled up the rusty, crooked antenna and switched to the shortwave channels. Adjusting the dial to search for a frequency with bearable audibility—most channels simply buzzed either because the machine was too old or because the signals had, as often happened in the Cold War years, been scrambled by the government—I suddenly came to a spot where, after a few snarls of static, a clear, slow, and manly voice in English rang out: "This is VOA, the Voice of America, broadcasting in Special English ..."

This encounter—some media theorists would call it "wireless rapture"—became a turning point in my life.[2] In the ensuing high school years, I regularly tuned in to the daily half-hour broadcast, which began with ten minutes of the latest news, followed by twenty minutes of feature programming in American culture, history, science, or short stories. My favorite was the short program called "Words and Their Stories," which introduced American idioms and their colorful etymologies. That's how I learned, for instance, the meanings of *gerrymander*, *powwow*, *bogus*, and *gobbledygook*. The language is called Special English because its vocabulary is limited to fifteen hundred words, written in short and simple sentences that supposedly contain only one idea and spoken at a slower pace, about two-thirds the speed of standard English.

Completely oblivious to the ideological agendas of the VOA, a propaganda machine controlled by the US State Department in the Cold War era (and also, as I now realize, at the risk of sending my parents to jail, because listening to "politically subversive" foreign radio programs was illegal at the time, and parents would be held responsible for any political "crimes" committed by their preadult children), I learned from the broadcasts a great deal of English.

Only years later, when I became a student of literature and started to look closely into the work of some twentieth-century writers, did I begin to see the connections between the VOA programs I had been listening to as a teenager and the modern literature I was studying as my field of expertise. The VOA's Special English, I learned, was modeled after Basic English, the brainchild of C. K. Ogden and I. A. Richards, coauthors of one of the most important books in modern criticism, *The Meaning of Meaning: A Study of the Influence of Language upon Thought and of the Science of Symbolism* (1925). Ogden was also responsible for the first English translation of Ludwig Wittgenstein's *Tractatus Logico-Philosophicus*, and Richards was arguably the founder of Anglo-American academic literary criticism. Furthermore, since its inception in 1929, Basic English had drawn the attention of a number of modernists, including Ezra Pound, James Joyce, Louis Zukofsky, Laura (Riding) Jackson, and Wittgenstein. Pound, Joyce, and Zukofsky were all simultaneously fascinated and troubled by the implications of Basic for their modernist poetry and poetics. Jackson launched a sustained attack on Basic and its underlying linguistic principles in her magnum opus, *Rational Meaning*. Wittgenstein constantly belittled Ogden and Richards in his lectures and notes.

When my gaze turned to Chinese modernism, however, I was surprised to find that my encounter with Special English and, by implication, with Basic English was by no means unique to China. History, as opposed to a linear procession, is often a strange palimpsest. Half a century before my wireless encounter with the VOA, China had already heard the buzz of Basic English. And like its Anglo-American counterpart, Chinese modernism also had a strange love-hate relationship with this onetime Esperanto. Moreover, some Chinese writers, such as Lin Yutang, would straddle at least two literary traditions, Chinese and American, forming what Richard Jean So has called a transpacific literary community.[3] Their transpacific trajectories further complicate my study of Basic English, making it impossible for me to draw a distinct line between the two bodies of literature and to tell stories from "both sides"—the Anglo-American side and the Chinese side. In fact, as we shall see, in the battle between Basic English and Chinglish, between a desire for control through linguistic standardization and a push for multitude through hybridization, it is sometimes hard to distinguish between friends and foes. In this "global race toward language dominance,"[4] while the proponents of Basic English dreamed of debabelization, their opponents advocated what I would call the translocal dialect. Between the two sides of the looking glass there lie myriad positions and practices, including Anglo-American modernism's desire for control and coherence on the one hand and for polyvocality and indeterminacy on the other; or Chinese modernism's rejection of its linguistic heritage on the one hand and the embracing of a more fluid, open approach anchored in Chinese as a rising star in the Babel of languages on the other.

* * *

The conclusion that I came to then was that it seemed impossible to be on both sides of the looking glass at once. That is, it made me think how much more dependent one was than one had suspected, upon a particular *tradition of thought from Thales down, so that I came to wonder how much* understanding *anything (a term, a system etc.) meant* merely being used *to it.... And it seemed to me that all I was trying to do and that any of the pundits had succeeded in doing, was to attempt to translate one terminology with a long tradition into another; and that however cleverly one did it, one would never produce anything better than an ingenious deformation.*

T. S. ELIOT, letter to I. A. Richards, August 9, 1930

Eliot in his letter was using his own studies in Indian philosophy and Sanskrit as evidence to cast doubt on Richards's efforts to translate Mencius and promote Basic English in China. In response to Richards's invitation to him to visit China and experience Confucian culture in person, Eliot wrote, "I do not care to visit any land which has no native cheese."[5] Cultural traditions, then, just like cheese, would have to be native products before any authentic understanding could take place; attempts at translation would be equivalent to desires for occupying an impossible position—"on both sides of the looking glass at once," which would produce only an "ingenious deformation." Sharing Eliot's appreciation for the difficulty of translation, Richards, however, believed that a solution exists: Basic English is a tool to combat the "ingenious deformation"; as a universal language, it is a transparent looking glass that renders both sides completely visible and translatable to each other.

Basic English was invented by C. K. Ogden in 1929 as an attempt to "give to everyone a second, or international, language which will take as little of the learner's time as possible." "Basic" is an acronym for British, American, Scientific, International, and Commercial. With a carefully selected vocabulary of 850 words, it is designed to cover all the essential requirements of communication in English. Of these 850, the first hundred consist of "operators," including eighteen verbs (*come, get, give, go, keep, let, make, put, seem, take, be, do, have, say, see, send, may*, and *will*) and words like *if, because, so, as, just, only, but, to, for, through, yes*, and *no*. There are 400 "general names," like *copper, cork, copy, cook, cotton*; 200 "common things" or "picturables," like *cake, camera, card, cart, cat*; and 150 "qualifiers," or adjectives, like *common, complex*, and *conscious*.[6]

According to Ogden and Richards, the idea of Basic came from their collaborative work on *The Meaning of Meaning*. This book was motivated in part by an idealistic desire to prevent the kind of abuse of language the co-authors had witnessed during World War I. The Great War was portrayed both in Britain and abroad as largely a war of propaganda, in which the distortion of abstract words like *freedom, democracy*, and *victory* was a key weapon.[7] They wanted to dispel so-called Word Magic, a relic of a primitive habit of mind in which words substitute themselves for the power of things. Opposing such verbal superstition, Ogden and Richards propose that words are not part of and do not inherently correspond to things, that words "mean" nothing by themselves, and that only when we make use of words do they stand for things and have "meaning." They object to Saussure's notion that meaning is generated by the language system and inseparable from the symbolization process in which a thought (signified) is expressed as a term (signifier). Instead, they cling to a more traditional view of meaning as standing apart from the language in which it is symbolized and insist that a crucial component of meaning does exist in advance of symbolization: the referent, the Thing. In other words, Ogden and Richards see the referent as meaning itself, whereas Saussure does not regard meaning as deriving from the referent.[8] Hence they characterize the Saussurean definition of meaning as merely "verbal definition," while calling their own "real definition."[9]

The instrumental view of language adopted by *The Meaning of Meaning* would result in the conception of Basic as the application of their theory. As Richards recalled the genesis of Basic, "When [Ogden] wrote a chapter, in *The Meaning of Meaning*, 'On Definition,' at the end of it we suddenly stared at one another and said, 'Do you know this means that with under a thousand words you can say everything?'"[10] In 1929, four years after the publication of *The Meaning of Meaning*, Ogden introduced his first list of Basic vocabulary.[11] He declared that "it is the business of all internationally-minded persons to make Basic English part of the system of education in every country, so that there may be less chance of war, and less learning of languages."[12] Echoing Henry Ford's peace slogan, "Make everybody speak English," Ogden suggested that "Basic English for all" was a counterpart of Ford's pacifist prescription for avoidance of another world war: "The so-called national barriers of today are ultimately language barriers. The absence of a common medium of communication is the chief obstacle of international understanding, and therefore the chief underlying cause of war."[13]

Pacifist utopianism aside, this proposal for a language-centered social reform must have appealed to Anglo-American modernists, who, like Ogden and Richards, had also responded to post–World War I cultural fragmentation by rethinking the function of language and imagining the power of the poetic language to change the world. But before turning to the modernists, let me dig a bit deeper into the Basic program and explain the process of vocabulary selection that may provide an even stronger link between Basic and Anglo-American modernism, a link manifested in their shared desire for control.

Basic, as Richards put it, "is a technical innovation in the deliberate control of language."[14] Ogden called his method for reducing the size of the vocabulary "panoptic conjugation," a term he had derived from Jeremy Bentham's model prison, the Panopticon.[15] Editor and advocate of Bentham's work, Ogden ascribed to the famous Utilitarianist the inspiration for his own work on Basic. The intellectual debts were incurred in two ways: one is the concept of fiction and the other the Panopticon. At the core of Bentham's theory on language lies the notion of fictions, by which he meant the patterns and norms that impute concrete qualities to entities where none exists. The sentence "Music moves the soul," for instance, conceals three fictions. Neither "music" nor "soul" is the name of a thing, nor is any physical movement involved in the relation between them, which the sentence is intended to express. Language is forced to introduce fictions by a form of predication, and verbs are especially guilty of composing fictions because of their work in predication, making us talk about qualities as if they were there while in fact they are merely linguistic ghosts and bogeys.[16] Compared by Bentham to the serpents of Eden because of their evanescent, slippery meanings, verbs find their population drastically reduced to only eighteen on Ogden's list, and, in fact, they are no longer called "verbs" but "operators."

Whereas Bentham's concept of fiction equipped Ogden with a theoretical basis for Basic English, the idea of the Panopticon lent him the inspiration for building the vocabulary list. The Panopticon was Bentham's design for a model prison, a circular building in which the inspector occupies the center and the cells the circumference. By blinds and other devices, the inspector conceals himself from the observation of the prisoners, creating the sense of an invisible omnipresence. The essence of such architectural design is to enable the supervisor to command a perfect, panoptic view of all the cells, *panoptic* meaning "seen at a glance."

Ogden developed the Basic vocabulary according to the panoptic principle. For example, he would put the word *house* in the center of a circle with spokes at the ends of which were *hut*, *cottage*, *mansion*, *bungalow*, *sky-scraper*, *log-cabin*, *habitation*, *residence*, *domicile*, *dwelling*, and so on. If the center word could, with appropriate adjectives on the Basic list, replace the other words, then the other words were dropped. In this way, the center word occupies what in Bentham's Panopticon is called the Inspector's Lodge and oversees the other words that are now excluded from "normative" use, or in a sense imprisoned. As Ogden puts it, the Panopticon "enables the entire vocabulary imprisoned in [its] procrustean structure to be envisaged at a glance."[17]

In *Discipline and Punish: The Birth of the Prison*, Michel Foucault identifies Bentham's design as a prime example of a modern society that is built upon the principle of discipline and panopticism. "'Discipline,'" writes Foucault, "may be identified neither with an institution nor with an apparatus; it is a type of power, a modality for its exercise, comprising a whole set of instruments.... It is a 'physics' or 'anatomy' of power, a technology.... We can speak of the formation of a disciplinary society in this movement that stretches from the enclosed discipline, a sort of social 'quarantine,' to an indefinitely generalizable mechanism of 'panopticism.'"[18] The selection of Basic vocabulary enacts exactly such disciplinarism and panopticism. A brief glance at Bentham's drawing for the Panopticon and an illustration of Ogden's method of vocabulary selection yields a striking resemblance as well as a similarity between the controlling mechanisms at work in both enterprises (figs. 3 and 4).

Linking the Inspector's Lodge or the center word to the cells or the periphery words is a panoptic vision or the spoke, which Foucault characterizes as "an uninterrupted work of writing" and Richards sees as the function of "vertical translation." "At the heart of language control," write Richards and Gibson, "is the use of words (or, better, senses) as instruments in looking closely at or into the senses of other words."[19] And Richards extends the panoptic, inspector/prisoner metaphor to describe the relation between words: "This selection, this language within language, can thus serve as a sort of caretaker, an inspectorate, a maintenance, repair and remedial staff, able to examine, criticize, deputize and demonstrate where needed: in brief be a control upon the rest. And not a control merely over its lexical performance, the efficiency of its vocabulary in use, the choice, justice and comprehensibility of its terms. The possible control covers the implications, the requirements and exclusions."[20] As I discuss later, this concept of language control will become complementary to Richards's account of poetry as a technical control of meaning and thus provide a linguistic and philosophical justification for the method of "close reading," the hallmark of New Criticism.

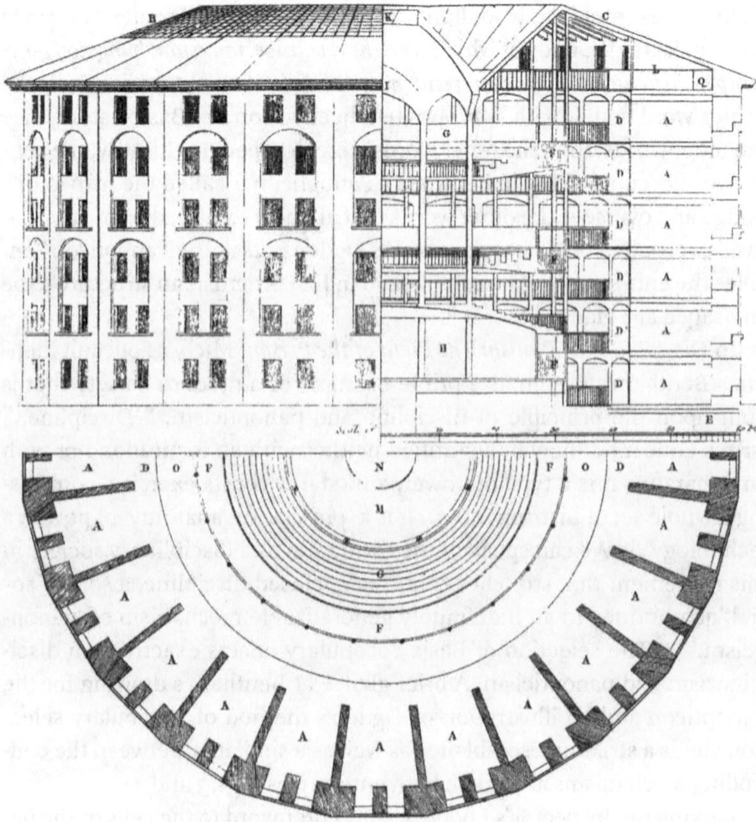

3. Plan of the Panopticon, eighteenth century.

The panoptic technology is used not only in the building of vocabulary, but also in the teaching of language. On April 30, 1961, the *New York Times* published a story about a mobile classroom designed by Richards and his assistant to aid foreign language education. The so-called Arlington Instruction Van is described as follows:

> The van itself, the type of trailer employed by a construction company as a building-site office, has positions for a total of 18 students along either wall of the 8-foot wide classroom on wheels. Each student has a clear view of the screen at the front of the van. The instructor, from the rear of the van, controls the film projector and the Inter-Com console through which he can instruct the students individually or as a group. The students hear the tapes and the voice of the teacher through headsets and all is quiet in the acoustically treated instruction van.... Since the student's work can be

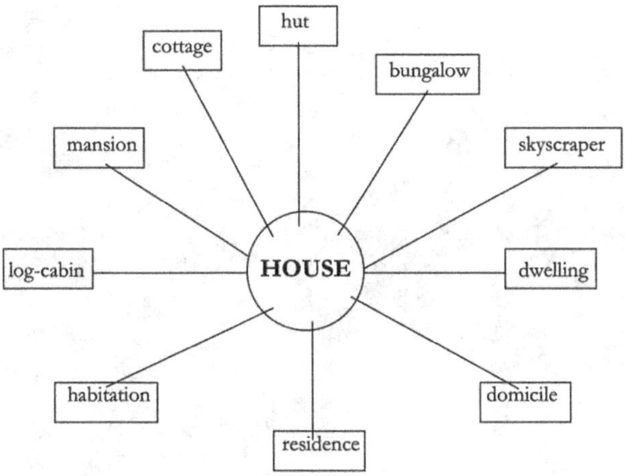

4. C. K. Ogden's method of vocabulary selection, early twentieth century.

> monitored without his realizing it, the instructor is fully able to analyze and correct the student's efforts.[21]

Interestingly, according to the reports by Richards and Gibson on the results of their instructional experiment, the Instruction Van sessions were aimed exclusively at underachieving students, or those whom the reports call "problem" boys and girls. The analogy is all too obvious between the van segregating academically delinquent pupils and the prison quarantining behaviorally delinquent members of a society.

It is not my purpose here to demonize the use of modern technology for more efficient language teaching. If you look at some of the pictures of the Arlington Instruction Van (figs. 5 and 6), the interior of the mobile classroom is not really so different from that of an ordinary language lab, with cubicle privacy for each student as well as monitoring power for the teacher. But we would be naive not to see classroom settings as reflections of the mode of production of a society and of the cultural ideology implied in the mode. Jesus, let me remind you, preached from the mountaintop and by the lake, Buddha taught in a garden full of flowers, and Confucius often gave lessons to his disciples at crowded, noisy marketplaces. The location and setup of the instructional venue are inevitably bound up with the conception of knowledge: in the cases of Jesus, Buddha, and Confucius, knowledge is embodied, inseparable from personality, whereas in the modern conception, knowledge is disembodied, objective, and instrumental. The degree to which knowledge is disembodied in our modern age can be seen in the very description of the Arlington Instruction Van.

5. Interior of the Arlington Instruction Van, mid-twentieth century. HUG(B) R461, Box 2, Folder: Instruction Van. Photograph: Harvard University Archives.

6. Exterior of the Arlington Instruction Van. HUG(B) R461, Box 2, Folder: Instruction Van. Photograph: Harvard University Archives.

As Richards and Gibson explain, one great advantage of using the van is that the learning process no longer hinges solely on a teacher's linguistic competence, because the projector and tapes will do the work for the teacher. As we move further in the current volume, especially when we get to chapter 5, we will see that the Arlington Instruction Van was just another instance of the cybernetic revolution that was taking shape in post–World War II Anglo-America, a technological imagination that intends to separate meaning from message, body from information.

As Foucault has reminded us, discipline should not be identified merely with an institution or apparatus; it manifests itself above all as a technology. Bentham's Panopticon, after all, originated from his brother's architectural drawings for a rotunda-shaped workshop in which the laborers are put under complete supervision by an invisible inspector.[22] Hence prisons, workshops, classrooms, and vocabulary lists have all become institutions where the cultural logic of panopticism is manifested and the technology of control applied.

* * *

Your heart would have responded
Gaily, when invited, beating obedient
To controlling hands
. . .
Datta. Dayadhvam. Damyata.

T. S. ELIOT, *The Waste Land*

In these lines, which end Eliot's famous poetic response to post–World War I cultural fragmentation, two words stand out: *controlling* and *Damyata*, Sanskrit for "control" (the Sanskrit triad translated: "Give, sympathize, control"). Eliot, who earlier objected to Richards's efforts in translating Chinese texts and promoting Basic in China, has now come to share with Richards a desire for the control of meaning. Although Eliot uses many foreign phrases and sentences in the poem, including the very Sanskrit word for "control," the appearance of openness, fragmentation, or multilingualism is immediately undercut not only by the thematic coherence of the poem but also by the use of endnotes by the poet, who apparently wants to aid and ensure proper understanding of the poem. The endnotes thus work as a control mechanism, although the choice of poetic vocabulary veers in the opposite direction from Basic.

It is actually no surprise that despite his objection to Basic, Eliot is Richards's kindred spirit in literary ideology. New Criticism, of which both of them remained founts of inspiration, is to a large extent predicated on the reader's ability to control textual meaning. New Criticism's notorious distaste for biographical information and historical background, focusing instead on the text itself, had an early rehearsal in Richards's *Practical Criticism*, which was published in 1929, the same year when Basic English was invented. The book was primarily based upon the results of experiments he had conducted with his students at Cambridge. He issued printed sheets of poems to his students, who were asked to comment freely on them; the authorship of the poems was not revealed and with rare exceptions was not recognized. The students' comments, therefore, would focus only on the texts themselves—a trademark of New Criticism.[23] Such a distaste for contextuality finds its parallel in the kind of decontextualization in Basic.

The other feature of New Criticism, "close reading," is an attempt not only to decontextualize but also to contain the multiplicity and ambiguity of meaning. In this sense, close reading is a panoptic technique. But the New Critical panopticism is manifested even more clearly in Richards's account of poetry, an account according to which poetry *is* Basic English and vice versa. A student of Romanticism, Richards sees poetry as, to quote Coleridge's dictum, "the best words in the best order," that is, the "best language." This "best language," otherwise called "poetic diction" in Romanticism, is a prototype for Basic as "a language within language"; and Richards's accounts of poetry and of Basic are often interchangeable. The technique of poetry, writes Richards, lies in "managing the variable connections between words and what they mean: what they might mean, can't mean, and should mean—that—not as a theoretical study only or chiefly, but as a matter of actual control."[24] Likewise, Basic is "a pioneer prototype for many of the inquiries into symbolic similarities and differences," or a "vertical translation from unrestricted into restricted language."[25] Hence, when Richards maintains that "this capacity of a small segment of the language to exercise such a wide and deep supervision over the rest is the ground for believing that an effective heightening in men's ability to understand one another can—given an adequate attempt—be brought about," we can be quite certain that the "small segment of the language" refers to both poetry and Basic English.[26]

But the New Criticism of Richards and Eliot tells only a partial truth about Anglo-American modernism. If Basic English is a program for decreasing difficulty and ambiguity and New Criticism introduces methods for controlling them, not every modernist shared such a desire for control. On the contrary, as Marjorie Perloff and others have argued, the desire for indeterminacy has been equally strong in the twentieth century.[27] "In the poetry of this 'other tradition,'" as Perloff argues, "ambiguity and complexity give way to inherent contradiction and undecidability, metaphor and symbol to metonymy and synecdoche, the well-wrought urn to what Ashbery calls 'an open field of narrative possibilities,' and the coherent structure of images to 'mysteries of construction,' nonsense, and free play."[28] Susan Sontag famously argues "against interpretation," maintaining that our obsession with codes of interpretation is motivated by "an open aggressiveness, an overt contempt for appearance," and that "the modern style of interpretation excavates, and as it excavates, destroys."[29] John Cage, whose work exemplifies for Perloff the poetics of indeterminacy and who figures later, in chapter 4, shares with Sontag the antipathy to interpretive control. Adopting the method of chance operation in writing as a way to free himself from authorial intention and egocentric interest, Cage also prefers the reader-as-mushroom-hunter to the reader-as-ragpicker, characterizing his ideal reader "as an unsystematic browser, one who is on the lookout for unexpected delights but who will not alter the landscape too much in search of hidden order."[30] In fact, Cage was inspired by the modernists, such as Ezra Pound and James Joyce, who were torn between their desire for control and aspiration for indeterminacy, a fact that is evidenced not only in their work but also in their mixed responses to Basic English.

In 1935, Ezra Pound wrote a review of Ogden's *Debabelization*, a book that seemingly argues against the kind of polyvocality that defines Pound's *Cantos*. Pound begins the review with an admission of guilt followed immediately by a self-defense.

> If mere extensions of vocabulary, or use of foreign words is a sin, I surely am chief among all sinners living. Yet, to the best of my knowledge, I have never used a Greek word or a Latin one where English would have served. I mean that I have never intentionally used, or wittingly left unexpurgated, any classic or foreign form save where I asserted: this concept, this rhythm is so solid, so embedded in the consciousness of humanity, so durable in its justness that it has lasted 2,000 years, or nearly three thousand. When it has been an Italian or French word, it has asserted or I have meant it to assert some meaning not current in English, some shade or gradation.[31]

On the one hand, Pound favored the use of Basic as a means of "weeding out bluffs . . . [and] fancy trimmings," "chucking out useless verbiage," and creating an effect resonant with his Imagistic aesthetics: "direct treatment of the thing," and "use absolutely no word that does not contribute to the presentation."[32] Consider also Pound's famous aphorism *Dichten = Condensare*, with its corollary call for condensation, which jibes well with the spirit of Basic. One the other hand, as he made clear in the above passage, his poetry taps into linguistic resources spanning continents and ages, a poetic desire that counters Basic's intention to limit and fix the tool of meaning, the tool being not just English, but a limited, controlled version thereof. As Pound insists in *ABC of Reading*, "The sum of human wisdom is not contained in any one language, and no single language is CAPABLE of expressing all forms and degrees of human comprehension. This is a very unpalatable and bitter doctrine. But I cannot omit it."[33]

In spite of his advocacy of polyvocality, however, Pound is also notorious for his manifest desire for the control of meaning and value. His pro-fascist ideology has often been interpreted as a symptom for such a desire. Pound's goal is to use as many linguistic resources as possible but also to arrive at a unified picture, a moment of absolute luminosity, or, to use his own term, "the great ball of crystal."[34] Pound's Imagism, with its emphasis on visual clarity, echoes Richards's description of Basic's panopticism: "*Clear* is one of the key words for any controlled language and we may note here that it has a surprising number of variously relevant senses: bright, unclouded, free from blotches; easily and distinctly heard; able to see or be see distinctly; free from doubt, from guilt; innocent; free from burden, from charges, as in 'clear profit.'"[35]

Speaking of profit, Pound apparently sees a connection between Basic's analytic economy and his own Social Credit theory. The latter is a proposal for the control of monetary value by an authoritarian government. It calls for the replacement of paper money by certificates issued by the government as payment for work. Pound believes that in this way social evils, such as usury, which obscures the nature of monetary and linguistic values, could be rooted out. In this sense, usury would be equivalent to what Bentham has condemned as "fiction," a concept that provided the theoretical foundation for Basic English; and Pound's prescription for social reform is similar to the ones provided by Bentham and his followers, namely, Ogden and Richards. Hence, Pound makes a connection between his economic theory and Basic in his review of Ogden's book.

> My recent condensed recommendation for Social Credit Policy as follows:
>
> 1. Simplification of terminology.
> 2. Articulation of terminology.
> 3. AS MUCH PROPAGANDA AS POSSIBLE SHOULD BE WRITTEN IN BASIC ENGLISH.
> 4. Less tolerance toward converging movements.
> 5. Hammer on root ideas.[36]

By "articulation of terminology," Pound means the ability to "distinguish the root from the branch," a reference to the panoptic design of the Basic vocabulary, in which the center word is the root and the periphery words are merely branches—"hammer on root ideas." In his letter to Ogden on January 28, 1935, Pound wrote, "I proposed starting a nice lively heresy, to effek, that gimme 50 more words and I can make Basic into a real licherary and mule-drivin' language, capable of blowin Freud to hell and gettin' a team from Soap Gulch over Hogback. You watch ole Ez do a basic Canto."[37]

Although Pound's proposed Basic Canto never materialized, some have argued that the principle of Basic is implied in *The Cantos*. The Brazilian poet Haroldo de Campos, whose concretism takes Pound's dictum *Dichten*

= *Condensare* to a new height, sees a clear connection between Pound's poetic work and Basic English. Following Ernest Fenollosa's advocacy of pictorialism embedded in Chinese characters, Pound's ideogrammatic method of composition, as de Campos suggests, brings him close to Basic English. In his preface to Fenollosa's monograph *The Chinese Written Character as a Medium for Poetry*, Pound compares Chinese ideograms to Ogden's Basic vocabulary: "Many of the nouns in the Ogden list of 850 words could very well serve as verbs, thereby giving considerably greater force to that brief vocabulary.... I suggest also that the limited gamut of actions included by Ogden in this essential vocabulary might be considered almost a declension of a yet briefer set of main root possibilities."[38] In this passage, de Campos believes, Pound is making a case for a "basic poetry," one that, modeled on Basic English, "has its lexical potential not as a function of a reduction in language to facilitate semantic communication but as a function of the communication of a poetic product for the accomplishment of which this basic concision is a structural principle." Referring to Pound's letter to Ogden about doing a "basic Cantos," de Campos goes further to suggest:

> This "basic Canto" is implicit in the very ideogrammatic macrostructure of *The Cantos*, where discursive language (from which Pound has not completely dissociated himself) is criticized. As the work progresses, however, along with a stylistic plurality, which aspires to monumental craftsmanship, there occurs a parallel fragmentation of discourse. The device of ideogrammatic montage invades the microstructure of the composition and—beginning with the Pisan Cantos—it can be said that the tension for the "basic Cantos" constantly shows up in details.[39]

Whether or not Pound, in reality or in essence, did strive for a Basic Canto, a similar project, one of welding the simplest language to a literary text whose linguistic complexity resembles *The Cantos*, did work out; and that is the Basic version of James Joyce's *Finnegans Wake*. The Basic English translation of the last four pages of the Anna Livia Plurabelle chapter of *Finnegans Wake* first appeared in Ogden's journal *Psyche* in 1931 and then was republished the next year in the avant-garde literary journal *transition*. Joyce's book, as we know, mixes words from sixty or seventy other languages into its "basically English" vocabulary, and like Pound's Cantos, the novel is excessively allusive in style, referring to everything from the content of the 11th *Britannica* to popular songs, jokes, and gags culled from comic books.[40] As Marshall McLuhan put it, "Joyce is making a mosaic, an Achilles shield, as it were, of all the themes and modes of human speech and communication."[41] To tame such a linguistically diverse text, then, would be the ultimate victory for Basic. The result, however, is far from being what Ogden claims in the introduction to the piece, that "the simplest and most complex languages of man are placed side by side" and that Basic succeeds in being an international language "in which everything may be said."[42] Let's examine some passages.

> *Joyce's original*: Wait till the honeying of the lune, love! Die eve, little eve, die! We see that wonder in your eye.
> *Ogden's translation*: Do not go till the moon is up love. She's dead, little Eve, little Eve she's dead. We see that strange look in your eye.
>
> *Joyce*: Sudds for me and supper for you and the doctor's bill for Joe John.
> *Ogden*: Washing for me, a good meal for you and the chemist's account for Joe John.
>
> *Joyce*: Flittering bats, fieldmice bawk talk.
> *Ogden*: Winged things in flight, field-rats louder than talk.
>
> *Joyce*: Tell me, tell me, tell me, elm! Night night! Telmetale of stem or stone.
> *Ogden*: Say it, say it, tree! Night night! The story say of stem or stone.[43]

In the aforementioned review of Ogden, Pound asserts, "If a novelist can survive translation into Basic, there is something solid under his language."[44] In the case of the Basic translation of *Finnegans Wake*, I leave it to the reader to appraise its success or failure, to decide whether the poetic effects of "the honeying of the lune, love," of "Tell me, tell me, tell me, elm!... Telmetale of stem or stone," and the ambiguity between the German "die" and English "die" have all survived translation; or whether "that strange look in your eye," "a good meal," "the chemist's account," and "winged things in flight" sound more like word riddles than actual translations of "the wonder in your eye," "supper," "the doctor's bill," and "flittering bats," respectively. Joyce's book itself, after all, relies on "punns and reedles" (239). And that may explain Joyce's willingness to cooperate with Ogden on this translation project; that is, rather than seeing the polyvocality of his work absorbed into the neutrality of Basic, Joyce regarded the Basic rendition as a new fragment of the linguistic multiplicity his text intends to incorporate. With its catholic appeal, made possible by its inclusion of something for everyone—a German word here, a French phrase there, even some Chinese pidgin sprinkled into the mix—*Finnegans Wake* seems to have realized the dream that gave birth to Basic: the dream of a universal language. And it has done so by running the opposite course: to be open to all languages, to rebuild Babel.

"Ogden is against 'Babel,' the confusion of many languages," writes Louis Zukofsky in a 1943 essay on Basic.[45] Earlier in his career, Zukofsky had already experimented with a literary project similar to Basic English. Between 1932 and 1934, he worked on a story titled "Thanks to the Dictionary," with its vocabulary limited to page samplings from two dictionaries.[46] In his study of Zukofsky's relation to Basic English, Barret Watten sees "Thanks to the Dictionary" as a reflection of what lies in common between Zukofsky's trademark Objectivism and Basic English: concrete visuality and objectivity of meaning. Watten shrewdly maintains that despite Zukofsky's fondness for poetic objectivity, he was also drawn to the competing aspect of modernist poetics: polysemy.[47] Zukofsky, in his own essay, has already identified the shortcoming of Basic in this respect: "The refreshing differences to be got from different ways of handling facts in the sound and peculiar expressions of different tongues is not to be overlooked, precisely because they have *international* worth."[48] The word stressed by Zukofsky, *international*, was first coined, as Ogden tells us, by Bentham. If Bentham's internationalism, which comes down to us via Basic, relies on the erasure of differences, the kind of internationalism advocated and practiced by Anglo-American modernists, as we see in Eliot, Pound, and Joyce, draws on those very linguistic differences. The poetic language of these modernist texts is often, to use Joyce's words, "a maundarin tongue in a pounderin jowl" (89). I am not quoting Joyce in vain; Mandarin Chinese in a Poundian jowl has continually fascinated these modernists. If Basic targets Word Magic, the poetics of the Chinese language, according to these modernists, draws precisely upon it. Zukofsky, in the same essay, tells a story about the magic effect of the Chinese written characters as an antidote to Basic's instrumentalization of language.

> It was a cold winter afternoon toward sunset. The Chinese laundryman had brought back the week's wash and left. When the package was opened, none of his patron's handkerchiefs were in it. The patron walked back in the cold to tell the laundryman. Without looking up the Chinese laundryman said merely: "Go home, you find." "Maybe you come, you find," the patron answered. "All light," the laundryman said gaily. He went out into the cold without bothering to put on a coat and this move troubled the patron.
>
> In any case, in the house of the man who gives him a week's wash the first act of the Chinese was to go over to the mantelpiece, look at the lot of books and ask: "How much?" "It doesn't much matter," he was told. The laundryman was not interested in looking at the man's linen. "You read English?" the man queried. "No, no savvy."
>
> The man had another kind of book on his desk shelf, one of the pages

> opened to a few Chinese ideographs—the characters resembling men standing with legs apart. The English under the Chinese writing read: "Knowledge is to know men; Humanity is to love them." The man thrust the book onto the laundryman, who responded gaily: "Heh, heh, yeh, handkerchiefs tomorrow!"

Zukofsky draws a moral lesson from the story, with a jab at Basic:

> Evidently the Chinese was not interested in the handkerchiefs that day. And the other man was not a little impressed by the effect on the Chinese of a force that might be sensed as active in the Chinese characters. At any rate, something more active than the man could find that day in a list of 400 *general things* and 200 *picturable*.[49]

The notion of "a force that might be sensed as active in the Chinese characters" would be conceived by Ogden as verbal superstition. But Anglo-American modernists did believe in such a magic force at work in Chinese characters, "something more active" than Basic words. Pound was no Chinese laundryman, and neither was Zukofsky. But the former made a career out of his dealings in Chinese—or laundering Chinese, some might say—and the latter founded the school of Objectivism, which treats words like objects just as the Chinese characters are regarded as natural signs. The question is, Do the Chinese themselves actually believe in the alleged magic of their language? What happens when the Chinese come into contact with a language like Basic, which regards Word Magic as its enemy? To answer these questions, we need to turn to Chinese modernism and witness its encounter with Basic English.

* * *

A better medium should, from the beginning, recognize that disparity (due to differences between Chinese and Western intellectual traditions) between Chinese and Western attitudes to language and its meaning.... It should aim at giving the Chinese learner of English what his own language does not (and perhaps never will) provide him with, an instrument of analytical discrimination between meanings.... The only way in which false and misleading approximations to Western units of meaning with Chinese "equivalents" can be avoided is by giving these meanings through, and together with, an apparatus for comparing meanings—through an explicit analytic language. Such a language is Basic English.

I. A. RICHARDS, *Basic in Teaching: East and West*

The introduction of Basic English to China began with Richards's arrival at Tsing Hua University in 1929. He had been invited as visiting professor to teach freshman English and other subjects in Peking. Paradoxically, Richards's Basic enterprise could not have been launched at a better or worse time in China. The Chinese language reform movement, which had begun in the late nineteenth century, was entering a new era in the late 1920s and early 1930s. The alphabetization of Chinese called for by native Chinese scholars would have dovetailed with the adoption of an imported alphabetic language like Basic. But the problem lies exactly in that it is an imported product, and the Chinese response to Basic reveals the Janus face of Chinese modernity: its simultaneous embracing of and resistance to the West.

Although the alphabetization of Chinese had started as early as 1605 when the Jesuit missionary Matteo Ricci wrote a book in which he annotated Chinese texts with pronunciations in the Roman alphabet, it was not until the late nineteenth century that, as a result of increasing contact and conflict with the West, the Chinese were compelled to rethink the nature of their language and its correlation with the future of Chinese civilization in the world. Diametrically opposite to Anglo-American modernists' idealization of the Chinese written characters, Chinese modernists saw the script as responsible in part for the backwardness of their culture. The lack of a correspondence between writing and speaking, they charged, had created an insurmountable obstacle for developments in rationality, science, and technology, developments direly needed to revitalize China. Unlike their later, more sophisticated views, the proposals they made in the first two decades of the twentieth century were strikingly radical. Qian Xuantong, for instance, a key player in the new cultural movement, called for total abolishment of the Chinese language and the adoption of an alphabetic world language as a lingua franca in China. Qian explained his rationale in this way:

> To abolish Confucianism and to eliminate Taoism is a fundamental way to prevent the fall of China and to allow the Chinese to become a civilized nation in the twentieth century. But a more fundamental way than this is to abolish the written Chinese language, in which Confucian thought and fallacious Taoist sayings are recorded.[50]

The most prominent writer, Lu Xun, had this to say about the very medium in which he wrote and excelled: "Chinese characters constitute a tubercle on the body of China's poor and laboring masses, inside of which the bacteria collect. If one does not clear them out, then one will die. If Chinese characters are not exterminated, there can be no doubt that China will perish."[51] Less radical proposals called for the creation of a system of "symbols for phonetic notation" that would parallel the Chinese script, or a Latin system of spelling that would replace the traditional script. The rationales behind these proposals remained the same: the Chinese language is outdated and therefore needs to be either modernized or abolished.

Such a view would actually fit well with the rationale for promoting Basic in China. As seen in this section's epigraph, Chinese is regarded as a linguistic instrument that is, unlike English, incapable of analytically discriminating between meanings. In *Debabelization*, Ogden quotes a Chinese scholar's characterization of the language to support his own cause.

> Dr. Yen points out that the Chinese language itself is very defective from the standpoint of clearness, accuracy, and logical consequence. "It is a language more appropriate for the expression of poetical and literary fancies than for the conveyance of legal and scientific thought." Time, place, and mode have to be largely implied, or left to the reader to supply. All this, of course, is apart from the well-known absence of scientific terms. (132–33)

Richards identifies another problem, that is, the Chinese attitude toward language and meaning. As Richards explains in the essay "Sources of Conflict":

> The root difficulty is that the fundamental Chinese attitude to statements is unlike that attitude to statements which in the West led to the development of an explicit logic and of that critical reflective examination of meanings which had produced modern scholarship. In brief, the difference is this: The modern Western scholar … devotes himself, first, to determining (as neutrally, consciously and explicitly as possible) what the meaning of a passage is, and second, to discussing by an open and verifiable technique whether it is true or false. But traditional Chinese scholarship has spent its immense resources of memory and ingenuity upon *fitting the passage into* an already accepted framework of meanings.[52]

Richards considers "this tendency to accommodating interpretations" as a formidable obstacle to understanding, resulting in that "the studies made by Chinese in Western subjects do not in general as yet give them … that power of critical neutral examination and understanding which should be their prime purpose." The solution to this problem, Richards believes, is for the Chinese to gain knowledge of Western ideas directly through a Western language rather than through Chinese (mis)translation. Basic English, since it is easy to learn and has a controlled vocabulary, emerges as the best candidate serving this purpose.[53]

In the years after his arrival in Peking in 1929 and before the outbreak of the Sino-Japanese War in 1937, Richards, with the help of his Western and Chinese colleagues at Tsing Hua University, promoted his Basic program quite successfully in China. With grants from the Rockefeller Foundation, which was pursuing its own interests in China at the time, Richards was able to establish the Orthological Institute of China, making connections with similar institutes that Ogden had founded in Britain, India, Japan, and other countries as regional headquarters for Basic English. The institute published Richards's Basic textbook, *First Book of English for Chinese Learners* (1937). A number of Chinese universities and middle schools adopted Basic into their curricula. In May 1937, Richards met with the minister of education and a government-appointed committee and successfully obtained their approval of his program for the teaching of Basic in middle schools nationwide. Were it not for the Japanese invasion two weeks later, which disrupted the work of the Chinese government and led to the abortion of the original plan, the fate of Basic in China might have been a different story.

But attributing the failure of Basic in China solely to an unforeseen historical event may only be wishful thinking. Before its demise in China, Basic had already run into obstacles created by a large number of Chinese modernists who aspired to the West on the one hand but remained loyal to the Chinese language on the other. Among them, Lin Yutang stood out as perhaps the most articulate opponent of Basic. In his November 16, 1933, letter to Richards, R. D. Jameson, director of the Orthological Institute in China, reported on the critical campaign that was being waged by some Chinese writers against Basic. Jameson cited Lin as the "leader of the Anti-Basic Movement" in the Chinese press. He did not provide Richards, who was back in Britain at the time, with details of Lin's objections on the grounds that "from his English articles it does not seem to me that his opposition is particularly serious."[54] But Jameson had apparently been fooled by Lin's idiosyncratically lighthearted, self-mocking style of prose. As I have argued elsewhere, behind Lin's humor lies his most profound critique of the West.[55]

The articles Jameson referred to were Lin's "'Basic English'" and "In Defense of Pidgin English," published a few months earlier in the Chinese-run English weekly, the *China Critic*. At the beginning of the first article, Lin seems willing to acknowledge some merits of Basic: "There is no question of the essential value of such a wise selection of vocabulary for people who must get along with what they have time for and who do not aspire to go into the niceties of the English language."[56] But he is quick to identify problems with Basic, and here he unleashes his sharp barbs of satire that will later earn him a sterling reputation in the United States with his English best sellers. Lin points out that because of the limitation of vocabulary, writing in Basic will inevitably fall into utter circumlocution: "The most fervent image of imagination" becomes "the most burning picture that has existence only in mind"; a "beard" becomes "growth of hair on the face"; and a woman's "breast" becomes a "milk vessel."[57] In terms of humor, however, nothing beats the restaurant menu that Lin designed by using Basic vocabulary.

A BASIC MENU
False soup of swimming animal with round
hard cover
or
Soup of end of male cow
Fish with suggestion of China or the
Peking language
Young cow inside thing nearest the heart
boiled in oil
Fowl that has red thing under mouth, that makes
funny, hard noise and is eaten by Americans on
certain day, taken with apple cooked with sugar
and water, but cold
meat with salt preparation that keeps long time
Hot drink makes heart jump or you don't go to sleep[58]

Imagine yourself sitting down at a Chinese restaurant in the United States and being presented with such a Basic menu. This imagined comical situation may only be compared to the one in which we face the crazy Chinese encyclopedia imagined by Jorge Luis Borges but made famous by Foucault in the preface to *The Order of Things*. In this encyclopedia, "animals are divided into: (a) belonging to the Emperor, (b) embalmed, (c) tame, (d) sucking pigs, (e) sirens, (f) fabulous, (g) stray dogs, (h) included in the present classification, (i) frenzied, (j) innumerable, (k) drawn with a very fine camelhair brush, (l) et cetera, (m) having just broken the water pitcher, (n) that from a long way off look like flies." The Basic Menu mocks the universalist desire to describe culture-specific objects such as turkey and coffee in a different cultural context by adopting a pseudo-universal language. Likewise, the imaginary Chinese encyclopedia supplies a cultural relativist lesson in laughter. "The wonderment of this taxonomy[,] … the exotic charm of another system of thought," writes Foucault, "is the limitation of our own, the stark impossibility of thinking *that*."[59] It is no wonder that Basic has drawn criticism from major proponents of linguistic and cultural relativism like Ludwig Wittgenstein and Benjamin Lee Whorf. The former has famously said that "to imagine a language means to imagine a form of life," and the latter maintains, along with Edward Sapir, that our understanding of the world is conditioned by our own linguistic structure.[60] But Lin's critique of Basic is not based simply on the grounds of linguistic relativism. His advocacy of pidgin, I argue, has outgrown the theoretical framework of linguistic relativism by projecting, in a manner not too dissimilar to *The Cantos* or *Finnegans Wake*, a world of cosmopolitan polyvocality, by reinventing a translocal dialect that has no single, identifiable cultural origin.

As an alternative to Basic, Lin advocates pidgin, which is a mixture of English and Chinese, or simply "Chinglish." According to Lin, Chinglish has at least three advantages over Basic. First, it is much more expressive, as Lin seconds Bernard Shaw's opinion that the pidgin "no can" is a more direct and forceful expression than the "unable" of standard English. "When a lady says she is 'unable' to come, you have a suspicion she may change her mind and perhaps come after all, but when she replies to your request with an abrupt, clear-cut 'no can,' you know you have to reckon without her company." Second, it will have a brighter future than Basic because of its wide base of support: "Advocates of English as an auxiliary international language have often advanced as an argument in its favor the fact that the language is now spoken by over five hundred million people. By this numerical standard, Chinese ought to stand a close second as an international language, since it is spoken by four hundred fifty million, or every fourth human being on earth." Therefore, a mixture of Chinese and English will defeat any language as the lingua franca of the world. Third, if being analytic is a prerequisite for an international language, Chinglish is more analytic than Basic: "The trouble with Basic English is that it is not analytic enough. We find the word 'gramophone,' for instance, circumlocuted in Basic English as 'a polished black disc with a picture of a dog in front of a horn.' In 2400 A.D., we could call it more simply in real pidgin as 'talking box.'" Likewise, "telescope" and "microscope" can simply be called "look-far-glass" and "show-small-glass"; "telegraph," "electric report"; "telephone," "electric talk"; "cinema," "electric picture"; and "radio," "no-wire-electricity."[61]

It is no wonder that, because of Lin's idiosyncratic prose style, Jameson had made light of his objections to Basic. But the notion that the pidginized "look-far-glass" and "no-wire-electricity" are better expressions than standard English's "telescope" and "radio" was a shared belief among Lin's fellow Chinese writers. T. F. Chu, in his essay "This Easy Chinese Language," published in the August 31, 1933, issue of the *China Critic*, also uses these two and other pidgin expressions as examples of Chinese's superiority over English. These new terms that have come into being during China's contact with the West, Chu writes, were all coined by using the principle of "expediency" of the Chinese language.[62] By "expediency," Chu apparently refers to what the linguist Otto Jespersen has characterized as Chinese's capacity for freely and regularly combining short elements of a phrase or sentence. This capacity, Jespersen argues in his influential *Progress in Language* (1894), places Chinese in an advanced stage of linguistic progression, more advanced even than English.[63] Both Chu and Lin concur with Jespersen's thesis, as Lin writes in "In Defense of Pidgin English":

> The whole trend of the development of the English language teaches us that it has been steadily advancing toward the Chinese type. English has triumphed over grammatical nonsense and refused to see sex in a tea cup or a writing desk, as modern French and German still do. It has practically abolished gender, and it has very nearly abolished case. It has now reached a stage where Chinese was perhaps ten thousand years ago.[64]

And Lin goes on to say that "James Joyce and pidgin English will do the rest and complete that historical process until English is as simple and as logical as Chinese."[65] Based on such a comparison, Chu even suggests that an equivalent to Basic English be created in Chinese, perhaps in the hope of making Basic Chinese, rather than Basic English, the international language.[66]

Chu's proposal seems to reveal the nationalist sentiments embedded in the campaign against Basic English, but the issue is more complicated. At the time when Basic was being promoted in China, the advocates of Chinese language reform had already given up their earlier, more radical stances, such as abolishing Chinese altogether and adopting Esperanto or French as China's official language. In the late 1920s and early 1930s, Chinese reformers had concentrated on two proposals: *Gwoyeu Romatzyh* and *Latinxua Sin Wenz*. Both proposals took a pragmatic, ambivalent approach to China's linguistic modernization: they call for, on the one hand, abandoning the Chinese script, which has been the bastion of traditional Chinese culture; but they want to preserve, on the other hand, the Chinese language in its spoken form, preventing any potential takeover by a foreign language, such as Basic English. Such an insistence on the vocal, the vernacular, even as the written script is being replaced in a wholesale manner by a Western alphabet, not only reveals the excruciating pain accompanying China's social modernization but also raises an interesting perspective on the alternative roads that lead to the linguistic modernity of different cultures, an important issue I address in chapter 5, where Lin appears again with his Chinese typewriter.[67]

I call Chinglish a "translocal dialect" because it not only transcends geographic boundaries but also unsettles the putative connection between a dialect and a localized, romanticized origin. Unlike Fukienese, Lin's native dialect, or Cantonese, the other dominant dialect among Chinese Americans, which often functions as a natural bond for the immigrant community, Chinglish is an invented vernacular in the sense that it only resembles various versions of pidgin that are used in real life. In fact, Chinglish, as Lin imagined, exists mostly as a literary language, which is not to say that it has no sociological basis or has no effect in real life—as if literature were not part of real life. In literature, the use of a specific language and style is often a result of a conscious decision made by the writer. But I am more interested in the creation of a particular literary code than the adoption of a preexisting one.

In his essay "Poetics of the Americas" in *My Way*, Charles Bernstein distinguishes between dialectical writing and ideolectical writing. By "dialectical writing," he means a language practice that refuses allegiance to, say, standard English but still bases its norm on an affiliation with a definable group's speaking practice. By "ideolectical writing," he refers to an ideologically informed nonstandard language practice that rejects both standard English and any localized, group-based linguistic norm. "Dialect," writes Bernstein, "has a centripetal force, regrouping often denigrated and dispirited language practices around a common center; ideolect, in contrast, suggests a centrifugal force, moving away from normative practices without necessarily replacing them with a new center of gravity."[68] Chinglish may be regarded as an example of ideolectical writing, which, as Bernstein insists, has no easily identifiable marker of group identity or authenticity. And that may indeed explain why for many years Lin Yutang has been criticized by the canon makers of Asian American literature for adopting a seemingly lighthearted, Chinglish style of writing, a style they believe to be symptomatic of his capitulation to the stereotype imposed on Asian Americans as weak-minded, incompetent speakers of English.[69] What they have missed is not only the critical edge of Chinglish against linguistic standardization, an issue to which I turn in a minute, but also the significant ways in which literature engages social reality, not by means of representation or reinforcement of identitarian representation, but by exploring the possibilities of such representation, refusing to be bound to the restrictions of rationalized ordering systems. Literature can be, in Bernstein's words, "a process of thinking rather than a report of things already settled; an investigation of figuration rather than a picture of something figured out."[70] The practice of dialectical writing may have its tremendous political edge against linguistic standardization, but its centripetal pull towards a new center reminds us of the very trap into which part of Anglo-American modernism is falling. As I discussed earlier, despite its desire for openness and fragmentation, Anglo-American modernism also has a penchant for control. If by "nonstandard" we only mean different but controllable, then I would rather it be different and exploratory.

Having discussed how Chinglish as a translocal dialect deviates from dialectism's local norms, I would now like to address how it deflates Basic English's global dreams. Chinglish, in short, goes against the grain of Basic English in two ways. First, it constitutes a Chinese response to English's linguistic imperialism, a response that originates in part from nationalism. But I am more interested in the second aspect, in Chinglish as a critique of English not from without but from within. That is, the question of Chinglish is not simply an issue of China versus the West, but a Chinese American issue. Basic, as I said, is a "controlled" language, and the word *control* should be understood by its etymology, "to check or verify, and hence regulate; or to check by comparison, and test the accuracy of" (*OED*). In other words, Basic is an extreme version of standardization, resembling in essence a project of linguistic purification that gained great momentum in modern Anglo-America. The publication of the *Oxford English Dictionary* was the best example of linguistic purification and codification against the onslaught on English by immigrants who flooded into the colonial centers and by the colonial subjects who had adopted and, in the eyes of the purists, "abused" the colonial language. Basic shared such a fear of contamination. In *Practical Criticism*, a book that paved the road for the founding of New Criticism, Richards already expressed concerns with the "decline in speech," which he believed was caused by the increased size of "communities" and the mixtures of culture. We must, writes Richards, "defend ourselves from the chaos that threatens us by stereotyping and standardizing both our utterances and our interpretations. And this threat, it must be insisted, can only grow greater as world communications, through the wireless and otherwise, improve."[71] And he repeated such a line of reasoning in *Basic English and Its Uses*, suggesting that "Basic English, by providing invulnerable but adequate substitutes for [those] more delicate instruments, can serve our language as a fender. It can guard full English from those who will blur all its lines and blunt all its edges if they try to write and talk it before they have learned to read it."[72]

When such a fear of linguistic contamination reaches an extreme, even Basic itself will be regarded as a potential danger to English. One objection that came from Western linguists was that Basic runs the risk of becoming a pidgin. Pidgin, by definition, "represents a language which has been stripped of everything but the bare essentials necessary for communication. There are few, if any, stylistic options. The emphasis is on the referential or communicative rather than the expressive function of language."[73] These features of pidgin eerily resemble those of Basic. Hence,

F. R. Leavis, who extolled his Cambridge mentor Richards as a locus classicus in literary criticism and a leader in the elitist campaign against popular culture, had this to say about Basic in *Mass Civilization and Minority Culture* (1930):

> No one aware of Shakespeare's language can view quite happily the interest taken by some of the most alert minds of our day in such a scheme as "Basic English." This instrument, embodying the extreme of analytical economy, is, of course, intended for a limited use. But what hope is there that the limits will be kept? If "Basic English" proves as efficacious as it promises it will not remain a mere transition language for the Chinese. What an excellent instrument of education it would make, for instance, in the English-speaking countries! And, if hopes are fulfilled, the demand for literature in "Basic English" will grow to vast dimensions as Asia learns how to use this means of access to the West. It seems incredible that the English language as used in the West should not be affected, especially in America, where it is so often written as if it were not native to the writer, and where the general use of it is so little subject to control by sentimental conservatism.[74]

I want to flatter myself by thinking that the frightening American scene Leavis alerts us to would include me and my writing at this moment in a language that *is*, rather than "as if it were," not native to me. In this sense, Leavis was quite prophetic, because after all, I *am* a product of Basic English, I have used what I learned from VOA's Special English programs to access the West, and now I am trying in my however limited way to tinker with Shakespeare's language. But I am humbled by the realization that my tinkering has not been as successful as what was done by those immigrants chastised by Henry James in his famous 1905 lecture, "The Question of Our Speech." These immigrants, James said, "play, to their heart's content, with the English language, or in other words, dump their mountain of promiscuous material into the foundations of the American."[75]

James's "mountain of promiscuous material" reminds me of what Milton Murayama has characterized as the "shit pyramid" in Hawaii. In *All I Asking for Is My Body*, Murayama describes a pyramidal structure that is at once monetary (different people receive wages according to different pay scales), spatially sanctioned in the layout of the plantation (a tiered housing system in which descending levels of the pyramid housed different ethnic groups), and linguistic (a scale that descends variously from standard English to pidgin English, from standard Japanese to pidgin Japanese, etc.). Even shit was organized according to the plantation pyramid, hence the term "shit pyramid."[76] But such linguistic stratification, which would have pleased James, is no longer stable. Let me refer you to a poem by the Hawaii-based Japanese American writer Lois-Ann Yamanaka. Yamanaka is well known for her use of pidgin. In this poem, titled "Tita: Boyfriends," the teenage speaker switches between Hawaiian Creole English and what might be called standard American California Valley Girl English (one can hear that accent in Yamanaka's oral performance of the poem).

> Richard wen' call me around 9:05 last night.
> Nah, I talk *real* nice to him.
> Tink I talk to him the way I talk to you?
> You cannot let boys know your true self.
> Here, this how I talk.
> *Hello, Richard. How are you?*
> *Oh, I'm just fine. How's school?*
> *My classes are just greeaat.*
> *Oh, really. Uh-huh, uh-huh.*
> *Oh, you're so funny.*
> *Yes, me too, I* love *C and K.*
> *Kalapana? Uh-huh, uh-huh.*

One of the effects of the dramatic code-switching is that the standard and Creole languages become opaque to each other: neither can the former claim to be the "better" language, one that stands at the top of the shit pyramid, nor can the latter celebrate its often-romanticized authenticity of local color.[77] In other words, both become marked, restricted languages, in the same way as Basic English loses its transparency as a lingua franca and runs the risk of becoming merely a pidgin, or yet another translocal dialect.

In *Bilingual Aesthetics*, Doris Sommer points out that linguists and anthropologists have often worried that code-switching is "a symptom of deficiency in one language or the other, since they assumed that switches are triggered by the demands of referential 'efficiency.'" What these experts fail to understand, Sommer argues, is that switches are often initiated not by virtue of a lack but as a performance. "Bilingualism makes mischief with meaning," she writes. "When more than one word point to a familiar thing, the excess shows that no one word can own or be that thing. Several contending words point, each imperfectly."[78] Or, as Gertrude Stein, a modernist poet who grew up speaking Yiddish and English, suggests in *Tender Buttons*, a work full of double entendres between English and French, "it is so earnest to have a green point not to red but to point again."[79]

Ultimately, the pitfall of a universalist project like Basic English lies not in its trust in language but in not trust enough. "Language is too much and not enough," Sommer reminds us, because no one language is enough.[80] In his study of parallel poetics as found in Mayan, Chinese, and other traditions, Dennis Tedlock shows that "a single proper name ... is likely to be denied self-sufficiency." Interestingly, Mayan poets dispel the properness of names by multiplying them. Working against the orthodox New Critical position of I. A. Richards and Cleanth Brooks of protecting the meaning of poems from the "heresy of paraphrase," Tedlock maintains that "for poets in other worlds, paraphrase has never been a heresy and translation has never been treasonous," because one way to conceptualize translation is to think of it as words from two different languages "dividing an object between them."[81] Dreaming to become a tool of perfect communication for all so that, as Ogden intends, "there may be less chance of war, and less learning of languages," Basic English sets out from the wrong premise of finding that one, single, unmistakable isomorphism between words and the world, failing to understand that, to quote Sommer again, "error is a part of meaning, not apart from it. From this perspective, knowing more than one language is humbling, because two languages make each other precarious." Contrary to the premise of Basic, which, as we will see later in the book, became an inspiration for the cybernetic imagination in the post–World War II era, literary scholars like Sommer, Tedlock, and Bernstein help us understand that "a level of ambivalence between or among intimate but precarious codes" might actually deter conflict rather than cause it.[82]

* * *

We have lingered in the chambers of the sea
By sea-girls wreathed with seaweed red and brown
Till human voices wake us, and we drown.

T. S. ELIOT, "The Love Song of J. Alfred Prufrock"

till other voices wake
us or we drown

GEORGE OPPEN, "Till Other Voices Wake Us"

Against Eliot's scene of awakening and drowning by human voices and in the spirit of Oppen's resolute revision by adding a conjunctive "or," I want to describe another scene, not again of my listening to the VOA as a teenager but after it. On hot summer nights in the South, I often slept outside our house, on a bamboo bed set up by the cobblestone street, canopied by a white, translucent mosquito net. At dawn, I was always awakened by the noise of fruit and vegetable farmers bargaining with traders at the nearby marketplace. Typical of southern China's linguistic diversity, these people used multiple dialects to haggle with one another, dialects that were not all comprehensible to me, although the morning air, reeking of overripe fruit, rotten vegetable, and the muddy tang of the river, remained a familiar mélange.

Somewhere in *Remembrance of Things Past*, Marcel Proust recalls himself lying awake at dawn and listening to the noises made by street vendors, a cacophony that penetrates his Parisian bedchamber: the horn of a china repairer, the trumpet of a chair mender, the flute of a goatherd, the intonation of an old clothes-man brandishing a whip, and the rattling refrain of a shepherd carrying a bull's pizzle in his hand. The noises remind Proust of Gregorian chants, causing him to weave a meandering passage of observations and recollections in the novel, comparing the Parisian street cries and those liturgical diversions.[83] In my case, however, at those almost Proustian moments when I hovered between dream and reality, I was not thinking of any liturgy, Gregorian or Buddhist. Instead, I was overcome by a weird feeling: I had just woken up in a foreign land, where its people spoke in foreign tongues.

As I discuss in the next chapter, when Marco Polo, the great medieval globetrotter, mentioned those foreign places with strange customs that he had visited, he repeatedly characterized them with a formulaic statement, almost like a refrain: "The people are idolaters, burn their dead, use paper money, and have a peculiar language." The peculiarity of a language or dialect, noticeable only to outsiders, is a line separating the insiders from the outsiders, the familiar from the foreign. For the younger me to realize the strangeness of our local dialects, in other words, the strangeness of home, even though I had not yet ventured once beyond the county line at that age, was probably not caused solely by the dreamy state I was in. Apparently, the English on the Voice of America, a truly foreign language to me, had begun, however subtly and slowly, to exert influence on me, turning the domestic and familiar into something foreign and uncanny. In some ways, if the VOA was transporting me to a world of cosmopolitanism that existed at the time only in my prepubescent imagination, the babbling noises from the local market had already revealed to me the truth about the cosmopolitan world in which I would one day wish to live. It is a world that speaks, if I may quote Joyce again, "a maundarin tongue in a pounderin jowl."

Listening to Marco Polo

[CHAPTER TWO]

Sound, Money, and Vernacular Imagination

To be listening is always to be on the edge of meaning . . . a resonant meaning, a meaning whose sense is supposed to be found in resonance, and only in resonance.

JEAN-LUC NANCY, *Listening*

Less an essay than a meditation, this chapter proceeds somewhat circuitously, like echoes bouncing off a wall, and ponders the poetics of sound and the increasingly acoustic quality of value, truth, and reality in the twenty-first century, what some have characterized as an auscultation of the world.[1]

I would begin with a return, or rather, re-tune, to the frequently read but seldom heard prologue to Marco Polo's famous book of travel to Asia, a passage in which the speaker makes a plea that we *listen* to the book. The acoustic truth, to which the book's narrator has begged us to attend, finds reverberations—not necessarily reconfirmations, mind you—throughout this chapter in Italo Calvino's *Invisible Cities*, Kublai Khan's paper money, the British Romantics' poetic imagination, twenty-first-century cryptocurrency, and, ultimately, in the idea and practice of cosmopolitanism. Whether in the case of cities that are invisible but audible where the emperor's words that have acquired gold-like quality or the financial market where reality is not objectively visible like signals but intersubjective like echoes, my primary concern is with the poetics of sound, or rather, a world of sounds out of the earshot of our logic-based, vision-biased, and tone-deaf rationality.

In the fantastic tales of Calvino, we see the pitfalls of an empire built on the principle of spatial conquest: the Great Khan insists on hearing the cities he has conquered, as if only sound could reveal the ultimate truth of places dotting the map of his sprawling empire. Poetic imagination as defined by the Romantics, as we will see, shares with imperial ambitions a preference for vision. To escape such vision-ary constraints, following the concept of translocal dialect formulated in the preceding chapter, I propose vernacular imagination as a gesturing toward a mode of being in the world built on both vision and sound, a mode of worlding that is both mimetic and methexic. As Jean-Luc Nancy asks in his profound meditation on the poetics of sound and art of listening, "Shouldn't truth 'itself,' as transitivity and incessant transition of a continual coming and going, be listened to rather than seen?"[2] Perhaps Plato's parable about shadows in a cave should be reevaluated. Rather than turn around, as Plato advises us to do, and hope to see the real, we need to listen to the echoes reverberating in the cave. In fact, scholars of prehistoric cave paintings have discovered an interesting phenomenon: a vast majority of those images (Platonic shadows?) are "in spots where the acoustics are particularly unusual." In other words, those prehistoric artists did not select rock surfaces by accident, but they chose the spots "where echoes are strongest or where sounds carry furthest."[3] In these acoustic spaces, we hear the sound bites of reality as echoes of dreams, moneyed thoughts uttered in local currencies, and clashes of empires as a result of a few misheard words.

Acoustic Truths

The book of Marco Polo, in the words of one of his most recent detractors, sounds like "a Chinese whisper translated from Persian." The strangeness of the language, which Frances Wood and others regard as part of the evidence that the infamous Merchant of Venice actually never went to China, speaks nonetheless to the acoustic truths of Marco Polo.[4] The genesis of the book, as we know, was an oral event, a dictation. While imprisoned in Genoa, Polo asked his fellow inmate, Messer Rusticiano, to commit his oral narratives to writing. In case the reader should miss the acoustics of the book, the prologue duly contains a recommendation and a caveat.

> Great Princes, Emperors, and Kings, Dukes and Marquises, Counts. Knights, and Burgesses! and People of all degrees who desire to get knowledge of the various races of mankind and of the diversities of the sundry regions of the World, take this Book and *cause it to be read to you*. For ye shall find therein all kinds of wonderful things . . . according to the description of Messer Marco Polo, a wise and noble citizen of Venice, as he *saw them with his own eyes*. Some things indeed there be therein which he *beheld not*; but these he *heard* from men of credit and veracity. And we shall set down things *seen as seen*, and things *heard as heard* only, so that no jot of falsehood may mar the truth of our Book, and that all who shall read it or *hear* it read may put full faith in the truth of all its contents.[5]

Undetected by most commentators, the speaker here is careful to distinguish between "things seen" and "things heard," between cognizable facts and reliable hearsays. Perhaps to intensify the effects of the latter, he recommends that it is best to hear the book with ears, as does the Great Khan in Italo Calvino's fantastic book, who prefers to listen to the "invisible cities." Being invisible does not condemn the cities to the realm of nowhere; cities, like truths, may be audible, or tactile, existing in the "soundscape," a term first popularized by the Canadian musician R. Murray Schafer in the 1970s, a more elegant variation of Marshall McLuhan's concept "acoustic space."

The book of Marco Polo, then, is built on acoustic signals as much as on visual signs. Names of places, persons, and objects are heard mostly in their Persian, Mongol, or Turkish sounds rather than their Chinese counterparts: *Cathay*, *Cambaluc*, *Pulisanghin*, *Tangut*, *Chagannor*, *Saianfu*, *Kenjanfu*, *Tenduc*, *Acbalec*, *Carajan*, *Zardandan*, *Zayton*, *Kemenfu*, *Brius*, *Caramoran*, *Chorcha*, and *Juju* (*Polo*, vol. 1, 111). The foreignness of the proper names creates tremendous difficulties for annotators to ascertain the exact reference, as if the referents existed only in sound. "Falsehood is never in words," asserts Calvino's Marco Polo, "it is in things."[6] Commenting on the French, supposedly the first, copy of the narrative, Henry Yule notices that in the book's style, apart from grammar or vocabulary, there is "a rude angularity, a rough dramatism like that of oral narrative." The frequent change in spelling of the same proper names, occurring sometimes within only a few lines, is especially indicative of "the unrevised product of dictation," a tale caught by ear first and fixed by pen later (*Polo*, vol. 1, 83–84).

The acoustic markers that draw us into the presence of the narration, that disappear faster than they appear, meet their echoes in "a marvelous thing" Polo describes that dwells in a Chinese desert.

> When travelers are on the move by night, and one of them chances to lag behind or to fall asleep or the like, when he tries to gain his company again he will hear spirits talking, and will suppose them to be his comrades. Sometimes the spirits will call him by name; and thus shall a traveler ofttimes be led astray so that he never finds his party. And in this way many have perished. [Sometimes the stray travelers will hear as it were the tramp and hum of a great cavalcade of people away from the real line of road, and taking this to be their own company they will follow the sound; and when day breaks they find that a cheat has been put on them and that they are in an ill plight.] Even in the day-time one hears those spirits talking. And sometimes you shall hear the sound of a variety of musical instruments, and still more commonly the sound of drums. (*Polo*, vol. 1, 197)

It is striking that Polo here describes an acoustic illusion rather than an optical one. A mirage, which travelers often encounter in deserts, is an illusory image of something that actually exists ("a deceptive image of a distant object formed by light that is refracted as it passes through air of varying temperature"—*OED*). But this "sound mirage," which occurs in a desert and is known in China by the name of *Lew-sha*, "Quicksand" or "Flowing Sands" (*Polo*, vol. 1, 198), cannot be seen but only heard in one's head, unverifiable and yet irresistibly hypnotizing.

In *The Global Village* (1989), Marshall McLuhan and Bruce R. Powers try to differentiate acoustic space from visual space: "The left-hemisphere [of the human brain] places information structurally in visual space, where things are connected sequentially—having separate centers with fixed boundaries. On the other hand, acoustic space structure, the function of the right brain in which processes are related simultaneously, has centers everywhere with boundaries nowhere." The nature of the human eye, which gave birth to linear logic, encourages reasoning by exclusion: something is either in that space or it isn't. By contrast, sounds can be neither inside nor outside, and they function less like signals than replies. If the visual space may be compared to a painting or a photograph, the acoustic space may be likened to a symphonic surround.[7]

The elusiveness of acoustic truth may be further fathomed by an ingenious mechanism that Jeremy Bentham envisaged along with his infamous Panopticon but never fully developed. As discussed in the preceding chapter, Bentham's Panopticon consists of a circular building where the observer occupies the center while the prisoners are placed in cells on the circumference separated from each other by the radii of the circle. By virtue of the architectural design, the Panopticon, in the words of Michel Foucault, "is a machine for dissociating the see/being seen dyad: in the peripheric ring, one is totally seen, without ever seeing; in the central tower, one sees everything without ever being seen."[8] It turns out that in tandem with the all-seeing machine, Bentham also attempted a design of an all-hearing apparatus, something that may be called the Panacousticon. He envisioned a small tin tube reaching from each cell to the Inspector's Lodge, and "by means of this implement, the slightest whisper of the one might be heard by the other." As Peter Szendy puts it in *All Ears*, "What Bentham imagines here as an addition or a supplementary accessory to his Panopticon is a simultaneously pandirectional and selective megaphone of sorts: a Panacousticon that facilitates communication and transmission between observer and observed in the context of efficiently organized labor."[9] Foucault also notices the panacoustic extension of the control mechanism, but more important, he identifies a fatal flaw in the design, which forced Bentham to abandon the idea: "Bentham had also imagined an acoustic surveillance, operated by means of pipes leading from the cells to the central tower. In the *Postscript* he abandoned the idea, perhaps because he could not introduce into it the principle of dissymmetry and prevent the prisoners from hearing the inspector as well as the inspector hears them."[10] In other words, Bentham had trouble with acoustically insulating those tin tubes so that sound would travel in only one direction, as did those visual sunbeams in a Panopticon. In relation to sound, as Szendy puts it, "there is no stable or stabilized point of listening fixed in a panacoustic edifice."[11] The acoustic truth remains as open-ended, relational as a two-way street.

From the Invisible (Cities) to the Intangible (Economy)

The visible world is no longer a reality and the unseen world is no longer a dream.

WILLIAM BUTLER YEATS

The Great Khan waged a war on uncertainties as they loom in the entanglement between an acoustic signal and its even more elusive referent. In Calvino's *Invisible Cities*, the Khan begins by listening to the Venetian Merchant's tales with some skepticism: "Kublai Khan does not necessarily believe everything Marco Polo says when he describes the cities visited on his expeditions, but the emperor of the Tartars does continue listening to the young Venetian with greater attention and curiosity than he shows any other messenger or explorer of his." Soon the emperor becomes impatient and interrupts Polo: "From now on I shall describe the cities and you will tell me if they exist and are as I have conceived them." If there still is something iffy in the Khan's conception—his voiced words may or may not materialize in real cities, because they are still subject to the listener's verification—then the other scheme of his would make his words "achieve cities too probable to be real."[12] And that scheme is the making of paper money.

In this famous chapter of Marco Polo's narrative, like in a modern-day techno-Orientalist fantasy, the Khan becomes an alchemist, a conjuror, who renders his words the equivalent to all the treasure in the world.

> The Emperor's Mint then is in this same city of Cambaluc, and the way it is wrought is such that you might say he hath the Secret of Alchemy in perfection, and you would be right! For he makes his money after this fashion.
>
> He makes them take of the bark of a certain tree, in fact of the Mulberry Tree, the leaves of which are the food of the silkworms,—these trees being so numerous that whole districts are full of them. What they take is a certain fine white bast or skin which lies between the wood of the tree and the thick outer bark, and this they make into something resembling sheets of paper, but black. When these sheets have been prepared they are

> cut up into pieces of different sizes. The smallest of these sizes is worth a half tornesel; the next, a little larger, one tornesel; one, a little larger still, is worth half a silver groat of Venice; another a whole groat; others yet two groats, five groats, and ten groats. There is also a kind worth one Bezant of gold, and others of three Bezants, and so up to ten. All these pieces of paper are [issued with as much solemnity and authority as if they were of pure gold or silver; and on every piece a variety of officials, whose duty it is, have to write their names, and to put their seals. And when all is prepared duly, the chief officer deputed by the Kaan smears the Seal entrusted to him with vermilion, and impresses it on the paper, so that the form of the Seal remains printed upon it in red; and Money is then authentic. Any one forging it would be punished with death.] And the Kaan causes every year to be made such a vast quantity of this money, which costs him nothing, that it must equal in amount all the treasure in the world. (*Polo*, vol. 1, 423–24)

The secret of the Khan's alchemy lies in the "as if" effect: "as if they were of pure gold or silver." And the key to the success of the poetic conflation is to rid of the "iffiness" and turn "as if" into simply "as." This is a verbal trickery Calvino's Khan is unable to perform because his futuristic descriptions of cities have yet to be verified by Marco Polo: "It is not the voice that commands the story: it is the ear."[13] In Polo's narrative, however, the Khan becomes King of Midas; his words, as deputed by his officials, change into gold when they fall onto sheets of paper. His voice is not just golden; it is as good as gold. It is gold.

It is not a sci-fi tale or speculative fiction that voices, words, and other intangible things acquire the power of creating wealth or become wealth itself.[14] A socioeconomic reality in Khan's empire or any society where there is an uneven power structure, it is an essential feature of what we in the twenty-first century have called the "intangible economy." In our postindustrial age, an identifiable shift from the tangible to the intangible has taken place. The economic landscape is no longer shaped by physical flows of material goods and products but by ethereal streams of data, images, and symbols. Whereas at the core of the agricultural economy was a relationship between man, nature, and natural products, and at the core of the industrial economy was a relationship between man, machine, and machine-created artificial objects, the intangible economy is structured around relationships between man and ideas and symbols. Ezra Pound, whose economic outlook is largely agrarian and industrial, not only promotes the image of 農精米 (Farmer pounds rice), but also writes the following in *The Cantos* to insist on the industrial production of value:

> A factory
> has also another aspect, which we call the financial aspect
> It gives people the power to buy (wages, dividends
> which are power to buy) but it is also the cause of prices
> or values, financial, I mean financial values.[15]

Today, however, the source of economic value and wealth is no longer the production of material goods but the creation and manipulation of intangible content.[16] In fact, most developed nations highly depend on intangible, information-based assets, information-intensive services (business and property services, communications, finance and insurance, and entertainment), and information-oriented public sectors (education, public administration, and health care). By 2010, in each member of the G7 group, at least 70 percent of its gross domestic product (GDP) depended on intangible goods, not on material goods.[17]

The Khan is apparently a forerunner of such intangible economy with his boundless ability to create and manipulate signs and their relationship to reality/value. In some sense, the name of the Khan is a most precious intangible asset. Like a name brand in our postindustrial age, the value of such an asset is beyond calculation, or is indeed, as Polo observes admiringly and jealously, "equal in amount to all the treasure in the world." In the case of the Khan, value is determined not by the weight of gold and silver but by his words, voices, seals, and so on; in the case of a postindustrial company, value is calculated not by its output of material production but by its brand, human capital, intellectual property, knowledge, and above all the ever-fickle pricing of its stocks. In the words of Christian Marazzi, as he tries to describe a post-Fordist world in which value is being generated by a linguistic machine through communication and interpretation:

> Communication and production overlap, and in fact they are now one and the same. In Fordism communication excluded production and the assembly line was silent, mechanically executing the directions established by the white collar managers. Now, however, in post-Fordism, we have a "speaking," "communicating" production process, and the technologies used in this system can be considered true "linguistic machines," whose main focus is to facilitate and accelerate the circulation of data.[18]

Such dematerialization of value is deeply unsettling because it runs squarely against some of the key tenets of the conventional logic of economy: "Conventional logic is concerned with scarcity, dematerialization logic with abundance. The former stresses equilibrium; the latter, disequilibrium. Obsolescence, redundancy and volatility, perceived in the past as pernicious epiphenomena, now constitute essential and necessary vectors."[19] The most unsettling thing about such dematerialization, however, is the emergence of the concept of truth that is no longer cognizable but fleeting, flying, audible, tactile, and, above all, participatory.

In his reflections upon the crisis of global capitalism, the billionaire and philanthropist George Soros points out that truth nowadays is not—even if it ever were—cognizable but instead is participatory: "We have come to treat correspondence as the hallmark of truth. But correspondence can be brought about in two ways: either by making true statements or by making an impact on the facts themselves. Correspondence is not the guarantor of truth." Especially in the world of global capital, cognizable truths, something the narrator in Polo's book painstakingly tries to differentiate from audible hearsays, become interactive mirages that change according to the actions of the observer. Soros writes, "Physical objects move the way they move irrespective of what anybody thinks. But financial markets attempt to predict a future that is contingent on the decisions people make in the present. Instead of just passively reflecting reality, financial markets are actively creating the reality that they, in turn, reflect. There is a two-way connection between present decisions and future events, which I call reflexivity."[20]

Such reflexivity would place value and truth less in the visual space, which is dominated by linear logic and abstraction, than in the acoustic space, where sounds, to quote McLuhan and Powers again, flow more like replies than signals. In their study of the history of media, McLuhan and Powers consider the invention of paper money as a major step toward the acoustic and intangible: "Cash money and the compass, leading technologies of the fifteenth century, illustrate early figure-ground transformations of visual space archetypes to the acoustic, from the tangible to the intangible, from hardware dominance to software dominance—analogous to the present role of the computer. The current shift from visual space to acoustic space technologies in society is accelerating."[21] And their investigation of the "global village" concludes with a description of the Electronic Funds Transfer System (EFTS) as an acoustic space, a world of the simultaneous, whose center is everywhere and margin nowhere. It is in this acoustic world that a modern-day Cinderella was born: virtual money.

From "Flying Money" to "Daylight Money"

When evening came Cinderella wanted to leave, and the prince tried to escort her, but she ran away from him so quickly that he could not follow her. The prince, however, had set a trap.

He had had the entire stairway smeared with pitch. When she ran down the stairs, her left slipper stuck in the pitch. The prince picked it up. It was small and dainty, and of pure gold.

JACOB AND WILHELM GRIMM, "Cinderella"

Virtual money is a kind of money that circles around the globe without a permanent, cognizable interface but whose effect is world-changing. It enabled, for instance, Soros to make a fortune of five billion dollars within a few months in 1992 by successfully shorting the British pounds. It is a money that is never to be touched, held, or seen, that is always in motion, "in the form of brief pulses of light that glide outward through cyberspace like ripples in a pond."[22] It also includes plastic money, credit and debit cards, the e-money used in the internet trade, and the quickly proliferating forms of cryptocurrency. Virtual money is often compared to a virtual particle in quantum mechanics, a particle that, according to Stephen Hawking, "can never be directly detected, but whose existence does have measurable effects."[23] And virtual money's effects are indeed astonishing if we would just consider these facts. The value of foreign currency trading, which is conducted almost exclusively in cyberspace, averaged $1.1 trillion a day in 2000, more than fifty times greater than the daily physical trade volume and thirty times greater than the combined volume of all US equity markets. At present, the relative weight of noncash monetary transactions exceeds the value of cash money by a factor of ten. Money and payments are almost entirely delivered via electronic networks as data bits and database entries.[24]

That mobile digital bits have replaced cash money is not, however, such a far cry from the invention of so-called flying money, which existed in China almost two thousand years ago and to which historians have attributed the origin of Khan's paper money. The Chinese 飛錢 *feiqian*, or flying money, was essentially a draft to transmit funds to distant places. In the Tang dynasty (618–907), there emerged large-scale commercial activities, of which the most spectacular was the tea trade between southern China and Chang'an, the Tang capital, in the north. The tea merchants wished to transfer profits realized from the sale of tea in the north back to the south but found the shipment of cash both cumbersome and perilous. The same problem of transfer faced the provincial authorities who were obliged to send monetary tribute and gifts to the imperial court. These authorities maintained in the capital liaison offices known as "memorial-presenting courts," whose duty in part was to expedite presentation of gifts. The transfer problem was solved by the institution flying money, whereby merchants deposited cash with the "memorial-presenting courts," in return for vouchers guaranteeing reimbursement in designated provinces.

Thereby a double transfer of cash was realized without an actual physical transfer. Hence the picturesque name "flying money."[25]

Almost all forms of modern-day virtual money are flying money of sorts because they all share the feature of mobility. But the queen among them, the form that represents the epitome of intangible economy, is "daylight money." Imagine a bank sending money by wire but being over its credit cap; in the United States (and in many other countries) the bank can borrow on overdraft but must pay back the sum within the day. These funds, existing only as figures on computer screens, live essentially on borrowed time. But before their inevitable end-of-day demise, they can buy and sell just as "real" money does. "Like Cinderella at the ball," writes Elinor Harris Solomon, the daylight money "has but a certain length of time in which to play. It buys and sells assets, whether currencies or thirty-year Treasury bonds. It stirs things up in markets and responds to expectation shifts. In a brief time span, it captures not a prince but a profits prize."[26] When the bell rings—not the midnight bell at the Prince's ball, but the closing bell of a business day—the virtual money vanishes in a cloud of settlement dust, only to arise again like the sun the next (business) morning.

Imagination: A Romantic Detour

In Xanadu did the Kubla Khan
A stately pleasure-dome decree:
Where Alph, the sacred river, ran
Through caverns measureless to man
  Down to a sunless sea.
So twice five miles of fertile ground
With walls and towers were girdled round:
And there were gardens bright with sinuous rills
Where blossomed many an incense-bearing tree;
And here were forests ancient as the hills,
Enfolding sunny spots of greenery.
SAMUEL TAYLOR COLERIDGE, "Kubla Khan"

Like money that is mobile, a romantic poet's mind can also travel long distances. For the poem "Kubla Khan," Coleridge provided a note of explanation: "In the summer of the year 1797, the Author, then in ill health, had retired to a lonely farm house between Porlock and Linton, on the Exmoor confines of Somerset and Devonshire. In consequence of a slight indisposition, an anodyne had been prescribed, from the effect of which he fell asleep in his chair at the moment that he was reading the following sentence, or words of the same substance, in *Purchas's Pilgrimage*: 'Here the

Khan Kubla commanded a palace to be built, and a stately garden thereunto: and thus ten miles of fertile ground were inclosed with a wall.'"[27]

The poet is meticulous about the local details, "a lonely farm house between Porlock and Linton, on the Exmoor confines of Somerset and Devonshire," partly because he wants to foreground the poetic mind's extraordinary capacity to travel across space and time and land itself in an Oriental palace centuries ago. Coleridge uses the phrase "words of the same substance" because his quote from Purchas is not exact.[28] If faithful duplication is the mode of validation of a culture of print, to which Coleridge rightly belongs, here he is apparently more concerned with the "substance" that underlies words, visions, dreams, and realities.[29] He disregards the laws of print for a good reason: he is following a higher law, the law of imagination. Coleridge is the one who has provided us with the quintessential Romantic definition of *imagination*, which he also calls the "esemplastic power." He coined the word *esemplastic* and used it to mean "molding into unity." Imagination, according to Coleridge, is "the living power and prime agent of all human perception" and "a repetition in the finite mind of the eternal act of creation in the infinite I AM.... It struggles to idealize and to unify. It is essentially vital, even as all objects (as objects) are essentially fixed and dead."[30]

That Coleridge in his opium reverie would dream of the palace of the Khan may be a result of his reading of Purchas's book, or it can be a staged performance of Romantic exoticism or Coleridge's trademark mysticism. But there could be an even deeper reason. If the Khan is, as I have suggested, a forerunner of intangible economy, the Romantics are certainly its early advocates. Intangible economy, as we know, is structured around relationships between man and ideas and symbols, rather than between man, nature, and natural products as in agricultural economy, or between man, machine, and machine-created artificial objects as in industrial economy. Likewise, the Romantics ran up against the centuries-old poetic theory of mimesis, which takes as its central concern the relationship between art and nature, and turned exclusively to imagination, whose interface is between man, his mind, and his poetic work. As M. H. Abrams puts it in his classic *The Mirror and the Lamp*, "Instead of imitation ... the orientation is now toward the artist, the focus of attention is upon the relation of the elements of the work to his state of mind."[31] A poet is, after all, literally a maker, someone who works with words. A poem, as Aristotle defines it (tautologically), "is a thing made." Marazzi quotes sympathetically Heidegger, who writes that "language, the field of 'the most innocent of all occupations,' is also 'the most dangerous of goods[,]' ... the danger of all dangers because it first creates the possibility of danger."[32]

Like the Great Khan, who envisions cities and wealth at will and in his mind, a Romantic poet, as Coleridge put it, expresses "intellectual purposes, thoughts, conceptions, sentiments, that have their origin in the human mind."[33] In his opium reverie, Coleridge describes his process of production of goods: "The author continued for about three hours in a profound sleep, at least of the external senses, during which time he has the most vivid confidence, that he could not have composed less than from two to three hundred lines; if that indeed can be called composition in which all the images rose up before him as things, with a parallel production of the correspondent expressions, without any sensation or consciousness of the effort."[34] Images, things, and expressions—all of them are interchangeable with each other.

Such a Romantic sublimity in the poet's head may now be re-created in a computer's brain: virtual money, information, access codes, and intellectual property all share a common technological substratum of digital storage in networked computers. It is, therefore, "easy and cheap to exchange money for information, information for access, access for intellectual property acknowledgement, and so on. Each of these can be used alternatively as a store of value and/or exchange medium."[35] Call that the digital sublime.

The Return of Polo: The Ear versus the Eye

"The other ambassadors warn me of famines, extortions, conspiracies, or else they inform me of newly discovered turquoise mines, advantageous prices in marten furs, suggestions for supplying damascened blades. And you?" the Great Khan asked Polo, "you return from lands equally distant and you can tell me only the thoughts that come to a man who sits on his doorstep at evening to enjoy the cool air. What is the use, then, of all your traveling?... My gaze is that of a man meditating, lost in thought—I admit it. But yours? You cross archipelagoes, tundras, mountain ranges. You would do as well never moving from here."

ITALO CALVINO, *Invisible Cities*

The Khan's skepticism about the worth of Polo's travel is easily understandable from a Romantic's viewpoint. Indeed, if Coleridge could see the Khan's palace without having to move an inch from his chair, "What is the use, then, of all your traveling?" It was in this context that the Khan told the Venetian, "From now on, I'll describe the cities to you.... [I]n your journeys you will see if they exist." Both the Khan and Coleridge turned inward to seek reality. "Perhaps, Kublai thought, the empire is nothing but a zodiac of the mind's phantasms."[36] Why, then, did the Khan want to hear Polo's stories? Could it be that there is something in hearing that even the most powerful imperial vision would not be able to, forgive the tautology, envision?

The Mongol emperor was a foreigner (who wouldn't be?) to the vast empire he had built; the dominant language in this empire, namely, Chinese, was a foreign tongue to him. "The foreignness of what you no longer are or no longer possess lies in wait for you in foreign, unpossessed places." An empire, boundless as it appears, exists in the visual space, which is ruled by boundaries; sound, however, is difficult to conquer. Could it be, then, that Polo's book, so far as it is a description of the empire, already exists in the Khan's mind, since he has indeed conquered all the cities, but it is the acoustic space, where cities exist in their invisibility, that constantly eludes his grasp? "'On the day when I know all the emblems,' he asked Marco, 'shall I be able to possess my empire, at last?' And the Venetian answered: 'Sire, do not believe it. On that day you will be an emblem among emblems.'"[37] Polo's answer is enigmatic; a clearer answer would be: it depends on what you mean by "know," because there is seeing, and then there is hearing. To echo Jacques Attali in *Noise*: "For twenty-five centuries, Western knowledge has tried to look upon the world. It has failed to understand that the world is not for beholding. It is for hearing. It is not legible, but audible."[38] Or, as Michael Hardt and Antonio Negri have most usefully reminded us, in contrast to old imperialism spreading its power linearly in closed spaces, today's new Empire rules in open space, through networks across an unbounded terrain. In other words, Empire is "a non-place."[39] Kublai Khan, the great conqueror who oversaw the birth of intangible economy as we know it today, seems to be aware of the limitation of imperial spatial conquest. Or, perhaps it was Calvino who, writing the book from the depth of European economic crisis and social turmoil in the early 1970s, when money was decoupled from gold, thereby rendering all currencies as floating fiat, ingeniously endowed a thirteenth-century Mongol emperor with the new kind of imperial mentality emerging after World War II. Either way, the Khan wants to listen to Marco Polo.

Curiously enough, the only piece of Chinese evidence—if that is indeed evidence—that may lend credibility to Polo's narrative exists in sound, or at least it requires one to listen across languages in order to hear the acoustic connections among a Chinese document, a Persian record, and Polo's narrative. Since the story of Marco Polo was first introduced into China in 1874, Chinese historians had tried in vain to uncover any evidence among the vast arrays of Chinese historical records to authenticate Polo as a reliable narrator. In 1941, the Chinese historian Zhijiu Yang published an article in which he announced his discovery of a passage in Chinese concerning Marco Polo's departure from China. On the basis of an official note recorded in the 19,148th volume of the encyclopedic *Yongle dadian*, Yang proves that the names of the three emissaries the note refers to are the same as those of the three emissaries dispatched by Argon mentioned in Polo's book.

In book 1, chapter XVII, of the Yule-Cordier edition, there is a passage that reads:

> Now it came to pass in those days that the Queen Bolgana, wife of Argon, Lord of the Levant, departed this life. And in her Will she had desired that no Lady should take her place, or succeed her as Argon's wife, except one of her own family [which existed in Cathay]. Argon therefore dispatched three of his Barons, by name respectively Qulatay, Apusca, and Coja, as ambassadors to the Great Khan, attended by a very gallant company, in order to bring back as his bride a lady of the family of Queen Bolgana, his late wife. (*Polo*, vol. 1, 32)

Polo told us that he, his father, and his uncle were able to persuade the Khan to allow them to accompany the three barons and the chosen lady, Cocachin, to travel back to the Levant, and from there they went back to Europe. In the Chinese record that Yang uncovered, the passage reads in English translation provided by Francis Woodman Cleaves, who published an article in the *Harvard Journal of Asiatic Studies* in 1976 to reassess Yang's evidence: "In the 3rd moon of this year there was received an Imperial Directive [to the effect] that Wu-lu-tai, A-pi-shih-ha, and Huo-che be dispatched to proceed to the domain of the Ta-wang, A-lu-hun, via Ma-pa-erh." Cleaves further quotes a crucial passage from a Persian text: "And after one moon the royal flags faced in the direction of Xurasan and into the city of Abhar came Xwajah and the party of messengers whom Aryun Xan had sent to the servitude of Qa'an in order that they bring one of the kinswomen of the Great Buluyan and seat her in her place."[40]

If the eye cannot find traces of connection when gliding over the vast terrain of scriptural differences, the ear can hear the echoes in *Coja*, *Huo-che*, and *Xwajah*. Coja, it seems, was the sole survivor of the three emissaries sent by the Great Khan after the long journey, and Polo's narrative also speaks of the loss of many lives on this journey. The Sinologists who are willing to lend Polo a sympathetic ear seem to concur that no one who has not heard the name spoken can provide such a seemingly flimsy but acoustically unmistaken line of connection despite the name's different appearances in different texts and languages.

Of all the episodes of Polo's adventure, it is this voyage from China to Persia that Eugene O'Neill chose as the basis for his 1927 play, *Marco Millions*. In the foreword, O'Neill laments that his protagonist has been called a liar in history. But he blames Polo himself for such an injustice: "The failure to appraise Polo at a fair valuation is his own fault. He dictated the book of his travels but left the traveler out. He was no author. He stuck to a recital of what he considered facts and the world called him a liar for his pains."[41] The undervaluation only shows the extent to which O'Neill himself is a prisoner of print culture and its attendant visual biases. Even Henry Yule, Polo's most sympathetic editor, admits that "in his Book impersonality is carried to excess; and we are often driven to discern by indirect and doubtful indications alone, whether he is speaking of a place from personal knowledge or only from hearsay" (*Polo*, vol. 1, 107–8).

In a culture of vision and silent reading, repetitions of such formulaic descriptions as "the people are idolaters, burn their dead, use paper money, and have a peculiar language" in a series of chapters not only appear to be unbearably verbose and monotonous, but they also expose the dire lack of visual evidence. But in a culture of orality and vocalized reading, they sound rhythmic and reverberant like an echo chamber. "One can look at seeing," says Marcel Duchamp, "[but] one can't hear hearing."[42] If applied to Polo, Duchamp's statement would sound more like a lament than a description. In a world where vision is predominant, hearing is not personal witness. As if he had foreseen such a future verdict on him, Polo's prologue begs us to hear the book read to us, to sound it out: Huo-che, Xwajah, Coja. Indeed, "a Chinese whisper translated from Persian."

Vernacular Imagination

Huo-che, 火者, the Chinese version of Coja, literally means "fire person," a person who carries a fire, a Prometheus. This fire is the verbal energy, an electrical current that flows through an otherwise fractured landscape of multiple graphic signs. Our ability to listen across linguistic boundaries constitutes what I would call "vernacular imagination." The Romantic notion of imagination as "the living power and prime agent of all human *perception*" carries a profound preference for vision; "transcendence" is above all a visualized, spatial metaphor, and so is "sublime." While the Romantics may have taken us a step closer to the world of intangibility (you *see*, I am using a visual metaphor, "a step closer," to describe the intangible), they also have left us a legacy of imperialist vision, an esemplastic power that molds everything into unity. The coupling of "vernacular" with "imagination," then, is my attempt to describe a relationship to the world that is predicated as much on vision as on listening, a mode of worlding that is at once local and global, harking back to the notion of the translocal dialect in chapter 1.

In his influential study of the cosmopolitan and the vernacular, Sheldon Pollock describes the different historical trajectories of two cosmopolitan vernaculars, Latin and Sanskrit, and comes to the conclusion that "if the cosmopolitanisms [of the two vernaculars] were similar in transcending the local and stimulating feelings of living in a large world, their modalities were radically different: the one coercive, the other voluntaristic." What justifies Pollock's conclusion is a small but telling sign, "the graphic sign itself": "Roman script was constitutive of Latin literature: *arma virumque cano* could be written in only a single alphabet. The graphic forms of Sanskrit literature, by contrast, were innumerable: *vagarthau iva samprktau* could be inscribed in Javanese script; in Thai, Sinhala, and Grantha in Tamil country; and in Sharada in Kashmir." In other words, whereas Latin imposed universality in both sound and vision, Sanskrit at least allowed graphic variations. Whereas Latin "traveled where it did as the language of a conquest state," Sanskrit "never sought to theorize its own universality," a feature Pollock deems consistent with Sanskrit being "an alternative form of cosmopolitanism in which 'here,' instead of being equated with 'everywhere,' is equated with 'nowhere in particular.'" It seems that the world of Sanskrit is such an invisible empire built in the acoustic space.[43]

In addition to differentiating two models of cosmopolitanism, Pollock challenges the perspective that sees the vernacular and the cosmopolitan as stable categories, urging us instead to see them "as a congeries of constantly changing repertoires of practices."[44] Which brings us to the ongoing debate over the virtue or vice of cosmopolitanism, as it has been advocated or opposed, practiced or shunned, by intellectuals and immigrants of all stripes and colors.

The idea of cosmopolitanism has been with us since the dawn of humanity. In the West, the Stoics of ancient Greece espoused the notion of being a person with allegiance to the worldwide community of human beings. When asked who he was, Diogenes replied, "I am a citizen of the world," thus refusing to be defined by the accident of where one is born and by the fortuity of local origins and group affiliations. Diogenes fully recognized that becoming a cosmopolitan is often a lonely business, a kind of exile "from the comfort of local truths, from the warm, nestling feeling of patriotism, from the absorbing drama of pride in oneself and one's own." However, as Martha Nussbaum points out, the Stoics also stress that to be a citizen of the world, one does not need to give up completely one's local identifications. Instead, they suggest that we are surrounded by a series of concentric circles: "The first one encircles the self, the next takes in the immediate family, then follows the extended family, then, in order, neighbors or local groups, fellow city-dwellers, and fellow countrymen.... Outside all these circles is the largest one, humanity as a whole."[45] In the East, Daoism advocates a worldview that is, if not strictly cosmopolitan, at least universal and translocal. Confucianism, in particular, shares with the

Stoics the idea of concentric circles with regard to one's self-positioning, expanding the spheres from self to family, nation, and then the world.

The critique of cosmopolitanism comes mainly from two camps: the postcolonialists and the constitutionalists. Taking issues with the kind of Eurocentric worldviews as formulated by Kant and Hegel, the postcolonialists put forward the concept of vernacular cosmopolitanism as a way to reach toward global contexts and responsibilities, at the same time recognizing that "these are always rooted in and permeated by local concerns."[46] Homi Bhabha, who is often credited with coining the term "vernacular cosmopolitanism," uses the concept to capture the "growing, global gulf between political citizenship, still largely negotiated in 'national' and statist terms, and cultural citizenship which is often community-based, transnational, diasporic, hybrid," an identitarian practice of "translating across cultures in an economy marked by iteration rather than teleology."[47] Paul Gilroy, in contrast, prefers what he terms "demotic cosmopolitanism," which involves "the principled and methodical cultivation of a degree of estrangement from one's own culture and history."[48] And Peter Nyer proposes "abject cosmopolitanism," which he defines as something that "does not aim for a higher ground so much as to burrow into the apparatuses and technologies of exclusion in order to disrupt the administrative routines, the day-to-day perceptions and constructions of normality."[49] All of these articulations, in the words of Stuart Hall, gesture toward "a cosmopolitanism that is aware of the limitations of any one culture or any one identity and that is radically aware of its insufficiency in governing a wider society, but which nevertheless is not prepared to rescind its claims to the traces of difference, which makes its life important."[50]

A more lucid and convincing critique of cosmopolitanism comes from constitutionalists such as Elaine Scarry. In her thoughtful response to Martha Nussbaum's "Patriotism and Cosmopolitanism," Scarry anchors her argument on the insufficiency of what she terms "generous imaginings" and the need for legal provisions and constitutional procedures rather than the goodwill of other people. Scarry warns against reliance on the imagination as a guarantor of political generosity, giving us a reality check by stating that "the human capacity to injure other people is very great precisely because our capacity to imagine other people is very small." The root cause for the human frailty is, in her words, "when we seek equality through generous imaginings, we start with our own weight, then attempt to acquire knowledge about the weight and complexity of others." As an alternative, she proposes that we try to "achieve equality between self and other not by trying to make one's knowledge of others as weighty as one's self knowledge, but by making one ignorant about oneself, and therefore as weightless as all others." Her constitutional argument, then, is exactly based on this strategy of "imagined weightlessness," since legal provisions "define rights and powers that are independent of any one person's personal features."[51]

Of course, the key word *weight* is used here, not in the literal sense of a person's physical mass or heft, but in the metaphorical sense of importance, power, clout, or worth. But in Marco Polo we encounter acts of imagining the other by referring to our own weight or worth almost in the literal sense, and it has to do with money.

Money may be a universal language, but it turns out that currencies speak vernaculars of their own, almost analogous to what Scarry says about universal rights: "Human rights are universal in content, but they are particular in their base of authorization and enforcement."[52] Curiously enough, currencies are usually called in their native tongues: dollar, pound, yuan, yen, won, mark, franc, lira, ruble, baht, and so on. We may change their graphic appearance when we transliterate them into English, but their sounds remain. It is as if we must have our own *terms*, with their sounds as measure and weight, in order to understand, to *come to terms* with the world and its meaning. In Polo's narrative, the reader/listener is constantly asked to look at things in terms of Venetian currency:

> The smallest of these sizes is worth a half tornsel; the next, a little larger, one tornsel; one, a little larger still, is worth half a silver groat of Venice; another a whole groat; others yet two groats, five groats, and ten groats. There is also a kind worth one Bezant of gold, and others of three Bezants, and so up to ten. (*Polo*, vol. 1, 423–24)

Or:

> First there is the salt, which brings in a great revenue. For it produces every year, in round numbers, fourscore tomans of gold; and the toman is worth 70,000 saggi of gold, so that the total value of the fourscore tomans will be five millions and six hundred thousand saggi of gold, each saggio being worth more than a gold florin or ducat. (*Polo*, vol. 2, 171)

Or:

> And you must know that Messer Marco Polo, who relates all this, was several times sent by the Great Kaan to inspect the amount of his customs and revenue from this ninth part of Manzi, and he found it to be, exclusive of the salt revenue which we have mentioned already, 210 tomans of gold, equivalent to 14,700,000 saggi of gold. (*Polo*, vol. 2, 172)

It seems that unless Polo renders everything in Venetian terms, such as tornsels, groats, saggi, florins, and ducats, his European contemporaries will have no way of imagining what he has seen. Monetary terms, besides being called in their vernacular sounds, are often themselves related to sounds. The Venetian ducat of Polo's times, for instance, bears an inscription, "SIT.T.XRE.DAT.Q.TV.REGIS.ISTE.DUCAT," which is meant to be read aloud as "Sit tibi Christe datus, quem tu Regis, iste ducatus" (Let this duchy, which thou rulest, be dedicated to thee, O Christ).[53] The issuing of a new coin is technically called an "utterance." To utter, according to the *Oxford English Dictionary*, means "to give currency to; to put into circulation," as well as "to send forth as a sound; to speak, say, or pronounce."

Rhubarb, Opium, and Coleridge's Dysentery: A Loose End

This fragment with a good deal more, not recoverable, composed, in a sort of Reverie brought on by two grains of opium, taken to check a dysentery, at a Farm House between Porlock & Linton, a quarter of a mile from Culbone Church, in the fall of the year, 1797.

Coleridge's note found on a manuscript copy of "Kubla Khan"

By his own admission, Coleridge took the poetically inspiring opium to cure his dysentery.[54] In 1839, on the eve of the first Opium War, China was imagining the opposite problem for the British people: constipation. In his official letter to Queen Victoria, the high imperial commissioner Lin Zexu tried to persuade Her Majesty to stop dumping opium in the Chinese market; the British had engaged in such aggressive drug dealing in order to balance the huge trade deficit created by their addiction to Chinese tea. Couched within the diplomatic niceties of the letter was a threat: "Has China (we should like to ask) ever yet sent forth a noxious article from its soil? Not to speak of our tea and rhubarb, things which your foreign countries could not exist a single day without, if we of the Central Land were to grudge you what is beneficial, and not to compassionate your wants, then wherewithal could you foreigners manage to exist?"[55] In other words, if you don't stop selling opium in China, we will stop exporting tea and rhubarb to you. Lin was imagining that with all the excessive consumption of tea, the British populace must be suffering from constipation, which may be alleviated by rhubarb, a medicinal root whose great abundance in China was keenly noted by Marco Polo.[56]

If Lin's threat may be construed as a one-sided perception of the problem, the British were not any better: they willfully misread the letter and heard something far more offensive. Lin's letter was written in Chinese, and the above-quoted passage can be translated differently as: "Is there a single article from China which has done any harm to foreign countries? Take tea and rhubarb, for example; the foreign countries cannot get along for a single day without them. If China cuts off these benefits with no sympathy for those who are to suffer, then what can the *barbarians* rely upon to keep themselves alive?" The crucial substitution of "barbarians" for "foreigners" as the translation of the Chinese term in Lin's letter, "yiren," could be deeply offensive to the queen. As Lydia H. Liu argues in her study of the politics of translation during China's clash with the West in the nineteenth century, yiren was a supersign that has entangled and embattled etymologies. While the Chinese term may be neutral and can be simply translated as "foreigner," the Western countries often translated it as "barbarian" and thereby regarded Chinese documents that used this word in their originals as deeply insulting.[57] One nation exaggerated the other's bowel problem, and one nation misheard the other's speech (the Greek term *barbaros* mimics the sound of incomprehensible speech). So the war broke out and we know the rest of the story.

Fast forward one and a half centuries, and we have another story that also makes use of vernacular imagination but with a happy ending. On April 1, 2001, while doing reconnaissance in the South China Sea, a US Navy spy plane collided with a Chinese military aircraft. The Chinese plane disappeared, and its pilot was supposedly dead. The US plane was damaged and had to perform an emergency landing in China without authorization. The US crew was detained by the Chinese, triggering a diplomatic crisis. What eventually resolved the issue was an intentional mistranslation, a purposeful realignment of the equivalence of words in English and Chinese as they are used in diplomatic exchanges. In his halfhearted letter of apology to the Chinese government, the US ambassador, Joseph W. Prueher, states, "Please convey to the Chinese people and to the family of pilot Wang Wei that we are very sorry for their loss.... We are very sorry the entering of China's airspace and the landing did not have verbal clearance."[58] When reported in Chinese media, however, the English phrase "very sorry," which sounds almost too simple or casual for an event of such magnitude, was translated into Chinese as "shenbiaoqianyi." Meaning literally "expressing the deepest regret," the Chinese phrase carries a weight of formality that goes way beyond the English colloquial term. It was this Chinese phrase that was published in bold as headlines in Chinese media, and it effectively quieted the raging anti-US sentiments. The crew was released and the spy plane returned. Despite the perennial US complaint of China's pegging of its currency against the dollar (as of today, August 21, 2021), the exchange rate of one US dollar to one Chinese yuan is 1:6.50), this is one pegged, uneven linguistic trade that the United States is more than happy to allow: "very sorry" for "shenbiaoqianyi."[59]

Somewhere the Merchant of Venice is whispering to the ears of his listeners because the secret is almost too good to be true: "In the mountains belonging to this city, rhubarb and ginger grow in great abundance; insomuch that you may get some 40 pounds of excellent fresh ginger for a Venice groat" (*Polo*, vol. 2, 181). We can almost hear the jingle and jangle of the moneyed mind, some susurrous hearsay of a mellifluent cosmopolite who tries to lure the locals into a world of wonder audible in their own terms.

Marco.

Polo.

Words Made in China

[CHAPTER THREE]

Ezra Pound as a Translational Poet

Whether or not Marco Polo actually went to China, there is no question that another famous Sinophile, Ezra Pound, never set his foot in the Middle Kingdom. But, as we saw in the previous chapter, ideas travel, words translate, money flies, and people walk in dreams.

At the Eighteenth International Ezra Pound Conference in Beijing in 1999, the Chinese poet Yang Lian said, "I am luckier than Pound—I was born into Chinese. He had to struggle against what his language imposed. *The Cantos* are complete only in their Chinese translation."[1] As the Chinese translator of *The Cantos*, I find Yang's extraordinary statement both absurd and inspiring. It is absurd because Yang seemed to be proposing a linguistic hierarchy, ranking Chinese higher than English as a poetic medium. Unless one wants to wax ethnocentric, it makes no sense on aesthetic ground to claim that one's native language, or any language, is more poetic than others. Even Pound, who spent his lifetime promoting the ideogrammic method, had to admit at one point that his cherished method speaks to "the fundamentals of all aesthetics," not just Chinese.[2] Or, if we follow Lacanian psychoanalytic supposition that we are all prisoners inside our languages, then Yang would be no luckier than Pound since he would have to struggle against the symbolic order imposed by Chinese as much as Pound would against English. The literary history of twentieth-century China provides ample examples of Chinese writers feeling imprisoned by their native language and wanting to find a new medium. Some of those writers have already been studied in chapter 1. But since when do poets give a damn about what linguists or psychoanalysts have to say? Certainly not Pound, skeptical as he was of academic Sinologists, who attacked his "amateurish" Chinese work, and of the psychiatrists who tried in vain to treat him during his decade-long incarceration at St. Elizabeths Hospital.

That is why I find Yang's counterintuitive statement fascinating, especially his idea that "*The Cantos* are complete only in their Chinese translation." A few years after he made that statement, Yang coauthored with John Cayley an essay titled "Hallucination and Coherence," in which they state, "After finishing and considering his reading of Huang Yunte's recently published translation of *The Pisan Cantos* into Chinese, Yang Lian commented that, for him, Ezra Pound's poetic project seemed to have been realized—he goes so far as to say that it is 'completed' (wancheng)—in the language of the translation, that is, in Chinese."[3] As the one responsible for the translation mentioned here, I wish I could say that my work has indeed realized Pound's poetic dream. But it is not humility, Charlie Chanish or not, that has prevented me from making such a grand and bogus claim. Instead, it is something that I have learned from translating and reading Pound, something that Yang has indicated but not quite pinpointed. To me, Pound's poetic project is realized not in the language of *the* translation but in the language of *translation*. Ezra Pound, to paraphrase Marjorie Perloff, is a translational poet, whose *Cantos*, interspersed with "Chinese characters, Greek and Latin phrases, lines from Guido Cavalcanti, [and] passages of American dialect and phonetic spelling," use over twenty languages.[4] Pound writes, I argue, in the poetic language of translationese, which is neither completely English nor exotically Chinese, or any one language in particular. In some ways, it is comparable to a translocal dialect like Chinglish, as discussed in chapter 1. His ideogrammic method, imported from Chinese, ultimately transcends Chinese and turns itself into what Haroldo de Campos calls a poetic intracode.[5] To understand how Pound's made-in-China poetics became a model of modernism as well as twenty-first-century poetry, we need to look again at his adventures into Chinese and see where his translational poetics got its inspiration.

Here I would like to skip the familiar story of how Pound came into possession of Fenollosa's papers and how the grand master of modernism worked like an alchemist, creating gems of Imagism out of Fenollosa's voluminous notes. Instead, I'd like to segue to my own experience as Pound's Chinese translator trying to back-translate Pound's ideogrammic poetics into Chinese. I believe my unique experience may shed some light on Pound's poetics by reversing the journey, not for a happy homecoming, but to show what happens between English and Chinese (and the twenty or so other languages) in Pound's work.

I began my translation of *The Pisan Cantos* when I was still a struggling Chinese restaurateur in the Deep South of the United States in the early 1990s. I remember the days when I sat on the greasy floor of the Chinese kitchen, trying to make heads or tails of *The Cantos*. After three years, I finally finished translating the eleven *Pisan Cantos*, and my work was subsequently published in 1998 by Lijiang Publishing House in China, with a print run of ten thousand. It sold out within six months.

It goes without saying that translating *The Cantos* was a herculean task. Pound was, after all, no Robert Frost. I don't mean to say that Frost, often credited with the infamous saying "Poetry is what's lost in translation," is easy to translate. But there is a technical distinction between translating Pound and, say, Frost. The distinction lies in that Pound's work is inherently multilingual whereas Frost's is apparently not. In the current debate over the concept of world literature, whether one agrees with David Damrosch or Emily Apter, the critical focus most likely remains on the circulation of literature out of its linguistic and cultural point of origin and into the broader world. As I have argued elsewhere, Pound presents a different paradigm of world literature due to its inherent global infrastructure at the level of the text.[6]

To translate Pound is often to translate his translations of others' translations. In my case, in translating *The Cantos* into Chinese, I seemed to be translating something back into Chinese. All those ancient Chinese characters, whose spirit, as they say, has been carried away by Pound and scattered into his poetic furrows, are now supposedly back on their home turf. So are those luminous or obscure passages from Confucian Classics. These passages, unlike Charlie Chan's fortune cookie witticisms mostly cooked up in gilded Hollywood, can all locate their roots in the voluminous Classics. The question is: What to do with Pound's translations in my own translation? Especially what to do with Pound's translations of the Chinese material in my Chinese translation? I am dealing with a text that originally contains, shall we say, an exotic other, but now in translation, after the text is rendered into the language of its former other, it experiences an uncanny familiarity with the other: they are now both in Chinese. Also, the translation targets readers for whom the text is supposedly foreign, but most of my readers intimately know the Chinese originals that *The Cantos* have relied upon; therefore, my back-translation creates a defamiliarization of the Chinese materials. They are translations from English! As a result, the Chinese readers experience the foreignness of what is their own.[7]

The Pisan Cantos, as Hugh Kenner puts it, is "a dialogue with Legge" about Confucius.[8] The Scottish missionary and Sinologist James Legge had translated the classical Chinese canon into English, and these translations were the main source for Pound's Confucius. Sitting in the outdoor cage, composing *The Pisan Cantos*, Pound had with him a book of Legge's *Confucius*, a pirated reprint from Shanghai's Commercial Press. Pound's daily life in prison involving poetry and Confucius is best described by Kenner in *The Pound Era*.

> He had begged for notebooks, and folded them down the center to make them pocket-size; with a very sharp pencil in a careful hand he wrote fair copies of the new *Cantos* on the right half of the right-hand page, the half to the left of the fold kept for second thoughts. When he chose to work at Confucius he turned the book around, so that the left-hand page became the right. So the *Pisan Cantos* run through the notebook in one direction, the *Great Digest* and *Unwobbling Pivot* in the other.[9]

The intricate interweaving between the *Cantos* and the Confucian texts creates a special demand on me as the translator, a demand for retaining the dialogical, translational quality of Pound's work. It might not be so difficult to replicate to a large extent the visual effects those Chinese characters have in the English version: the ideograms were originally taken by Pound directly from Legge's bilingual edition, and they were all calligraphed in an old style and typeset in a large font. Reproduced in my Chinese version, these ideograms still contrast sharply with the main body of poetry, which is printed in modernized, simplified Chinese characters in a much smaller font. Other tasks involving Chinese ideograms include inserting the right characters since Pound or the publisher sometimes misplaced them and setting the characters back to the right "posture" since the English version turned some characters upside down.

While it may be easy to fix the characters, it is much more complicated to deal with poetry lines related to Confucian Classics. This is where Pound's "creative translation" comes into play. A well-known example is these two lines from Canto 74:

> To study with the white wings of time passing
> Is not that our delight[10]

Legge's version, which Pound relied upon, had it as "Is it not pleasant to learn with a constant perseverance and application?" Legge also provided a footnote for the key character involved, 習 (xi): "the rapid and frequent motion of the wings of a bird in flying, used for 'to repeat,' 'to practice.'"[11] Using his ingenious "etymosinological" method, Pound evidently took much liberty with his rendition. As a translator, it is not my job to judge whether or not Pound was faithful to the original or to philosophize over what faithfulness means. What concerns me is how to represent in my translation the way Pound "etymosinologically" or "ideogrammatically" translated the Chinese. If rendered well, the Chinese version will be an intriguing mirroring, and the reading of it will become a process of defamiliarization mentioned above: Confucian wisdom will sound foreign and uncanny to a native ear. In order to achieve such an effect, I decided to follow Pound's etymosinological version of Confucius and use modern Mandarin (*baihua wen*) to translate those classical passages while providing in the footnotes the original Confucian texts, which were written in the ancient Literary Style (*wenyan wen*). The modern Mandarin version of Confucius, aided by Pound's poetic tinkering, may sound a bit strange to a native who knows the original by heart, but the strangeness is the desired effect of a back-translation of a translation, dare I say it again, of a translation.[12] This back-translation by no means leads to what Yang Lian has called the "completion" of the Cantos in Chinese. If anything, it actually demonstrates more clearly the inherent translational structure of Pound's work, suggesting that the poetic home of the Cantos lies, not in English or Chinese, but in the relational space of translation. Somewhere Susan Howe said, "The relational space is the thing that's alive with something from somewhere else."[13] It is to that "somewhere else" I now return.

It is worth noting that Pound's closest encounter with Chinese, or his boldest exploration, took place in a period when his mental health was most seriously in jeopardy or in question. I am referring to the time when he was jailed in Pisa while composing *The Pisan Cantos*, followed by about a dozen years at St. Elizabeths, where he was treated, or rather, resisted the treatment, by professional psychiatrists. It was in this period that Pound began systematically translating, or more precisely, retranslating, Confucian Classics, became obsessed with sound symbolism in the Chinese language, and eventually dabbled in composing Chinese lines by himself. A visitor to St. Elizabeths recalled Pound showing her a dog-eared copy of James Legge's *Confucius*, the same volume that, as Kenner described earlier, was vital to *The Pisan Cantos*. Pound told the visitor, "This little book has been my bible for years, the only thing I could hang onto during those hellish days at Pisa.... Had it not been for this book, from which I drew my strength, I would really have gone insane ... so you see how I am indebted to Kung."[14] It is easy to understand the spiritual support a Chinese book could provide for Pound in the form of the Confucian ideas it contains, ideas to which Pound wholeheartedly subscribed. But it is not so easy to see the other ways in which a Chinese book could help Pound as he struggled on the brink of insanity. Some of these other ways would include explorations into what psychoanalysts would call the frontiers of language, areas consigned to anagrams, puns, paronomasia, echolalia, and schizophrenia.

During his St. Elizabeths years, Pound kept close contact with Achilles Fang, a Harvard-trained Sinologist, who helped the poet with his Confucian translations as well as his Chinese studies. Unlike most Sinologists who would never take Pound's Chinese work seriously, Fang, eventually the author of an eight-hundred-page dissertation on Pound, was quite open and receptive to the poet's unconventional ideas. More than once, Fang even applauded Pound, the Chinese neophyte, for his brilliant insights and original interpretations of Confucian Classics. For instance, Pound's creative reading of the Chinese word 止 as meaning "the hitching post, position, place one is in, and works from" prompted Fang to write to Pound, "Your interpretation of 止 seems to solve a number of knotty problems in Kung's book. I have been looking through commentaries, but so far failed to come across any that lays emphasis on that term. Please accept my congratulations."[15] Emboldened by Fang's friendly words, Pound would try out with his Chinese confidant a series of "transcreative" readings.

In a letter to Fang in March 1951, Pound wrote in his usual idiosyncratic manner, "what has the hnbl/Fang to say to thick-headed occidental re/ the chinkese langwidG OR ideogram which is fer somethings the most precise and, in fact, only satisfactory medium for making certain statements, and IS in others the most damblasted and DAMbiguous modus loquendi, wot yu cant bust open with a meat AX??"[16] Pound then went on to list about a dozen Chinese characters along with his own creative interpretations, some of which he would eventually incorporate into the *Cantos*:

> [舍] she, 5699/shed
> [甘] kan as in CANdy and sugar CANE
> [恨] 2095/hen, as in french haine
> [落] lo, 4122/low, and LOC as in location
> [理] li, 3864, LIning[17]

As we see here, Pound was trying to make sense of Chinese words by linking them phonologically to words in alphabetic languages such as English and French. 甘, pronounced as *gan* or *kan*, meaning "sweet," seems both semantically and phonologically akin to "sweet" English words such as *candy* and *cane*. 恨, pronounced as *hen*, meaning "hate" or "hatred," reminds Pound of the French word *haine* (also meaning hatred). The same scenario goes for 落 and 理.

In particular, the word 舍 (pronounced as *she*, meaning "house, shed, or hut") does sound like the English word *shed*. The magic of coincidence does not stop here. In Canto 98, one of the *Thrones Cantos*, composed during this period of odyssey into Chinese, Pound wrote (707):

> Is the Bhud likely to return for these harridans?
>   having had his palace with court yards
> and a dragon verandah, plus a feng-ko

presumably furnished with phoenix
and he *ch'i'd* 'em or *shed* 'em
棄　捨

The speaker here, presumably a Chinese emperor, is chastising the priests for betraying the true teachings of the Buddha, who, originally a royal prince and heir apparent to the throne, grew weary of the cares of the world, gave up his harem, forsook the Dragon Chamber and Phoenix Hall, and abandoned his family, in order to hide himself in the heights of a snowy mountain to practice asceticism. The two Chinese characters 棄 (ch'i) and 捨 (she) both mean "abandon, neglect." Pound adopted the transliterations of Chinese words and used them directly as English verbs, as indicated by their past tense: *ch'i'd* and *shed*. More important, the word *shed* would make sense in both Chinese and English. 捨 is a variation of 舍, which can be both a noun (meaning, as we see earlier, house or shed) and a verb (meaning abandon, get rid of). Interestingly, the English word *shed* can also be both a noun (hut) and a verb (abandon, get rid of). Roman Jakobson once reminded us, "In poetry, any phonological coincidence is felt to mean semantic kinship."[18] Or, to follow Walter Benjamin, there is no translation more transparent or literal than the case of 舍 here. "A real translation," says Benjamin, "is transparent; it does not cover the original, does not block its light, but allows the pure language, as though reinforced by its own medium, to shine upon the original all the more fully."[19] But Pound's purpose is not translation itself. Instead, translation, which reveals the uncanny kinship—Ludwig Wittgenstein would call it "family resemblance"—between Chinese and English, is the foundational poetics of *The Cantos*.

Interestingly, around the time he wrote these cantos, Pound was not alone in noting, or tapping into, some of the etymological similarities between Chinese and English. Parallel across languages was not just the purview of poets. In the early 1950s, it was a major concern for a group of scientists, mathematicians, engineers, and linguists blazing the trails for what we now call the digital revolution. As we know, the computer was originally designed for the purpose of cryptography, using a machine to translate or decode intelligence. In the heyday of the Cold War, to process massive information data gathered in espionage operations, especially intelligence from Russian and Chinese sources, became a Herculean task that could no longer be accomplished by human agents alone. Cracking the Russian or Chinese code, literally or metaphorically, had always been on the minds of those cyberneticians. In a letter to Norbert Wiener on March 4, 1947, a text that would be distributed two years later as a memorandum widely regarded as the founding treatise of the digital revolution, the mathematician Warren Weaver wrote, "A most serious problem... for the constructive and peaceful future of the planet, is the problem of translation, as it unavoidably affects the communication between peoples.... It is very tempting to say that a book written in Chinese is simply a book written in English which was coded into the 'Chinese code.'"[20] While the implications of this memo will have to be discussed later in chapter 5, we should note here that Weaver's idea of the "Chinese code" and its translatability into English exerted profound influence on his colleagues, to whom he had sent the memo.

Starting with the first conference on machine translation at MIT in 1951, participating researchers actively pursued all aspects, theoretical or technical, of the problem of machine translation. One participant, in particular, took the possible translatability between Chinese and English literally. In a series of papers delivered at the Macy conferences in the early 1950s, Erwin Reifler, a Sinologist from the University of Washington, Seattle, reported his findings of certain etymological similarities between Chinese and English in a manner not so different from Pound's "etymosinological" imagination. For example, Reifler examines the Chinese character 射 (*she*, to shoot, to fire) and 谢 (*xie*, to thank, to resign). As the bent body is implied in both characters through the shared radicals of 身 and 寸, Reifler concludes that "they resonate with the two semantic meanings of the English word 'bow,' which means 'shooting an arrow' as well as 'bowing out' or 'dismissing oneself.'" In the same vein, Reifler argues that the character for pupil, 瞳 (*tong*), which is made up of the characters for "eye" 目 and "child" 童, also has both the meanings of "student" and "eye" in English. As Jing Tsu notes in her book *Sound and Script in Chinese Diaspora*, Reifler's research findings, which some might regard as a bit of a stretch, encouraged Weaver to explore broader parameters "to attempt a universal code for translating languages into one another."[21]

While his contemporaries in the technological world continued to search for universal translatability, Pound, incarcerated in the madhouse, pursued even more daring translingual dreams. In January 1951, Pound sent Fang a typescript of forty-five pages titled "Preliminary Survey," in which the poet systematically examines Chinese vocabulary for evidence of sound symbolism. The concept of sound symbolism found its earliest expression in Plato's *Dialogues*. In *Cratylus*, Socrates offers a classical explanation of how words acquire their meanings, a belief that "each consonant and vowel means something, and that meaning is its pronunciation. The sounds then pass on this meaning to every word that contains them." For instance, words containing /b/ may involve bulging, blocking, booming, and bursting. It may be no sheer coincidence that bud, bulb, bloom, and blossom are all plant "babies" that are bulging and ready to burst.[22]

An orphan of modern linguistics, sound symbolism, or phonosemantics, is a favorite topic for only a handful of linguists with a penchant for the poetic and irrational, such as Roman Jakobson, Otto Jespersen, Maurice Bloomfield, and Edward Sapir. Jakobson, in particular, likes to explore what he calls the "sound shape of language," an inmost, natural association between sound and meaning. It is Jakobson who, having cut his poetic teeth with the Futurists, gives us the most valuable concept in this regard, paronomasia, which he defines as "a semantic confrontation of phonemically similar words irrespective of any etymological connection." As opposed to Saussure (especially the early Saussure), who considered onomatopoeia, anagram, and other poetic features as negligible exceptions to the rule of arbitrariness, Jakobson maintains that paronomasia "plays a considerable role in the life of language." He believes that the semantic similarity among the words *crash*, *bash*, *splash*, *mash*, *dash*, *trash*, and *clash*, or the serial contiguity of *eleven* and *twelve*, despite the absence of any etymological connectivity or explanation, is undeniable evidence that there exists in language a contest between nature and convention.[23] Benjamin, who derives his language theories from the Gnostic and Kabbalistic traditions, is also no stranger to sound symbolism. In his essay "Doctrine of the Similar," Benjamin explores what he calls the "nonsensuous similarity," a correspondence between word and meaning that has become incomprehensible to us due to our incremental loss of a mimetic faculty. "For instance," Benjamin writes, "the letter beth [in Hebrew] is the root for the word meaning 'house,'" and all words beginning with that letter would then bear a semantic relation to house, even though empirical philology would deny that. Language, to Benjamin, is "an archive of nonsensuous similarities, of nonsensuous correspondences."[24]

Discarding empirical philology, Pound's "Preliminary Survey," based on his examination of *A Complete Chinese-English Dictionary*, edited by O. Z. Tsang, also yields clusters of phonetically related words sharing semantic values. In the introduction Pound states, "Understanding of the Chinese language has been perhaps retarded by the assumption that because the ideogrammic signs do not inflect, the spoken language, which children are said to acquire so much more readily than their foreign elders, is not inflected." Citing the Swedish Sinological authority Bernhard Karlgren, who believed that spoken Chinese preceded the ideogram, Pound postulated that the original Chinese speech "was not only inflected but also agglutinative."[25] Such a possibility provided grounds for Pound to make some astonishing observations regarding sound symbolism in Chinese. For instance, he claimed that "64 out of the 466 sounds in Mr. O. Z. Tsang's dictionary begin with ch, the commonest bird sound" (207). He listed a series of words that begin with the *ch* sound: *chu*, *chueh*, *ch'i*, *chi*, *chih*, *ching*, *chiang*, *cheng*, *chung*, *chiung*, all of which "can be read as indicative of place or of motion [of birds]" (208). For agglutinative suggestions, Pound believed that /ang/ is associated with "up," /iang/ with "down from above," /ao/ possibly with "high," and /ung/ possibly with "weight." "A certain number of 'an'," Pound suggested, "certainly agglutinate into words implying tranquility." He came up with a diagram, matching consonants with clusters of meaning:

hither and yon	CH
light and dark	M
the hard and soft	J
the branching and converging	Y
the wrapping and separating	P

In the case of M, for example, "Ming is bright," writes Pound, "the sun and moon, the total light process; MEI and MENG are in certain cases dark, from definite black ink to young ignorance" (220). He then expanded the scope of his investigation and reached into the area of comparative philology: "MA presents several probably fortuitous to common european words, the italian ma (but) ma and old lady MA means horse, and nothing phoneticly to do with a male horse, but the sound is indubitably initial in mare" (227).

In the case of Y words, Pound picked YA as an example. "YA in its simplicity is the forked stick or crotch that has come down in our own Y, what opens also shuts." In this cluster he cited 牙 (teeth), 衙 (law court), 鸦 (crow), 鸭 (duck), 芽 (bud), and 崖 (cliff). Conventional etymology would find little or no connection among these words, all pronounced /ya/. But Pound's etymosinological readings would reveal underlying paronomasiac relations: "the main radical in 16 ideograms is 'teeth' verbal sense being: what the teeth do, as in Ode 'we are the king's claws and teeth' it extends to the law court, and a bird's 'open and shut' is the neat beak. The buds come out like bright teeth. YA, the toothed cliff, precipice." In other words, the syllable /ya/, as well as the visional cypher, the radical 牙, holds together a chain of words semantically linked to "teeth," from 衙 as the teeth of law to the beaks of crows and ducks, the buds of plants like baby teeth, and cliffs protruding like sharp teeth (220).

Following the same principle, words whose sounds begin with /ya/ also carry the semantic connotation of diverging, converging, or rising like teeth. For instance, the /yang/ words: 仰, to look up; 央, middle, visually diverging and converging in the middle; 羊, sheep or goat, with "the Y of the horns thoroughly visible"; 洋, ocean, or in Pound's decipherment, "ocean water sheep, vast, wide spread." In the last three examples, 央, 羊,

and 洋, sound symbolisms and imagistic radicals work together to form ideograms. Or, as Pound put it, "the meaning fills up and extends over the space between graph and sound" (217). Years later, when the Brazilian Concrete poet Haroldo de Campos wrote "Poetic Function and Ideogram/The Sinological Argument," perhaps the most insightful essay in the Fenollosa-Pound tradition, he used 洋 as a prime example of how relational intracoding works in Chinese ideograms, poetically welding the phonic to the graphic plane and semantically magnetizing them both. De Campos correctly interpreted the radical 羊 as "the phonogram which indicates the pronunciation yang," but like Pound, he also recognized the iconic value of the radical and its accompanying semantic connotation: "This is also individually the pictogram for 'ewe' or 'sheep' (a zoomorphic head, detached from the animal's body by a stroke of synecdoche and stylized so as to represent the muzzle and horns with six brushstrokes)." As if taking a cue from Pound's insight into the sound symbolism of *yang*, de Campos postulated that "the idea of representing the ocean by means of this combination of characters originated precisely in the immemorial perceptive fact that 'a flock of sheep in motion reminds one of the rolling of white-capped waves on the open sea.'" De Campos characterized such a Poundian interpretation of Chinese characters as an opposition between etymological truth and poetic etymology.[26] Or, as Jean-Jacques Lecercle would say, it is "etymology gone mad."[27]

In his study of the remainder of language, Lecercle sees that "there is another side to language, one that escapes the linguist's attention, not because of his temporary failure or failings, but for necessary reasons."[28] It is the side that, as we shall see in chapter 5, haunted Saussure in his later years, seducing him into "a Chinese game" or "Chinese puzzle," as he ran his finger up and down the pages of ancient Greek and Latin texts, recognizing anagrams, hypograms, and anaphony like shadows in a Platonic cave.[29] Chinese, in the eyes of Pound, is certainly full of remainders. The ideogrammic method is above all a poetic game of excess, surplus, n+1. The remainder, says Lecercle, "is the place of excessive (that is, multiple) analysis and false synthesis. The delirious patient and the inspired poet do it."[30]

There is nothing new in comparing an inspired poet to a delirious patient. But in the case of Pound's obsession with Chinese, there is an undeniable logophiliac madness, perhaps the same kind that beset the late Saussure. How sound Pound's mind was in those Pisa and St. Elizabeths years has remained a puzzling question for scholars. With no expertise in psychology, I would not venture into this topic but would just quote an authority, Dr. Jerome Kavka, who once treated Pound at St. Elizabeths. In his posthumous article, "The Dreams of Ezra Pound," Kavka recalls the poet's answer to the question as to whether Pound thought himself insane: "No, I don't think I am insane but I am so shot to pieces that it will take me years to write a sensible piece of prose." According to Kavka, the poet/patient resisted psychotherapy, regarding it more or less as blackmail. But the doctor also noticed Pound's desperation to hang on by seeking his own therapy: "There was an air of tragic resignation on his part with some feeble assertion to hold onto that which for him had always spelled cohesion of the self—the capacity to write."[31] Claiming his inability to write any sensible prose, Pound ended up translating the Confucian Classics and writing some of his more heavily China-themed poems, the *Rock-Drill Cantos*, the *Thrones Cantos*, and, unknown to most, a Chinese poem.

On January 25, 1952, Pound sent Fang a letter, "enclose exercise/got to find some means of fixing approx sound in remains of disjecta mente [scattered mind]." The enclosed "exercise" turned out to be a quadruplet in Chinese:[32]

閒　成　使　敬
顯　至　周　花
先　在　栽　忠
仙　止　采　見

Read vertically, from right to left, the poem roughly translates, in the words of Angela Palandri:

1. Respect for the kind of intelligence that enables the cherrystone to grow cherries and uphold the cultural florescence with utmost sincerity and perception.
2. Based upon those aforesaid qualities the rulers of the Chou dynasty had cultivated and collected the fruit of their civilization.
3. Governmental and personal actions must proceed and progress to the ultimate goal and come to rest upon perfection.
4. Only then can one enjoy the leisurely life (by watching the moon at one's door), and manifest and glorify the immortality of men of the past.[33]

Palandri, still a young Chinese student when she first visited Pound at St. Elizabeths, is overly generous here in her paraphrase of this Chinese poem, because even Pound himself was not so sure about the meaning of his Chinese concoction, as he asked Fang:

1. does this make sense
2. does it scan, according to an accepted chinese ear?
3. wd/ 4th line be considered bad taste, stunt merely changing tone?

Fang's reply was frank and disappointing: "The four lines ... cannot mean what you intend (granted that I do understand you). As for the sounds, there are too many gutturals and too many of what the vorchristlicher Christ called snake sounds; one labial does not seem to relieve the overwrought alliteration. And rhyme? The fourth line sounds like a jeu d'esprit. Sorry to disappoint you."[34]

Pound, however, did not give up. He soon sent the poem to Palandri with a note: "I have a friend who really knows, & who says my little poem ... can't possibly mean what he thinks I want it to mean. If you really want to help me you might tell me what you think it means, if it makes sense @ all." Anticipating disapproval from yet another native Chinese, Pound quickly added, "The 4th line is a trick line, that I did not expect a chinese to approve ... AND then: people who speak a language are often incapable of either reading or singing a poem. The other problem would be: how many more ideograms would I have to add to make my meaning clear if it is possible to get @ it."[35] Pound's ambivalence is obvious here: on the one hand, he knew that his Chinese poem did not make too much sense to a native speaker, but on the other, he believed that a native speaker might not be the best reader of poetry in that particular language or the best judge of how poetic language works. The fourth line in Pound's Chinese poem is indeed tricky, with four words all pronounced as *xian*, albeit in different tones. Almost no Chinese would write a line like that, not because there is no avant-garde poetry in China, but because to write such a line is to explore the frontier or explode the limit of language, as the Chinese linguist Chao Yuen Ren did in his presentation at the Macy Conference in 1953 (see the coda of this book). Pound had thought about including this poem in *The Cantos*, but he never did. Instead, he composed another Chinese line in Canto 110, "yueh ming mo hsien peng" (月明莫顯朋). Approximately meaning "bright moon doesn't reveal friends," this line is barely idiomatic Chinese, but it is an ingenious play on the visual homology of the sun (日) and moon (月) radicals, reminiscent of the famous example of 日昇東 used in Fenollosa's article (see chap. 5).

"When I say that the orders 'Bring me sugar' and 'Bring me milk' make sense, but not the combination 'Milk me sugar,'" says Ludwig Wittgenstein in *Philosophical Investigations*, "that does not mean that the utterance of this combination of words has no effect." To Wittgenstein, who remained restless in language as well as between languages (i.e., German and English), to say a combination of words makes no sense merely "excludes it from the sphere of language and thereby bounds the domain of language."[36] Beyond that sphere or domain, in the words of Lecercle, "there is no chaos out there, only parts of language that are no longer or not yet acceptable—but that are potentially acceptable."[37] "Xian xian xian

xian" may be syntactically awkward or impossible, but the repetition commands a rhythmic competence, just as "yue ming mo xian peng" reveals visual rhymes like anagrams in an alphabetic language.

Make no mistake: I am not claiming that Pound was a genius who has composed superb Chinese lines. Instead, I see his adventure into Chinese as a poetic exploration of the rhizomatic, subterranean, nomadic, and unconscious zones of language, a project not so dissimilar to Khlebnikov's Zaum. Whereas Zaum takes us beyond sense by appealing to our "transrational," Pound's Chinese is a Joycean portmanteau whose meaning hovers between languages, between language and its own other. In this way, it makes no sense to speak of *The Cantos*' completion in Chinese, be it Pound's own Chinese composition or the translation of his work, because Pound's greatest achievement in *The Cantos* is his translational poetics, creating rhizomatic links among the twenty or so languages he used or quoted in the work, charging language with "meaning to the utmost possible degree."[38] Let's look at just a few lines from *The Cantos*:

> plowed in the sacred field and unwound the silk worms early
> in tensile 顯
> in the light of light is the virtu
> "sunt lumina" said Erigena Scotus
> As of Shun on Mt Taishan
> and in the hall of the forebears[39]

Here is an echo chamber of reverberations across languages, a silver screen of moving images fading in and out of diverse scripts. *Silk*, *tensile*, and the radical 絲 in the Chinese character 顯 all contain the syllable /si/. The English word *tensile* carries a double alliteration with the Chinese name "Taishan." The Latin word *sunt* in "sunt lumina" contains "sun," as do the Chinese name "Shun" and the character 顯, thus creating paragrams across Chinese, English, and Latin. 顯 (*xian*) also rhymes with Taishan in Chinese. If we want to dig even deeper or listen more closely, not only is 顯 the second word in the fourth line of Pound's Chinese poem, but "forebears" can easily be the literal translation of the last two words of the same line, "先仙," which would add a hidden rhyme with 顯 and Taishan.

In "The Task of the Translator," Benjamin warns of the enormous danger of literal translation: "The gates of language thus expanded and modified may slam shut and enclose the translator in silence.... [M]eaning plunges from abyss to abyss until it threatens to become lost in the bottomless depths of language." For Benjamin, the only way to stop such a fall to Babel is the Truth in Holy Scripture: "It is vouchsafed in Holy Writ alone."[40] For Pound, however, literal translation in the Benjaminian sense, but done through his own ideogrammic method, opens up rather than shuts down the gates of language. "The sum of human wisdom," says Pound in *ABC of Reading*, "is not contained in any one language, and no single language is CAPABLE of expressing all forms and degrees of human comprehension."[41] Whether or not *The Cantos* is truly "a great ball of crystal," whether or not it is even made in China, Pound at least points us in the direction of a world literature that is inherently translational and multilingual.

I began this chapter on a personal note, relating my own tribulations as Pound's Chinese translator. Please allow me to conclude in the same fashion. Despite the surprising success of the Chinese edition of *The Pisan Cantos*, I always have one regret: my inability to preserve the multilingual textuality of Pound's work, or rather, to protect it against the corrosion by monolingual interests on the part of publishers and readers. In my original manuscript, I provided Chinese translation for that part of Pound's text originally in English but reproduced those instances where the original was other than English. As a result, in my manuscript version, French, Italian, or Greek would appear as French, Italian, or Greek in the main text but with a translation in the footnote. That way I was hoping to reproduce the multilingual textuality that lies at the heart of Pound's poetics. Unfortunately, the Chinese publisher objected to my approach. Pound was already difficult enough, they said, and who's going to pick up a book full of foreign words on a page? Hard as I tried, I was unable to convince the publisher that monolingual pages would undermine, if not contradict, Pound's poetics. As a result, the published version was a monolingually Chinese edition, in which everything appears as Chinese, a sui generis "Made-in-China Ezra Pound." That monolingual effect might have strengthened Yang Lian's conviction about *The Cantos*' completion in Chinese.

In his assessment of Basic English, Ezra Pound, if we recall, said that he had never used a foreign word where English would have served: "When it has been an Italian or French word, it has asserted or I have meant it to assert some meaning not current in English, some shade or gradation."[42] If Pound still sounded a bit defensive here, his statement in *Guide to Kulchur* was blunt: "a monolingual culture will never breed anything but asses."[43] Publishers and readers alike would do well to listen to ole Ez.

Thirteen Ways of Looking at a Blackbird Too Big to Fail

[CHAPTER FOUR]

Wallace Stevens, John Cage, and the Poetics of Risk

Poetry and surety claims are not as unlikely a combination as they may seem.

WALLACE STEVENS

On the night of September 25, 2008, only days after the spectacular collapse of the Wall Street firm Lehman Brothers had sent the stock market into a tailspin, causing the worst financial catastrophe since the Great Depression, American poetry was celebrating its best at a gathering in New York City, to launch that year's edition of *Best American Poetry*. Addressing the series editor, David Lehman (perhaps no relation to the firm that had just gone bankrupt), and the evening event's emcee, Robert Polito, the poet and critic Charles Bernstein, whose work was also included in the volume, read a statement. It began as follows: "Chairman Lehman, Secretary Polito, distinguished poets and readers—I regret having to interrupt the celebrations tonight with an important announcement. As you know, the glut of illiquid, insolvent, and troubled poems is clogging the literary arteries of the West. These debt-ridden poems threaten to infect other areas of the literary sector and ultimately to topple our culture industry."

With a sly nod to the political leaders who had come together to propose a massive bailout known as TARP (Troubled Asset Relief Program), Bernstein went on to say, "Cultural leaders have come together to announce a massive poetry bailout: leveraged and unsecured poems, poetry derivatives, delinquent poems, and subprime poems will be removed from circulation in the biggest poetry bailout since the Victorian era." Parodying the Republican presidential candidate, John McCain, who had abruptly curtailed his election campaign, returned to Washington, and tried to reassure the panic-stricken nation with some awkwardly executed political sloganeering, Bernstein stated, "Let there be no mistake: the fundamentals of poetry are sound. The problem is not poetry but poems. The crisis has been precipitated by the escalation of poetry debt—poems that circulate in the market at an economic loss due to their difficulty, incompetence, or irrelevance. Illiquid poetry assets are choking off the flow of imagination that is so vital to our literature."[1]

No one familiar with Bernstein's humor would fail to recognize the tongue-in-cheek nature of his satirical statement, which would soon be printed in *Harper's Magazine* with the title, "Poetry Bailout Will Restore Confidence of Readers." Bernstein did not pull any punches as he took the historical occasion to ridicule what he had famously dubbed the Official Verse Culture, that is, mainstream literary establishments, including publishers, review journals, award committees, fellowship foundations, and MFA programs, that work together to promote a very narrow, myopic spectrum of poetry. The irony was hard to miss: just as the nation was reeling from an economic disaster caused in part by the three rating agencies, Moody, Standard and Poor, and Fitch, which conspired with greedy financial institutions to give false ratings to toxic, subprime assets, the leaders of the Official Verse Culture were gathering on that September night to give an "AAA" stamp to what they considered to be the "Best of American Poetry."

Technically speaking, what caused the 2008 financial meltdown was a problem of insurance. Rampant predatory lending in the subprime mortgage sector went unnoticed for long thanks to the so-called credit default swap, or CDS, an exotic species genetically engineered in the jungles of Wall Street. CDS is no more than an insurance scheme, an elaborate casino game masked and marketed as risk management. When AIG, the world's largest insurance company, was on the verge of going belly-up because it could no longer cover those risky CDS bets, the U.S. government had to step in and bailed out financial institutions deemed "too big to fail." Stretching Bernstein's analogy a bit further, we may ask: Is poetry too big to fail? Or, is it just some poems that are too big to fail? If those cornerstones of modern poetry, such as *The Waste Land* or *The Cantos*, were allowed to fail—in fact, many have seen them as "failures"—would it topple the Culture Industry, or would it doom the insurers of the Official Verse Culture? While these big questions will have to be explored on a different occasion, my immediate concern here is with the relationship between poetry and risk.

As Wallace Stevens puts it in the epigraph above, the art of poetry is not so different from the management of risk. In fact, as I show in this chapter by way of Stevens, who lived a double life as a poet and an insurance man, poetry is deeply invested in risk. Looking from the depth inside the post-crash crater of late-late capitalism in the twenty-first century, articulations made by Stevens in the early to mid-twentieth century, when capitalism was still young and raging, sound quite prescient, if not downright prophetic. Moreover, when Bernstein parodied the unsustainable poetic scene, he was careful to limit his remarks to the West. Even though both global capitalism and world literature have made it difficult to contain disasters within one region or hemisphere, there might be a glimmer of hope for an alternative way of worrying, if not fixing, the problems of risk management.

Risk, real or perceived, is ubiquitous today: terrorism, war, financial loss, currency crisis, pollution, natural disaster, global warming, airplane crash, car accident, nuclear meltdown, infectious diseases, poverty, unemployment, alien invasion, Donald Trump, and so on. In this chapter, I am trying to address the issue of risk by reading the work of Stevens, who as an insurance man knew a great deal about risk and risk management and who as a poet was also deeply concerned with the unexpected, uncertain, and risky. Above all, I want to showcase the intersection between poetic imagination and statistical imagination against a backdrop of a world that has become increasingly risky and where chance and uncertainty cannot be tamed. Further strengthening this connection between poetry and risk, I argue, is an imaginative and fruitful engagement with the East on the part of Stevens and other American poets.[2]

(1)

"Among twenty snowy mountains,
The only moving thing
Was the eye of the blackbird."

"Thirteen," says Helen Vendler in her authoritative study of "Thirteen Ways of Looking at a Blackbird," "is the eccentric number."[3] Mathematically, 13 is an indivisible, prime number with no stable root. In everyday English, 13 is the unlucky number, suggesting the likelihood of mishap. Even the seemingly benign expression "baker's dozen" indicates the possibility of an unwanted outcome. The cost of making an extra cookie or croissant is a bet against accident, a small attempt at risk management. Vendler, like most of the critics after her, regards the blackbird in the poem as a bad omen, a direct descendant of Edgar Allan Poe's raven in "Nevermore." Indeed, when "Thirteen Ways of Looking at a Blackbird" first appeared in December 1917, the world was in the throes of the Great War, haunted by Death, the Blackbird. The Spanish Flu would hit in two months and wipe out fifty million people worldwide. Against the backdrop of a still, frozen white mass of twenty snowy mountains, a decimated landscape that T. S. Eliot would in a few years down the road characterize as a "waste land," the only moving thing was the eye of a haunting blackbird.

However, such a symbolic reading of these thirteen minimalist, haiku-like stanzas must be counterbalanced, as Susan Howe suggests, by attention to the poet's "intricacies of form and measure." In her recent study of Stevens via the work of Howe, Marjorie Perloff remarks, "*Form* here refers, not only to a given poem's metrics or stanzaic structure but also to the internal 'frequencies' of sound and word repetition that bind phrase and line together." It is what Howe calls "word frequencies and zero zones" in Stevens's poetic work.[4] For us, we want to pay attention to the poem's latent arithmetic or algorithmic structure, something that an insurance man, or a surety poet, might well be toying with. Despite the number 20, this stanza actually contains twenty-one syllables:

Among twenty snowy mountains	8
The only moving thing	6
Was the eye of the blackbird	7
	21

As one critic keenly points out, the equation here "seems to be twenty [white] mountains, plus one black eye (a perpetual pun?)."[5] The number game encapsulates a black-and-white, or colorless, world of mathematical abstraction, an opening salvo in a poetic sequence full of numerical calculations, chance operations, and above all a deep concern with risk, an obsession with untamed chance and uncertainty.

"The most decisive conceptual event of twentieth-century physics," writes Ian Hacking in *The Taming of Chance*, "has been the discovery that the world is not deterministic. Causality, long the bastion of metaphysics, was toppled, or at least tilted: the past does not determine exactly what happens next." In the words of Immanuel Kant, a firm believer in rationality who nonetheless foresaw the grim future, "the dismal reign of chance replaces the guiding principle of reason." What Thomas Kuhn famously called a paradigm shift did not happen just in physics or other natural sciences but also in psychology when Freud uncovered the unconscious and in philosophy when in 1892 the iconoclastic American pragmatist Charles Sanders Peirce proposed "to examine the common belief that every single fact in the universe is determined by law." Peirce's conclusion was that "the world is irreducibly chancy." He believed that chance is ontological, not merely epistemological. Hence he called it, oxymoronically, absolute chance. Against the doctrine of necessity, the self-labeled "backwoodsman" of American philosophy pitched the doctrine of chance. To paraphrase Nietzsche, the most passionate critic of determinism, God as the ultimate guarantor and underwriter for the certainty of all meanings is dead.[6]

Paradoxically, in response to a world becoming chancy, random, and indeterminate, there was the rise of statistics and probability. Or, as Hacking puts it, "the more the indeterminism, the more the control." From census to crime data, from urban zoning to disease control, laws of probability relying on enumeration began to take over all aspects of human society since the late nineteenth century. Realism gave way to a new real, the statistical real. Charts, graphs, and other forms of numerical abstractions constitute a statistical society's response to the erosion of determinism. "Most professionals now believe that representative sampling gives more accurate information about a population than an exhaustive census. This was unthinkable during most of the 19th century."[7]

The insurance industry, hailing from its humble roots in maritime commerce, emerged as the Prince Charming in the Age of Indeterminacy and began to reign over our lives—health insurance, life insurance, auto insurance, property insurance, fire insurance, and in the context of the United States, Social Security, as a socialized, government-controlled public insurance program. By 1930, according to Jason Puskar, "many middle class Americans owned private insurance policies on their lives, health, automobiles, homes, travel, and livestock and crops, in addition to insurance against industrial accidents, business interruptions, or legal liability."[8] Hence, Stevens declared in 1937, "we may well be entering an insurance era" (*CPP* 793).

Mostly known as a modernist poet with a penchant for abstraction, Stevens had a "day job" at the Hartford Indemnity and Insurance Company, where he worked for the greater part of his life and rose to the high rank of vice president of the company. Hartford, Connecticut, I should add, was once America's capital of insurance, dubbed "a city of calculated risk." At his company, Stevens specialized in fidelity and surety. Fidelity bonds guarantee employees' honesty, and surety bonds guarantee a contractor's satisfactory completion of contracted work, say, a sewer line or road paving. Actually, Stevens did more work in surety than fidelity, thus earning him the epithet "surety poet." The company also covered fire insurance, a department where Benjamin Lee Whorf had worked until his early death in 1941. Whorf was that eccentric, self-taught linguist who gave us, among other things, the famous Whorfian Hypothesis about linguistic relativism, a notion that the structure of our language conditions the way we look at the world. In fact, some of the key examples Whorf used in his influential essay, "The Relation of Habitual Thought and Behavior to Language" (1941), came from his experience as a fire prevention engineer at Stevens's company. Whorf also acknowledged that the "indifference to the unexpectedness of life" built into Standard Average European language groups had motivated his writing of that landmark essay.[9] The other line of insurance is liability, or workers' compensation, a field in which the famous

Prague-born, German-language writer Franz Kafka was an expert. In *The Metamorphosis* (1915), a traveling salesman wakes up in the morning and is surprised to find that he has turned into a giant, monstrous bug. How do you insure against that kind of accident?[10]

Back to Stevens. Despite his dual career as a poet and insurance company executive, scholars of modern poetry, until recently, have long disregarded the insurance side of Stevens's work, treating it as if it had nothing to do with his poetry and poetics. Stories are legion as to how Stevens himself kept the two sides of his work separate from each other, like this one told by the Yale professor Louis Martz, who had invited Stevens to New Haven to give the prestigious Bergen lecture at the university.

> He came up from New York with a big briefcase because he had been down doing legal business and came directly here.... As he was arranging to give his lecture, I took him back to my office. He opened up the briefcase and said, "Now you see everything is neatly sorted out here. Over in this compartment is my insurance business with the farmers, and over in this compartment, this is my lecture and some poems that I want to read. I keep them completely separate."

Or, as in the following anecdote told by his colleague, Stevens was said to have kept his poetry and business affairs at the company completely separate as well.

> He'd be writing poems right there at his desk, because he would stop dictating to Mrs. Baldwin. He would stop right in the middle of dictating, and he would reach down in his right-hand drawer, and he would just write down something, put it back. I've seen him do that. He had a peculiar filing system. He always filed his poetry notes in his lower right corner of his desk, which opened most of the time to a degree. It seemed to me there were sheaves and sheaves. And sometimes he would reach down, and he'd shuffle through three or four. He'd scratch out something or put something in. Or he might take the top one and just add a line or two. All of a sudden, he'd be reading a case, and I've seen him reach down in his drawer and just pick something up. His private copies of his commercial work or his business letters would go in his lower left-hand drawer.[11]

In spite of these anecdotal and biographical facts that seem to support a time-honored critical consensus with regard to the separation of Stevens's poetry from his insurance work, the poet himself made statements to the effect that the idea and business logic of insurance in fact lies at the heart of his poetics. He acknowledged, as quoted above, "Poetry and surety claims are not as unlikely a combination as they may seem."[12] To take him seriously as a "surety poet," someone whose poetic imagination and statistical imagination are deeply intertwined, we need to explore the ways in which Stevens in his dual capacity as a poet and an insurance man exploits and manages risk in his writing and business. More important, we need to ponder the larger implications for our own understanding and management of risk today.

(2)

"I was of three minds,
Like a tree
In which there are three blackbirds."

Tree, three, there. There are three. A game of statistical probability: How many different meaningful combinations can you make out of the five letters, *t*, *h*, *e*, *r*, and *e*? Interestingly, the surety poet gives us only three—tree, there, three—although there are many more possibilities, such as he, her, here, the, tee, thee, and so on. In a stanza numbered 2, the poet chooses varying manifestations of trinity: three minds, three blackbirds, three combinations of letters, and, most notably, three lines. One may argue that Stevens was composing in the style of haiku, which is indeed a tercet in format. But a passing glance, or counting by fingers, would reveal no recognizable pattern in the correlation between sequence number of the stanza and the number of lines in that stanza: stanza 1 has three lines; 2 has three; 3, two; 4, four; 5, five; 6, seven; 7, five; 8, five; 9, three; and so on. Not chaos but unpredictability seems to be the matrix of the sequence. Looking this way, the choice of three in stanza 2, as well as the inversion in the next stanza—a couplet for stanza 3—appears deliberate, or deliberately off, like a person of three minds rather than the proverbial two, as in "I am of two minds."

In *The Modernist Response to Chinese Art*, Zhaoming Qian studies Stevens's debt to Zen Buddhism. He argues that "Thirteen Ways" illustrates the Zen preference for "informality over formality, irregularity over regularity, odd numbers over even numbers." Counting the line numbers, which vary from two, three, and four to five, six, and seven, Qian suggests that the poem betrays an irregularity that is typical of Zen art.[13] Taking a cue from Qian and others, we need to explore the triangulation of Stevens's poetry, risk discourse, and imaginative engagement with the East. In fact, Chinese philosophical understanding of risk and its unique brand of risk management have largely remained absent in contemporary thoughts on the subject, except in the field of poetry and poetics, where Zen Buddhism, Daoism, and the *I Ching* have exerted a profound impact. Via Stevens and other American poets, such as John Cage, who was clearly influenced by Asian thoughts, I hope to open up a new path toward worlding in a risky world.

I too am of three minds. The three blackbirds on the tree of my mind are Robert Frost, Edgar Allan Poe, and Aristotle.

(3)

"The blackbird whirled in the autumn winds.
It was a small part of the pantomime."

A poem, says Robert Frost, "runs a course of lucky events." In other words, for a poem to be born into the world, it needs luck. A good old pragmatist, Frost advocates a poetry that stakes its claim on the wayward, chancy, unexpected, surprising: "It is but a trick poem and no poem at all if the best of it was thought of first and saved for the last. It finds its own name as it goes and discovers the best waiting for it in some final phrase at once wise and sad.... No surprise for the writer, no surprise for the reader."[14] Nothing would better illustrate Frost's pragmatist approach to life and poetic experience as one of chance operation than his classic poem, "The Road Not Taken" (1916), written about the same time as "Thirteen Ways of Looking at a Blackbird":

Two roads diverged in a yellow wood,
And sorry I could not travel both
And be one traveler, long I stood
And looked down one as far as I could
To where it bent in the undergrowth;

Then took the other, as just as fair,
And having perhaps the better claim,
Because it was grassy and wanted wear;
Though as for that the passing there
Had worn them really about the same

In addition to the thematic concern with the wayward, unpredictable quality of life, "how way leads on to way" after one has made a choice between two probabilities, like 0 and 1, the words as building blocks of the poem are also charged with a pun-ish energy, an undercurrent of uncertainty, slipperiness, and vagueness: far/fair, black/back, wear/where, and ultimately, I/I, the same word but with a different reference.[15] As Gertrude Stein would say, "The difference is spreading."[16] I draw your special attention to the word *claim* in the line, "And having perhaps the better claim." Claim is an insurance term, a demand made after a loss has occurred. It is as if the traveler knows fully that there will be danger ahead, and the road he chooses will enable him to claim and recuperate his loss more sufficiently, to make good on the inevitable loss.

Poetry, just like life, also involves and invests in chance operation and risk taking. "It was chance," Frost says, "when the right subject matter and the right words came together."[17] It cannot be mechanically prearranged. In section 3 of Stevens's poem, the resonance of blackbird and whirled (ir), whirled and wind (w-i-d), autumn and pantomime (tum, tom), part and pant-, would exemplify what Roman Jakobson would call paronomasia: "a semantic confrontation of phonemically similar words irrespective of any etymological connection, plays a considerable role in the life of language."[18] The play on the chain of words, *there*, *three*, *tree*, in stanza 2 is also an example of paronomasia. These semantic confrontations of words are more or less chance encounters in a linguistic universe ruled or determined not by grammar, etymology, or rationality. "Like giants," Frost said, "we are always hurling experience ahead of us to pave the future with against the day when we may want to strike a line of purpose across it for somewhere. The line will have the more charm for not being mechanically straight. We enjoy the straight crookedness of a good walking stick."[19] Poetry, for Frost, is a private exercise in chance operation that inevitably and positively involves risk, a case of what Thoreau once called "to be wild with nothing to be wild about." In this sense, Frost stands solidly in the tradition of understanding risk as something worth taking. Especially in poetry, the risk of losing love either in the sense of unrequited love or losing a loved one is a time-honored theme. Shakespeare's "So long lives this, and this gives life to thee" and John Keats's "She cannot fade, though thou hast not thy bliss" are both poetic strategies of risk management, using poetry to ward off the hazard of time passing and the fair one getting old or getting away. The English word *risk*, I want to remind you, derives from the French word *risqué* and was spelled *risqué* until 1621. Contemporary studies of risk, understandably, also cover personal relationship, intimacy as a risky/risqué affair, or marriage as a risky commitment or investment. What is a prenuptial agreement if not risk management?

In the art of poetic management of love as a risk/risqué business, no one has invested more than did Edgar Allan Poe.

(4)

"A man and a woman
Are one.
A man and a woman and a blackbird
Are one."

"The Raven" is a poem about a man, a woman (Lenore), and a blackbird whose name is "Nevermore":

> Much I marvelled this ungainly fowl to hear discourse so plainly,
> Though its answer little meaning—little relevancy bore;
> For we cannot help agreeing that no living human being
> Ever yet was blessed with seeing bird above his chamber door—
> Bird or beast upon the sculptured bust above his chamber door,
> With such name as "Nevermore."[20]

Edgar Allan Poe is our first risk manager in poetry, one who regards risk as a hazard to avoid. He was one of the first major writers—Balzac being the other—who looked at literature through the modern prism of probability. Poe's manifesto, "The Philosophy of Composition," was a blueprint for insuring against the kind of risky poetic ventures launched by the likes of Frost, who contemplates the loss of poetry in prenatal meditation or postmortem translation. Recalling to mind the progressive steps of his composition of the poem "The Raven," Poe brags like an insurance agent making a sales pitch: "It is my design to render it manifest that no one point in its composition is referable either to accident or intuition—that the work proceeded, step by step, to its completion with the precision and rigid consequence of a mathematical problem."[21] He leaves, literally, nothing to chance, trying to ensure that all aspects of the poem, from intended effect, tone, and refrain to versification, are results of careful mathematical calculation, acquiring the sense of logical inevitability and certainty.

In some ways, Poe's fantastical essay was a nineteenth-century update on Aristotle's apology for poetry. Against Plato's accusation of poets as liars twice removed from truth, Aristotle defended poetry in three ways: first, imitation is human nature; second, poetry has the cathartic function; third, poetry dwells in probability.

> It is not the poet's function to narrate events that have actually happened, but rather, events such as might occur and have the capability of occurring in accordance with the laws of probability or necessity. For the historian and the poet do not differ by their writing in prose or verse ... [but rather]

> in the fact that the historian narrates events that have actually happened, whereas the poet writes about things as they might possibly occur. Poetry, therefore, is more philosophical and more significant than history, for poetry is more concerned with the universal, and history more with the individual. By universal I mean what sort of man turns out to say or do what sort of thing according to probability or necessity—this being the goal poetry aims at.[22]

History pertains to the individual; poetry to the universal, what may happen or have the higher probability or even certainty of happening. Aristotle, the best defender of poetry, has defended the universality of probability. Aristotle, it seems, was poetry's first actuary.

Following Aristotle, Poe's contemporary Emily Dickinson famously said, "I dwell in possibility." Doing it in a more pseudoscientific manner, Poe, in the wilderness of seemingly infinite variables, completes his poem by a principle recognizable to any insurance man looking at a chart or a table: "Everything is within the limits of the accountable—of the real."[23] Equating the accountable, mathematical or statistical, with the real or equating the actual with the actuarial is a twentieth-century invention. Counting a man and a woman together as one is actually and actuarially sound, and so is counting a man, a woman, and a blackbird together as one. Both are statistically real, depending on the metrics you use, and I don't just mean poetic metrics.

More important, counting a man, a woman, and a blackbird as one, as a collective, a population group, lies at the heart of the industrial logic of insurance. Let me explain.

(5)

"I do not know which to prefer,
The beauty of inflections
Or the beauty of innuendoes,
The blackbird whistling
Or just after."

Stevens, the poet, hesitates between inflections and innuendos, between the heard melodies of the blackbird and the sweet silence afterward. As he writes in "The Snow Man," "Nothing that is not there and the nothing that is" (*CPP* 8). Or, to quote from John Keats, "Heard melodies are sweet, but those unheard / Are sweeter." Besides the trick on the ear, appearance can be deceiving. Indeed, there is also an optical illusion one should be aware of here. As Perloff shrewdly points out, the word *innuendoes* may look longer than the word *inflections*, but in fact, it is actually shorter in the number of letters (ten), whereas its partner has eleven letters.[24] Before one chooses or prefers, some abstraction, mathematical or otherwise, seems necessary.

Stevens, the insurance man, studies the claims and charts, the particulars and abstractions. "It must be abstract," insists the poet in "Notes toward a Supreme Fiction" (*CPP* 329). Statistical abstraction is the backbone of the insurance industry, which looks at each accident, each event, through the lens of numerical probability. In the eye of an insurance agent, each accident, as real as it gets, with its nitty-gritty details, will eventually show up on the company report or the actuarial table as a number, a dot on a chart, or to pun on Frost, a figure (a figure a poem makes), that helps the company calculate future risk and adjust the premiums to charge. As Joseph Stalin once put it crudely, "One death is a tragedy, one million is a statistic."

The concept "major man" in Stevens's long poem "Notes toward a Supreme Fiction" gives us a clue as to what Stevens both as a poet and as an insurance man thinks about poetic and statistical abstraction:

> The major abstraction is the idea of man
> And major man is its exponent, abler
> In the abstract than in his singular (*CPP* 336)

As Stevens writes elsewhere in the poem, the so-called major man is an "abstraction blooded" (333), a man "of composite nature" (643). He is a descendant of the "average man" as conceptualized in the early nineteenth century when the theory of probability and the science of statistics began to influence social policies. According to Adolphe Quetelet, a powerhouse of the statistical movement in the 1830s and 1840s, the average man was divorced 0.17 times and had 2.2 children.[25] But of course there was no such a man in reality, except in the statistical real, consubstantial with the poetic real, which Stevens has dubbed "a supreme fiction." Many critics have noted Stevens's penchant for aloof abstraction, and some of the critiques have gone so far as to equate, mistakenly, the "abstract" with the "inhuman." Vendler, perhaps Stevens's most sympathetic reader, suggests that his poetry specializes in "second-order reflection" rather than "first-order personal narrative." Joseph Harrington observes that Stevens's poems are full of "theoretical people," or to pun on Emerson's phrase, "representative men." Mark Halliday mounts "a moral critique of Stevens as a writer whose work apparently embodies 'an objectionable withdrawal ... from caring about ... individual other persons.'" Against some of these readings, I want to suggest that Stevens's interest in what Anthony Hecht has called "the very beauty of the abstract things" should be understood in relation to the statistical imagination exercised by an insurance man.[26]

"At its heart," Michael Szalay points out, "risk identifies the frequency with which a given outcome will occur in a given target group. As a measure of probability, risk is not predictive for the individual per se."[27] When Quetelet claimed in 1815 that for any given year in the city of Paris "we know in advance how many individuals will dirty their hands with the blood of others, how many will be forgers, how many prisoners, nearly as well as one enumerate in advance the births and deaths that must take place," the Frenchman didn't mean that any Parisian in that specific year would have the same amount of likelihood of committing a murder, forgery, going to jail, etc.[28] As François Ewald reminded us, "Risk is collective, whereas an accident, as damage, misfortune and suffering, is always individual, striking at one and not another, a risk of accident affects a population. Strictly speaking, there is no such a thing as an individual risk."[29] In Szalay's words, "Insurance orders and systematizes what seem to be random events by studying those events as they occur in population groups; the population group alone is the subject of statistical analysis."[30]

Stevens says of insured risks, "There is no difference between the worm in the apple and the tack in the can of sardines, and not the slightest difference between the piano out of tune and a person disabled" (*CPP* 793). From the point of view of the insurance business, each instance can be abstracted into an actuarial table and a uniform premium affixed. "The beggar in Rome / Is the beggar in Bogota," as the poet writes in "Owl's Clover" (*CPP* 162). Connecticut, Tennessee, Florida. Place-names in Stevens's work are often proportionally too large for the context. "I placed a jar in Tennessee" (*CCP* 61). Where in Tennessee? Places devoid of specifics.

Here lies the secret of Stevens's aesthetics of abstraction, counting "a man and a woman" as one, counting "a man, a woman, and a blackbird" also as one. Such a supreme fiction, as mentioned earlier, has lent itself to attack by critics. Randall Jarrell, in particular, equated the Stevensian abstraction with solipsism, as he commented dismissively, "Little of Stevens' work has the dramatic immediacy, the mesmeric, involving humanity."[31] While the professional hazard of an insurance man may lend some intellectual justification for the kind of abstraction in Stevens's poetry, there is another source of inspiration his critics have often ignored, that is, his imaginative engagement with the East.

As a poet, Stevens first gained national recognition after winning a *Poetry* magazine contest in 1916, a $100 cash prize for his verse drama, *Three Travelers Watch a Sunrise*. The play features three Chinese, attended by two black servants, fixing tea in the Pennsylvania woods, waiting for sunrise.

Contemporaneous with Pound's *Cathay* (1915) and Amy Lowell's *Pictures of the Floating World* (1919), *Three Travelers* is yet another specimen of *chinoiserie* in vogue at the time. With a hint of the Japanese Noh theater, the minimalist play is almost devoid of plot development and characterization. In fact, as Richard Alan Schwartz points out in his examination of the textual history of the play, *Three Travelers* is designed only to demonstrate a concept. The artistic goal was explicated by Stevens himself in a letter to the editor of *Poetry*, Harriet Monroe, on May 29, 1916: "The play is simply intended to demonstrate that just as objects in nature affect us ... so, on the other hand, we affect objects in nature, by projecting our moods, emotions, etc."[32] In other words, the interaction between humans and nature, rather than human drama, remains Stevens's primary concern. This play, along with the two poems "Thirteen Ways" and "Six Significant Landscapes," was written in a period when Stevens was preoccupied with Oriental art and ideas. In a journal entry dating from this period, Stevens copied an unattributed observation: "It is in landscape and the themes allied to landscape, that the art of the East is superior to our own—the art of the West excels in the human drama."[33] In the same letter to Monroe, Stevens further explained the intentional lack of human drama in his play, rejecting what he called "the invasion of humanity."[34] In *Three Travelers* there is a hint of a story about an Italian tragedian who ran away with his neighbor's daughter and then ended up hanging himself from a tree. But Stevens chose not to develop the narrative and left it hanging, as he wrote to Monroe, "To some extent, this is intentional, because I do not desire to become involved in the story or characters of the man and the girl."[35] Such a stance of resisting humanity's invasion would lead to the kind of meditative detachment from the human world characteristic of Stevens's poetry. In "The Snow Man," for instance, the poet asks the listener not to think of any misery in the sound of the wind and become "nothing himself" (*CPP* 8).

Likewise, the three Chinese in the play are never fully developed as characters. They are described only at the beginning: "The first is short, fat, quizzical, and of middle age. The second is of middle height, thin and turning gray; a man of sense and sympathy. The third is a young man, intent, detached. They wear European clothes." Having satisfied the minimum requirement of casting, the play quickly moves on and spends no more ink on characterization. As Schwartz shrewdly points out, the characters are merely agents toward the goal of demonstrating a concept. The three Chinese remain samples of an "abstract man" discussed earlier. They are, in Stevens's own words, "as abstract as porcelain." Or, to adopt the lingo of Stevens's time (remember that unfortunate title "Like Decorations in a Nigger Cemetery"?), the three Chinamen are as abstract as china. Critics who, as did Jarrell, find a lack of "dramatic immediacy" or "mesmeric, involving humanity" in Stevens's work, should remember these lines from the play: "There is a seclusion of porcelain / That humanity never invades" (*CPP* 601–14).

(6)

"Icicles filled the long window
With barbaric glass.
The shadow of the blackbird
Crossed it, to and fro.
The mood
Traced in the shadow
An indecipherable cause."

While "It must be abstract" constitutes the first credo in "Notes toward a Supreme Fiction," we ought to remember that "It must change" is the second (*CPP* 336). Despite his penchant for abstraction, which often gives his work an appearance of inhumanity, as an insurance man and a poet, Stevens never wards off risk, chaos, the nitty-gritty, the irrational. If anything, the insurance industry is by nature reliant on calculated risk to make money and therefore simultaneously embraces capitalist abstraction and the dynamism of change. Similarly, poetry, as Frost and others have suggested, is an exercise in risk management, which feeds on chance and the irrational.

While Stevens must be acquainted with the basic principles of actuarial math, which looks at the world and events through the cold eye of numbers and probability, the particular kind of insurance he specialized in, that is, surety claims, almost never relies on actuarial work. As Jason Puskar reminds us, "The surety business differs significantly from all other forms of insurance. Indeed, there has even been debate about whether surety bonds should be considered insurance at all."[36] A surety bond is an insurance against a broken contract, which always involves messy lawsuits and court filings more than an actuarial table. "There is nothing cut and dried about any of these things," Stevens wrote. "You adapt yourself to each case" (*CPP* 797). And each case requires attention to its particulars, not some mathematical generality. In other words, each surety case "is the cry of its occasion," to quote a line from "An Ordinary Evening in New Haven" (*CPP* 404). If poetry and surety claims share the principle of abstraction, they are also linked, in Stevens's mind, for their attention to the concrete, mundane, particular.

In December 1936, as the Spanish Civil War was raging and the world was edging closer to yet another catastrophe, Stevens gave a lecture at

Harvard titled "The Irrational Element in Poetry." Feeling the palpable pressure of contemporary events, the poet spoke about the irrational as the fountainhead of poetry. By "irrational," Stevens did not mean it in a pathological sense. "Fuseli," Stevens said, "used to eat raw beef at night before going to bed in order that his dreams might attain a beefy violence otherwise lacking. Nor are we concerned with that sort of thing; nor with irrationality provoked by prayer, whisky, fasting, opium, or the hope of publicity. . . . What interests us is a particular process in the rational mind which we recognize as irrational in the sense that it takes place unaccountably." With a nod to Freud, who Stevens said had "given the irrational a legitimacy that it never had before," the poet regarded the irrational, the unaccountable, as the saving grace of humanity. "We expect," Stevens said, "the irrational to liberate us from the rational," because "rational beings are canaille." Poetry traffics in the unknown, "an indecipherable cause," like the crisscrossing shadow of the blackbird on the window, tracing a mood. Unlike Poe, the moody mystic who pretends to manage risk in poetry by means of reasoning and probability (but learns that reason fails), Stevens the surety poet welcomes the unpredictable into his work. "We no longer like Poe's tintinnabulations," he announced. "Just as the choice of subject is unpredictable at the outset, so its development, after it has been chosen, is unpredictable." He paid tribute in "The Irrational Element in Poetry" to Stephane Mallarmé, the French poet whose 1897 poem "A Throw of the Dice" begins with a declaration that we "never will abolish chance" (*CPP* 781–92). Stevens's avowal of the irrational and unpredictable should take us back to Frost, who, as I quoted above, celebrated the crookedness of a walking stick, an odd shape created by chance and randomness rather than by rational design. For Frost, as it is for Charles Sanders Peirce, William James, and other American pragmatists, chance is "equivalent to freedom, in both a philosophical sense and in a political sense closely tied to the values of liberalism." As James put it in his diatribe against determinism, chance "is the vital air which lets the world live, the salt which keeps it sweet."[37]

Similarly, insurance welcomes the unpredictable, as long as it is quantifiable and manageable, as evidenced in the following definition of risk by the insurance industry: "A probability or threat of damage, injury, liability, loss, or any other negative occurrence that is caused by external or internal vulnerabilities, and that may be avoided through preemptive action."[38] When Stevens said in his Harvard lecture that "resistance to the pressure of ominous and destructive circumstance consists of its conversion, so far as possible, into a different, an explicable, an amenable circumstance" (*CPP* 789), we don't know if it's the poet or the insurance man speaking. Chances are, and I bet, it's both.

(7)

"O thin men of Haddam,
Why do you imagine golden birds?
Do you not see how the blackbird
Walks around the feet
Of the women about you?"

They say, what they don't know won't hurt them. But in this case, it will hurt. The blackbird that walks menacingly around the feet of the Haddam women has a name: risk. Unlike the speaker in Emily Dickinson's poem that goes, "My Life had stood – a Loaded Gun – / in Corners," a speaker who fully anticipates and desires the risks in life (hunting deer and killing humans), the thin men in a town with a pseudobiblical name, Haddam, are so caught up with the logic of desire and production that they fail to see the threat that has already descended upon their wives and lives.

In his pioneering work, *Risk Society*, Ulrich Beck sees risk as a crisis of modernity: "Risk may be defined as a systematic way of dealing with hazards and insecurities induced and introduced by modernization itself. Risks, as opposed to older dangers, are consequences which relate to the threatening force of modernization and to its globalization of doubt." Beck declares that we have entered an era of risk society, which is fundamentally different from an industrial society, with its functional principles. While in classical industrial society the logic of wealth production dominates the logic of risk production, in risk society this relationship is reversed. The gain in power from technoeconomic progress is being increasingly overshadowed by the production of risk. In an early stage, risks can be legitimated as latent side effects. As they become globalized, and subject to public criticism and scientific investigation, they come out of the closet and achieve a central importance in social and political debates.

> At the center lie the risks and consequences of modernization, which are revealed as irreversible threats to the life of plants, animals, and human beings. Unlike the factory-related or occupational hazards of the nineteenth and the first half of the twentieth centuries, these can no longer be limited to certain localities or groups, but rather exhibit a tendency to globalization which spans production and reproduction as much as national borders, and in this sense brings into being supra-national and non-class-specific global hazards with a new type of social and political dynamisms.

More important, the normative bases of calculating risks, such as the concept of accident and insurance, medical precautions, and so on, do not fit the basic dimensions of these modern threats. This means that "the calculation of risk as it has been established so far by science and legal institutions collapses." In other words, "in the risk society the unknown and unintended consequences come to be a dominant force in history and society."[39]

Writing at the dawn of risk society, Stevens seemed to be fully aware of the inability of the insurance industry or any industry or government program to eliminate risk. In his article "Insurance and Social Change," published in 1937, two years after the passage of the Social Security Act in the United States, Stevens distinguished the newly instituted government program designed to protect people against economic catastrophe from a hypothetical insurance that would cover all risks: "To be certain of a regular income, as in the case of social security, is not the same thing as to be able to repair any damage, or to meet any emergency. Obviously, in a world in which insurance had become perfect, the case of social security would be a minor case. In short, universal insurance or insurance for all is not the same thing as ubiquitous insurance or insurance for everything" (*CPP* 792). With the idea that "it helps us to see the actual world to visualize a fantastic world," Stevens goes on to draw a picture of "a world in which insurance had been made perfect."

> In such a world we should be certain of an income. Out of the income we should be able, by the payment of a trivial premium, to protect ourselves, our families and our property against everything. The procedure would necessarily be simple: Probably the dropping of a penny each morning in a box at the corner nearest one's place of residence on the way to one's place of employment. Each of us would have a personal or peculiar penny. What is the difference between a personal penny and social security number? The circle just stated: income, insurance, the thing that happens and income again, would widen and soon become income, insurance, the thing that fails to happen and income again. In other words, not only would all our losses be made good, but all our wishes would come true. (*CPP* 793)

Such a perfect world covered by a perfect insurance of course does not exist, and Stevens knew that, as he went on to say, "The objective of us is to live in a world in which nothing unpleasant can happen. Our prime instinct is to go on indefinitely like the wax flowers on the mantelpiece" (*CPP* 793). As Joseph Harrington points out, the lifeless wax flowers symbolize "a utopia, a nowhere, a nothing."[40] It seems that rather than a metaphysical and even logocentric poet some critics have tried to make him out to be, Stevens has a full grasp of reality and understands fully well the material base for imagination, whether poetic or statistical. In "Esthetique du Mal," Stevens writes, "The greatest poverty is not to live / In a physical world" (*CPP* 286). A physical world is always full of risk, hazard, change, and unpredictability, whereas paradise, as Stevens points out in "Sunday Morning," never changes and is therefore static, lifeless. What Stevens looks for, as Puskar puts it, is "a balance between stability and instability."[41]

(8)

"I know noble accents
And lucid, inescapable rhythms;
But I know, too,
That the blackbird is involved
In what I know."

In "The Noble Rider and the Sound of Words," Stevens writes, "the relation between the imagination and reality is a question, more or less, of precise equilibrium" rather than "a question of the difference between grotesque extremes." The foregoing sections about statistical society and its identical twin, risk society, speak to Stevens's persistent acknowledgment that the relation between imagination and reality is not one of isomorphism or domination, but of imbrication. On the one hand, reality, as represented by accidents, wars, or even "noble accents" are inescapable. On the other, imagination, be it poetic or statistical, sharpens our ability to cope with the blackbird of reality that "is involved in what I know." As Stevens says, "The real [is] made more acute by an unreal" (*CPP* 386).

In her influential book on risk, Deborah Lupton describes three major epistemological approaches to risk in social and cultural theory. First is the technical-scientific perspective that regards risk as an objective hazard, threat, or danger that exists and can be measured independently of social and cultural processes. She calls this approach "naïve realism." Second is the risk society perspective and cultural/symbolic perspective that regards risk as an objective hazard, threat, or danger that is inevitably mediated through social and cultural processes and can never be known in isolation from these processes. She calls this approach "critical realism." And third is the Foucauldian governmentality approach that holds that nothing is a risk in itself; what we understand to be a "risk" is the product of historically, socially, and culturally contingent "ways of seeing." She labels this the "strong constructionist approach."[42]

Judging by Lupton's useful categories, it seems that Stevens's understanding of risk encompasses the entire spectrum of all these three positions. As an insurance man, he certainly saw risk from a technical-scientific perspective, treating it as an objective hazard. Given his philosophical views on imagination versus reality, it appears that he would also be open to the critical realist approach, seeing risk as an objective hazard mediated by language and imagination. In "Adagia," Stevens writes, "Reality is a cliché / From which we escape by metaphor," and "The real is only the base. But it is the base" (*CPP* 917). Fully acknowledging reality as the material base, Stevens also prioritizes imagination through metaphor or description: "Description is revelation. It is not / The thing described, nor false facsimile" (*CPP* 301). And finally, Stevens was also sympathetic to the view that imagination is a supreme fiction, a position that Foucauldian poststructuralists would affirm. "The final belief," Stevens writes in "Adagia," "is to believe in a fiction, which you know to be a fiction, there being nothing else. The exquisite truth is to know that it is a fiction and that you believe in it willingly" (*CPP* 903).

(9)

"When the blackbird flew out of sight,
It marked the edge
Of one of many circles."

Emerson says that the circle is "the highest emblem in the cipher of the world": "The eye is the first circle; the horizon which it forms is the second; and throughout nature this primary figure is repeated without end."[43] On the desk of the insurance man lie charts, graphs, circles, and other geometric figures designed to rein in reality whose escape, like a blackbird flying out of sight, spells trouble, loss, and risk for the company. The mind cannot be divorced from reality, but to know it on a higher level, a technical mandate for any statistical enterprise, the mind must maintain a sort of meditative detachment. Hence, as in "The Snow Man," "One must have a mind of winter / To regard the frost and the boughs / Of the pine-trees crusted with snow; / And have been cold a long time / To behold the junipers shagged with ice" (*CPP* 8). To "regard" and "behold" is to keep things in sight. In *Things Merely Are*, Simon Critchley observes, "Far from any otherworldly sophism, in a language free from mysticism, Stevens' poetry can teach a certain disposition of *calm*, an insight into things that comes from having them in sight."[44]

Such meditative regarding or beholding is akin to the concept of perception in Zen Buddhism, which undergirds "The Snow Man" and other works by Stevens. "Before one is enlightened," Zen masters often say, "one sees a mountain as a mountain and a river as a river; in the process of attaining enlightenment, mountains are no longer mountains, rivers no longer rivers; but when one has finally achieved enlightenment, mountains are once more mountains, rivers once more rivers." As Zhaoming Qian explains, "What they mean is that before enlightenment one tends to confuse seeing/hearing with cogitating, whereas with enlightenment one loses all cogitating (misery, joy, and so on), hence perception of the thing itself and the nothing."[45]

(10)

"At the sight of blackbirds
Flying in a green light,
Even the bawds of euphony
Would cry out sharply."

Of all the blackbirds haunting the world today, of all the risks threatening human affairs at present, there is one, according to Nassim Taleb, that is most serious and most unpredictable: a black swan. What the *New York Times* best-selling author and a professor of the science of risk and uncertainty calls "a black swan event" has three distinct features: rarity, extreme impact, and retrospective predictability: "First, it is an *outlier*, as it lies outside the realm of regular expectations, because nothing in the past can convincingly point to its possibility. Second, it carries an extreme impact. Third, in spite of its outlier status, human nature makes us concoct explanations for its occurrence *after* the fact, making it explainable and predictable." The astonishing success of Google was a black swan; so was 9/11. If Taleb's book had been published a year or so later, he would certainly have counted the 2008 financial meltdown as a black swan as well. Taleb believes that the effect of these blackbirds has been increasing since the dawn of humanity. "It started accelerating during the industrial revolution, as the world started getting more complicated, while ordinary events, the ones we study and discuss and try to predict from reading the newspapers, have become increasingly inconsequential."[46]

In *The Matter of Capital*, Christopher Nealon astutely points out that perceptive as his analysis of the black swan is, Taleb actually represents "a kind of apotheosis of risk encouragement." That is, Taleb is "not a critic of risk orientation per se, just a critic of the idea that risk can be predicted." According to Randy Martin, since the 1970s there has been a process of "socialization of risk," which seeps into all aspects of our lives. Two key developments that have reoriented our subjective experience of risk take place in the labor market and the financial sector: First, the restructuring of pension plans from defined-benefit to defined-contribution model effectively hitched millions of future retirees to the ups and downs of the marketplace. Second, the financial sector's race to securitize debt (i.e., bundle and disperse it) and sell it, epitomized by the CDS, played out in full view to a disastrous end during the 2008–9 financial crisis. As a result of this ideology of risk, people have been given advice that risk needs to be not only embraced, but made into a universal causal principle of the unforeseeable. Nealon thus sees Taleb as the prophet of what Naomi Klein has called "disaster capitalism," by which she means "a stage of capitalist history in which the demands of liquidity achieve a scale and intensity that puts states, economies, and ecosystems in danger." At this stage of capital, Klein argues, "liquidity seeks out disaster, because disaster is the only instrument capable of producing truly 'free' conditions for capital expansion." As Milton Friedman, the guru of free-market economics, candidly acknowledges, "Only crisis—actual or perceived—produces real change."[47]

(11)

"He rode over Connecticut
In a glass coach.
Once, a fear pierced him,
In that he mistook
The shadow of his equipage
For blackbirds."

Against a background where risk is not only increasing, but is also ideologically embraced or financially leveraged, we need to return to Stevens the surety poet, who has long thought about poetry in tandem with risk. In panel 11, Stevens gives us a poetic representation of the conflation of real risk and perceived risk. A misapprehension, mistaking the shadow of a vehicle for a flock of blackbirds, leads to apprehension, a piercing fear. "Perceived risk or subjective risk," writes Nicholas Rescher, "is something different from risk itself. A person who has an eccentric idea about the probability of a possible threat or about the character of the harm at issue will confront a subjective risk based on a misconception." And the eminent scholar on the theory of risk evaluation and management readily admits, "To be sure, such misconceptions can play a role in human affairs every bit as significant as an apprehension of the real facts."[48]

When all is said and done, Stevens does not really provide us a clear answer as to how to avoid risk, partly because as an insurance man he knows that risk is unavoidable. For an American pragmatist, waywardness is part of human experience. What we need is an alternative way of conceptualizing risk, a way of being in the world that takes full cognizance, pardon the seeming tautology, of our place in the risky world. In "Of Mere Being," very likely his last poem, Stevens gives us an inkling of what's on his mind.

The palm at the end of the mind,
Beyond the last thought, rises
In the bronze décor,

A gold-feathered bird
Sings in the palm, without human meaning,

Without human feeling, a foreign song.

......

(*CPP* 476)

In a letter to Paul Henry Lang in 1954, John Cage wrote, "'Art' and 'music,' when anthropocentric (involved in self-expression), seems trivial and lacking in urgency to me. We live in a world where there are things as well as people. Trees, stones, water, everything is expressive."[49] The gold-feathered bird in Stevens's poem is anti-anthropocentric, as it sings "without human meaning," "without human feeling." Its "foreign song" has nothing to do with human happiness or unhappiness. It just sings, and its feathers shine. By "Of Mere Being," Stevens seems to point us in a direction where, as Cage puts it, "everything is expressive."

(12)

"The river is moving.
The blackbird must be flying."

Relativity. The word *must* signals causality, the backbone upon which science is built. Against causality and statistical truth, Carl G. Jung proposes synchronicity as "a psychically conditioned relativity of space and time," which "takes the coincidence of events in space and time as meaning something more than mere chance."[50] Jung tells us a story involving birds:

> The wife of one of my patients, a man in his fifties, once told me in conversation that, at the deaths of her mother and her grandmother, a number of birds gathered outside the windows of the death-chamber. I had heard similar stories from other people. When her husband's treatment was nearing its end, his neurosis having been cleared up, he developed some apparently quite innocuous symptoms which seemed to me, however, to be those of heart-disease. I sent him along to a specialist, who after examining him told me in writing that he could find no cause for anxiety. On the way back from this consultation (with the medical report in his pocket) my patient collapsed in the street. As he was brought home dying, his wife was already in a great state of anxiety because, soon after her husband had gone to the doctor, a whole flock of birds alighted on their house. She naturally remembered the similar incidents that had happened at the death of her own relatives, and feared the worst.[51]

A skeptic of modern science, Jung believes that causality is "a merely statistical truth and not absolute, it is a sort of working hypothesis of how events evolve one out of another." Synchronicity, by contrast, suggests "a peculiar interdependence of objective events among themselves as well as with the subjective (psychic) states of the observer or observers."[52] In Jung's story, the connection between the flock of birds and death is neither causal nor symbolic; it seems chancy, but it is more than coincidence.

In his influential foreword to Richard Wilhelm's translation of the *I Ching*, Jung sees the Chinese use of the *Book of Changes* as an example of synchronicity. "The manner in which the *I Ching* tends to look upon reality," Jung writes, "seems to disfavor our causalistic procedures. The moment under actual observation appears to the ancient Chinese view more of a chance hit than a clearly defined result of concurring causal chain processes. The matter of interest seems to be the configuration formed by chance events in the moment of observation, and not at all the hypothetical reasons that seemingly account for the coincidence." To Jung, the hexagram, which one gets from the book after the seemingly random tossing of coins or sticks, is an indicator of the essential situation prevailing in the moment, a true rendering of the questioner's psychic condition.[53] By matching the answer received with the questioner's psychological blind spot, Jung understands that synchronicity functions in the Chinese *Book of Changes* as a form of self-knowledge. But it is not the kind of self-knowledge of a Cartesian ego; instead, it is an opening up of self to chance, coincidence, that lies out there.

Deeply sympathetic with Jung's interpretation of the *I Ching*, John Cage maintains that a mind emptied by chance operation would generate an experimental action that "does not move in terms of approximations and errors, as 'informed' action by its nature must," but rather "sees things directly as they are."[54] Forsaking intention, as Cage famously does in his work, leads to the prize of direct, undistorted experience of the world; it "leads to the world of nature, where, gradually or suddenly, one sees that humanity and nature, not separate, are in this world together; that nothing was lost when everything was given away."[55]

(13)

"It was evening all afternoon.
It was snowing
And it was going to snow.
The blackbird sat
In the cedar-limbs."

Event ("It was snowing") and probability ("it was going to snow"). The present/event bears no causal relationship with the future/probability. Temporalities are linked by a paratactic "and," the same paradigmatic word that opens Ezra Pound's modern epic, *The Cantos*. If anything, the future has already unfolded in the present: "It was evening all afternoon." Risk lies in the future, which is already here. Jungian synchronicity runs rampant. Insouciant to human time, to the fusion and confusion of anthropocentric temporalities, "the blackbird sat in the cedar-limbs," much like the gold-feathered bird in "Of Mere Being," singing "a foreign song," oblivious to human meaning or human feeling. A somewhat romanticized Nature, an antidote to ills of the Anthropocene.

"Language," says Emerson, "is fossil poetry. As the limestone of the continent consists of infinite masses of the shells of animalcules, so language is made up of images, or tropes, which now, in their secondary use, have long ceased to remind us of their poetic origin."[56] The etymology of the Chinese word 西 (west), as revealed in the ancient script 𠧧, is a bird sitting on its nest. When birds return to their nests, it is usually sunset time, and the sun sets in the "west." It stands in contrast to 東 (east), which in Pound's creative interpretation is an image of the rising sun caught in the branches of a tree—a topic addressed in the next chapter.

Unlike the gold-feathered bird or Taleb's black swan, the Chinese bird, as an ideographic component, has no color. Only a philosopher as unconventional—some would say zany—as Ludwig Wittgenstein could ask a quixotic question like, "What's the color of seven?" But Wittgenstein has also taught us that to imagine a language is to imagine a form of life. To find a way out of the dilemma of risk, we need to find a new language, a new direction. To do that, we need to take a cue from Stevens and then look beyond his legacy in American poetry to identify kindred or varying ways of managing risk through poetic imagination.

As we have seen, Stevens's prescription is "mere being," a meditative "nothing." The word *nothing* is almost a verb here, in the sense of Ernest Fenollosa, who insists that all nouns are verbal in origin, because thinking *things*; *thing* being a verb, one more *-ing* word.[57] Indeed, the Chinese character for nothing, 無, is an image of footprints lost in the forest. As a surety poet, Stevens embraces risk as the irrational elements in poetry that he works to tame through abstraction and as the commodity that enables the workings of the industry he works in.

Risk, real or perceived, is a problem of probability, a situation created when chance cannot be tamed, or a commodity transacted in the financial market. In contrast to Stevens's poetics of risk, a poet like Cage has a very different approach to the issue, a way of busting, as he quips, out of "whatever cage you find yourself in."[58]

An innovative composer who first scandalized the world with a Zen-inspired, silent piece titled *4'33"*, Cage is also an experimental poet who played with chance in writing. Throughout his long career, Cage adopted a variety of compositional methods that could free him from authorial intention, from what he dismissed as "the tyranny of the ego and of personal taste." Sometimes he would use the *I Ching* as the oracle, tossing coins or sticks to decide, step by step, what words or texts to include in his work. At other times, he would compose so-called mesostic poems according to rules he had set. Either way, chance is the primary mechanism by which Cage generates his composition.

For Cage, chance worked in a double capacity: on the one hand, chance operation was a way to remove intention and allow him to become receptive to nature, and, on the other, it was also, as Cage recognized, the way nature works. In other words, "In addition to serving as a technique of silencing the ego, chance was also the manner of operation of nature itself."[59] As Cage explains the creation of one of his texts, *Roaratorio*:

> Taking the name of the author and/or the title of the book as their subject (the row), write a series of mesostics beginning on the first page and continuing to the last. Mesostics means a row down the middle. In this circumstance a mesostic is written by finding the first word in the book that contains the first letter of the row that is not followed in the same word by the second letter of the row. The second letter belongs on the second line and is to be found in the next word that contains it that is not followed in the same word by the third letter of the row.[60]

In this case, using *Finnegans Wake* as the source and the author's name JAMES JOYCE as the spine word or the mesostic, Cage produced a poetic text that looks like this:

wroth with twone nathandJoe
A
Malt
jhEm
Shen

pftJschute
sOlid man
that the humptYhillhead of humself
is at the knoCk out
in thE park

Strictly speaking, the mesostic rule Cage has used to generate the text should, as Perloff has astutely pointed out, be called "constraint" or "procedurality." A rule in traditional metrics "creates a certain stasis, in that the projected poem must fit into a particular preexistent mold"; for instance, a Petrarchan sonnet must have fourteen lines made up of an octave and a variable sestet. In contrast, a constraint tends toward multiplicity, because it prompts the author "to let the concealed phonemes and morphemes of a given text come to the surface and create their own configurations." Perloff's virtuoso reading of *Roaratorio* helps us see and hear the almost rhizomatic configuration that resonates through Cage's text, the aural and visual elements that refuse to cohere: "The name JAMES JOYCE, visible as a column on the page, is not heard at all when the poem is read aloud; conversely, the sounded *e* in 'jhEm' or 'hEaven' transforms the silent *e* of *James*, just as the /*z*/ phoneme of *James* can become the /*s*/ of 'Skysign' and the diphthong /*oy*/ of *Joyce* can supply both the open /*o*/ of 'sOlid' and the short /*i*/ of 'humptYhillhead.'"[61]

Perloff regards Cage's chance operation as a continuation of a poetic tradition of indeterminacy that goes from Rimbaud and Mallarmé through Pound and Joyce to Cage, David Antin, and others. Measured against those modernist giants, however, Cage seems to show a more profound understanding of the world from the perspective of chance and risk; or, at least, Cage offers a different antidote. As I discussed in chapter 1, in tandem with the tradition of indeterminacy, there was also a strong desire for control in Anglo-American modernism. Stevens's well-known poem "Anecdote of a Jar," as it is often interpreted, is exemplary of such a yearning for control and order. When a man-made object, a jar, is placed in Nature, the wilderness surrounds it and makes a shrine out of art, thus creating order in the dominion. Another example of the modernist desire for control is, as seen earlier, the Basic English rendition of *Finnegans Wake*. Promoting Basic English as a tool to combat the Babel, C. K. Ogden tried his hand at translating Joyce's great work of portmanteau into the limited vocabulary of Basic. And the result, as I described, was a work of utter absurdity. With its extreme circumlocution, Ogden's version achieved the opposite of his stated intention of facilitating human communication with a simplified language. A quick glance at the difference between Ogden's Basic translation and Cage's mesostic writing through Joyce's text will tell us that Ogden's redundancy (a loaded term in the field of informatics, discussed in the next chapter) is a far cry from Cage's multitude.

Rather than control, Cage, paraphrasing the Sri Lankan metaphysician Ananda Coomaraswamy, proposed that art is the imitation of nature in her manner of operation. And nature, the wilderness in Stevens's poem, is chance, noise, nonintention, and multiplicity. For Cage, the more we seek to order what is essentially unordered, the more we are behaving in a manner contrary to nature. This design for risk management runs contrary to the situation Ian Hacking has succinctly described as "the more the indeterminism, the more the control." Such a desire for control makes for what Bruno Latour defines as the Modern Constitution. Latour points out that since the seventeenth century, with the rise of science, modernity has been predicated on the division between nature and society, between human and thing.[62] Across the great divide, as Graham Harman explicates, "modernity is the attempt to cleanse of each half of the residue of the other, freeing facts from any contamination with personal value judgments, while liberating values and perspectives from the test of hard reality."[63] But in fact, this discourse of modernity covers up the reality of how science and politics work, that is, through the construction of hybrids of human and nonhuman entities, interpenetrating systems that mix politics, science, technology, and nature. In Latour's call for an end to the old dichotomy between nature and culture, we hear a resonance with Cage's pronouncement that "a measuring mind can never finally measure nature."[64]

Moreover, against Stevens's "The Idea of Order at Key West," if I may pun on "West," Cage looked eastward for ideas of randomness, chance, and indeterminacy. As Peter Jaeger shows in *John Cage and Buddhist Ecopoetics*, the indeterminacy in Cage's work is akin to the Buddhist concept of *anupalabdhatva*, or incomprehensibility, "a term which refers to the ultimate nature of things as incomprehensible and ungraspable to the ordinary mind." More important, indeterminacy, in Jaeger's words, "calls into question the subject's illusory sense of certainty about phenomena or about the self. In Buddhist terms, the conditioned, subjective mind is unable to comprehend its own inability to comprehend, although it is able to cultivate a sense of tolerance towards the incomprehensible."[65] Such an open-minded acceptance of uncertainty is not akin to the risk theory promoted in finance capitalism, nor is Cage's chance operation a model for risk management trumpeted by the business world, although the latter may indeed have much to learn from Cagean ideas. In the age of big data, when statistical truth passes for fact and constitutes our comprehension of phenomena, Cage, influenced by Zen Buddhism, advised against any attempt to control ambiguity and uncertainty by clasping onto a fleeting and fictitious sense of conviction or assurance.

Cage did not just try to give up his own authorial control and let chance and nature take over his work, as he did once when he pushed open the gate and allowed the street noise of a city to pour into the concert hall, or at another time when he recorded natural sounds as music. He also tried to help others attain the freedom after forgoing the ego in writing. His trademark mesostic poetry, writing through the source texts by a few of his select authors, became the major route toward freedom for him and others alike. Henry David Thoreau, one of Cage's favorites, once said that when he heard a sentence, he heard feet marching. Not a fan of syntax as an imposition lording over a sentence, Cage regarded *Finnegans Wake* as a work that still uses sentence as its basic structure. "In ancient Chinese language," Cage said, "the sentence—as we know it—doesn't to my mind exist, because you're uncertain ... whether a noun is a noun, or whether it's a verb or ... an adjective. So you don't know the relationship of the words." The mesostic, then, was really Cage's way of making "it less like sentences," rejecting the stability and predictability of syntax.[66] In his rewriting of Pound's *The Cantos*, for instance, Cage followed what he called a method of "the rolling of a metal ball," that is, the name EZRA POUND through the cantos, thereby producing lines such as

and th**E**n with bron**Z**e lance heads bea**R**ing yet **A**rms
sheep**P** slain **O**f pl**U**to stro**N**g prasie**D**[67]

As Perloff has noted, this recourse to rule-based choice of words is akin to an Oulipian clinamen, introducing the spontaneous and unexpected.[68] Cage made it very clear that such a method serves to free him and the reader not only of his intentions but also those of Pound and Joyce. "I am confident," he said, "that Joyce would have been delighted by what happens when intention is removed from the *Wake*, and I hazard that Pound, if not delighted, would have been relieved. *Canto CXX*: 'Let those I love try to forgive what I have made.'"[69]

As we will see in the next chapter, inside the echo chamber of Chinese whispers, we will experience again the spontaneous and unexpected, the opening up of the virtual inside the actual, Oulipian clinamen claiming, not presence, but proximity, like an echo preceding the sound of a voice.

Chinese Whispers

[CHAPTER FIVE]

The Future of Meaning in the Age of Information

Literature is news that STAYS news.

EZRA POUND

In the game of Chinese whispers, also known as the telephone game, players line up in a circle and whisper to their immediate neighbors, not hearing any other players farther away. The player at the beginning of the line picks a phrase and whispers it as quietly as possible to his or her neighbor. The neighbor then passes the message on to the next player. The passing continues in this fashion until it reaches the player at the end of the line, who calls out the message. If the game has been "successful," the final message will bear little or no resemblance to the original, due to the cumulative effect of mistakes made along the way.

What lies at the heart of this game is the unreliability of hearsay. Or, as John Ashbery puts it in a poem titled "Chinese Whispers," "Finally the rumors grew more fabulous than the real thing."[1] What's fabulous and virtual has become more real than the factual and objective. But why "Chinese"? What is so Chinese in "Chinese whispers"?

Harking back to Europeans' inability to understand China in earlier centuries, the phrase "Chinese whispers" actually gained currency in the English language in the mid-twentieth century, and the eponymous game became popular among American children in the dark ages of Cold War propaganda. The term's connection to geopolitics is evident in its variations: Russian Scandal, Russian Gossip, or Russian Telephone. A metaphor for inaccuracy of communication, "Chinese whispers," at a time when everything Chinese or Chinese-sounding seemed suspicious, carried with it a sense of paranoia caused by espionage, counterespionage, the Red Scare, the arms race, and other war games, real or imaginary, cold or hot.

It was in the same period that we saw the birth of the computer. As we know, the original purpose of the computer was for use in translation or cryptography, relying on machines to translate or decode massive information data gathered in intelligence operations, a Herculean task that could no longer be accomplished by human agents alone. The technical work of translation or cryptography demanded that noise, in the form of whisper, chatter, gossip, disinformation—all forms of communication essential to propaganda—be separated from real intelligence, or meaningful information. In other words, Chinese whispers, or rather the desire to get rid of such an echo chamber of misinformation and uncertainty, stood right there at the dawn of the Information Age.

As aforementioned, after Warren Weaver, a trailblazer of information theory, first broached the topic in a personal letter in 1947, he circulated in 1949 among two hundred mathematicians, scientists, linguists, and public policy makers in the United States a memorandum, in which he wrote, "It is very tempting to say that a book written in Chinese is simply a book written in English which was coded into the 'Chinese code.'"[2] Such a statement reveals the entangled roots of Orientalism and technology in the quest of universal intelligibility, a search that dates back to the dawn of Western modernity, to Leibniz's *clavis sinica*, John Wilkins's Real Character, and John Webb's pre-Babelian lingua franca.[3] What distinguishes Weaver's wish from all the earlier "Chinese dreams" is the technical tool provided by the emergent digital technology. Alphabet-based and alphabet-biased, the computer has brought the earlier search for the universal language to its seemingly logical conclusion, reaching a stage where, as Weaver imagines, a Chinese book is merely an English book that happens to be "coded into the 'Chinese code.'" Regarding a natural language, whether Chinese or English, as a code that can be decoded and recoded is the modus operandi of the computer. What ensures such a universal translatability is the definition of information as a disembodied, discrete unit.

As we shall see below, at the beginning of the digital age, leading scientists like Weaver, Claude Shannon, and others envisioned ways to patrol and control the borders of language. By separating materiality from information, turning "meaning" into computable data, they tried to filter out noise from message and avoid the echolalia a la Chinese whispers. John Keats's conception of "Negative Capability," the bedrock of humanism favoring intellectual ambiguity over philosophical certainty, is thus turned into a game of quantitative probability.

* * *

Information can be considered as order wrenched from disorder.

HEINZ VON FOERSTER

In 1947, the same year that Warren Weaver first aired privately his notion about the "Chinese code," Claude Shannon published an article titled "A

Mathematical Theory of Communication," arguably the most important and influential treatise on information technology.[4] In the article, Shannon approaches the concept of information with a clear intention of achieving maximum efficiency in the channel of communication, as he explains:

> The fundamental problem of communication is that of reproducing at one point either exactly or approximately a message selected at another point. Frequently the messages have *meaning*; that is, they refer to or are correlated according to some system with certain physical or conceptual entities. These semantic aspects of communication are irrelevant to the engineering problem. The significant aspect is that the actual message is one *selected from a set* of possible messages.[5]

Here Shannon purposefully defines *message*, that is, information, as a probability function with no semantic meaning. "To be sure," Shannon writes, "the word information in communication theory relates not so much to what you *do* say, as to what you *could* say" (8; emphasis original). They want to design a discrete system of communication in which "both the message and the signal are a sequence of discrete symbols." Telegraphy, for instance, is a discrete system "where the message is a sequence of letters and the signal a sequence of dots, dashes and spaces" (3). Norbert Wiener, another chief architect of cybernetics, also thought of information as representing "a choice of one message from among a range of possible messages," defining *information* as a probability function "with no dimensions, no materiality, and no necessary connection with meaning." Wiener declared, "Information is information, not matter or energy."[6]

By divorcing information from meaning and conceiving it as a medium with no material dimensions, these theorists achieve the reification of information. That was how, in the words of N. Katherine Hayles, "information lost its body." In *How We Became Posthuman* (1999), Hayles traces the troubling history of conceptualizing information as a disembodied medium. She describes how participants of the Macy conferences from the late 1940s to the early 1950s fought over cybernetic models and artifacts, especially with respect to the definition of information.[7] In fact, there were alternative models of conceptualizing information, such as conceiving it as matter or energy or defining it in terms of what it does rather than what it is. A small group led by the anthropologists Gregory Bateson and Margaret Mead tried to explore the feedback loop for its participatory potential rather than centralized information engineering. Unlike the unidirectional model of communication visioned by Shannon, Bateson noted, "because the [feedback] system is circular, effects at any point in the circuit can be carried all around to produce changes at that point of origin." In other words, in the nascent cybernetic technology, some saw a powerful symbol for democratic imagination, an informatics of liberation as opposed to an informatics of control.[8]

But ultimately, the model proposed by Weaver, Shannon, and Wiener et al. won the day, thanks in part to the circumstances of the US technoscientific culture in those postwar decades. That culture, as Hayles points out, "had a conservative bias that privileges stasis over change." In the eye of the designers, the apparent technical advantage of freeing information from semantics is that information would have a stable value as it moves from context to context, from the information source to the destination. Otherwise, if it was tied to meaning, information "would potentially have to change values every time it was embedded in a new context, because context affects meaning."[9] In other words, the mathematical model is designed to prevent the kind of semantic shifts that inevitably occur in a communication channel like Chinese whispers.

"In the process of being transmitted," Shannon writes, "it is characteristic that certain things are added to the signal which were not intended by the information source. These unwanted additions may be distortions or sound (in telephony, for example) or static (in radio), or distortions in shape or shading of picture (television), or errors in transmission (telegraphy or facsimile), etc. All of these changes in the transmitted signal are called noise."[10] In Shannon's mathematical theory of communication (MTC), noise is the opposite of redundancy, which is defined as "the difference between the physical representation of a message and the mathematical representation of the same message that uses no more bits than necessary."[11] The redundancy of the English language, for instance, is about 50 percent, which means that "about half of the letters or words we choose in writing or speaking are under our free choice, and about half (although we are not ordinarily aware of it) are really controlled by the statistical structure of the language."[12] Redundancy may sound bad, but in MTC it is actually an effective way to counteract noise. As Luciano Floridi explains:

> A message + noise contains more data than the original message by itself, but the aim of a communication process is fidelity, the accurate transfer of the original message from sender to receiver, not data increase. We are more likely to reconstruct a message correctly at the end of the transmission if some degree of redundancy counterbalances the inevitable noise and equivocation introduced by the physical process of communication and the environment.[13]

Interestingly, Shannon cites Basic English and James Joyce's *Finnegans Wake*, both of which I have discussed in chapter 1, as two extremes of redundancy: "The Basic English vocabulary is limited to 850 words and the redundancy is very high. This is reflected in the expansion that occurs when a passage is translated into Basic English. Joyce on the other hand enlarges the vocabulary and is alleged to achieve a compression of semantic content."[14] In other words, Basic English, consisting of restricted vocabulary, commands a high degree of redundancy, which in turn ensures the stability of information, leaving little room for ambiguity or equivocation. In contrast, *Finnegans Wake* mixes words from sixty or seventy languages and expands the "basically English" vocabulary, creating a potpourri of portmanteaus that are statistically random and unpredictable. To architects of MTC, the Joycean language of "a maundarin tongue in a poundering jowl" is full of noises, loaded with information as well as undesirable freedom, for noise extends the reader's freedom of choice in selecting a message. As Alice would say about her jabberwocky, "I mean what I say and I say what I mean." Or, in the words of Gilles Deleuze in his study of portmanteau, quoting Michel Butor, "Each of these words can act as a switch, and we can move from one to another by means of many passages; hence the idea of a book which does not simply narrate one story, but a whole ocean of stories."[15] Such multichannel communication with a pelagic body of stories, something Jean-François Lyotard characterizes as not channels but drifts, would produce too much noise for the MTC model.[16]

In fact, to counteract noise and ensure stability, Weaver even considered Basic English as a blueprint for an input language in machine translation. He presented the plan to I. A. Richards and Norbert Wiener, but they rebuffed the idea, because they were concerned that "the boundaries of words in different languages are too vague and the emotional and international connotations are too extensive to make any quasi mechanical translation scheme very hopeful."[17] Richards's skepticism notwithstanding, we can see that the underlying rationales of Basic English dovetail with those of MTC. As seen in chapter 1, Basic English, relying on panoptic conjugation, is what Richards calls "a technical innovation in the deliberate control of language." Promoted as a common medium that facilitates international communication, Basic represents an instrumental view of language. In *The Meaning of Meaning*, Ogden and Richards are adamant that "words 'mean' nothing by themselves.... It is only when a thinker makes use of them that they stand for anything, or, in one sense, have 'meaning.'" Denigrating as "superstition" the notion that "words are in some way parts of things or always imply things correspondent to them," they separate words from their materiality, in the same way that in MTC information is decoupled from its material support, rendering the actual format and medium irrelevant to its "meaning."[18]

In addition to dematerialization, Basic shares with MTC the penchant for stability and control. In the mechanics of panoptic conjugation, we already saw how Ogden and Richards deliberately chose "a set of referents which is common to all concerned" and thereby reduced the English vocabulary to 850 words. By relying on these most common referents, they conceived linguistic communication exactly the same way as MTC. Ogden and Richards write in *The Meaning of Meaning*, "Thus a language transaction or a communication may be defined as a use of symbols in such a way that acts of reference occur in a hearer which are similar in all relevant aspects to those which are symbolized by them in the speaker."[19] If MTC is, as Floridi puts it, "a theory of information without meaning,"[20] Basic is a dry run, or a forerunner, of the cybernetic dream of dematerialization and control, to prevent the kind of metaphorical shifts, linguistic accidents, and other forms of disequilibrium and displacement that fill the echo chamber of Chinese whispers. Cybernetic vision, as Robert von Hallberg explains, is a "steering method, the goal of which is to control uncertainty by manipulation of information."[21] After all, as Jean-Pierre Dupuy reminds us, etymologically speaking, "cybernetics is meant to signify control, mastery, governance—in short, the philosophical project associated with Descartes, who assigned mankind the mission of exercising dominion over the world, and over mankind itself."[22]

* * *

I make no secret of the fact that I myself am perplexed—about the most important point: that is, how one should judge the reality or phantasmagoria of the whole question.

FERDINAND DE SAUSSURE, letter to Leopold Gautier, 1908

While Weaver's idea of the "Chinese code" represents one node of the entangled roots of Orientalism and technology, there is, in fact, an alternative route on this Silk Road of meaning. Or, as Hayles puts it, "Conceptualizing information as a disembodied entity was not an arbitrary decision, but neither was it inevitable."[23] Along the same genealogy dating back to Leibniz's monad and fold, we can trace the line down to the modern era, reaching the twentieth century, which features an article that is as foundational as Claude Shannon's "Mathematical Theory of Communication," that is, "The Chinese Written Character as a Medium for Poetry" by Ernest Fenollosa. Despite its vital importance to Anglo-American poetic modernism and visual culture (a la Pound, Imagism, and film), we have failed to see what is really at stake in Fenollosa's seminal essay. Especially in the midst of the rising dominance of alphabetic technology, it may be worthwhile to revisit Fenollosa's essay and address an issue that concerns us the most: What can we learn from the Chinese mode of coding? Or, what can we learn from the seemingly childish game of Chinese whispers?

Conceived at the turn of the twentieth century, Fenollosa's article calls for a convergence of East and West by uncovering the mystery of language, especially the ways in which the Chinese characters reveal the magical workings of the universal grammar. Fenollosa maintains that Chinese writing is "something much more than arbitrary symbols. It is based upon a vivid shorthand picture of the operations of nature." In alphabetic languages, poetry, like music, "is a time art, weaving its unities out of successive impressions of sound," as in the following famous line from Thomas Gray's "Elegy Written in a Country Churchyard":

> The curfew tolls the knell of a parting day

The series of explosive consonants, /k/, /t/, /p/, /d/, and the softness of the /l/ in "toll" and "knell," all contribute to the resonating sounds of a church bell. In contrast, Chinese poetry, using a linguistic medium "consisting largely of semi-pictorial appeals to the eye," gives us lines such as this:

人	見	馬
Man	see	horse

Here 人 has two legs, 見 two legs, and 馬 four hooves. So the sentence is mobile, as if running on legs. Or, in the next sentence,

日	昇	東
Sun	rise	east

One can see the word for "sun" moving through the entire sentence, creating what the Russian filmmaker Sergei Eisenstein called "montage."[24] Eisenstein, who was enamored with Fenollosa's essay, regarded each of these Chinese words in the two examples above as a frame in film. In his groundbreaking essay, "The Cinematographic Principle and the Ideogram" (1929), Eisenstein writes, "This is exactly what we do in the cinema, combining shots that are deceptive, single in meaning, neutral in content—into intellectual contexts and series."[25] Thus, Fenollosa believed that Chinese poetry has the unique advantage of combining both the visual and the temporal: "It speaks at once with the vividness of painting, and with the mobility of sounds."[26]

Whether or not Fenollosa and his followers, such as Ezra Pound, steeped in their Emersonian transcendentalism, stand on solid linguistic or Sinological ground is not really an issue here. As the Brazilian concrete poet Haroldo de Campos puts it, Fenollosa's greatest discovery is to give us a glimpse in Chinese writing of the "workings of a relational intracode," by which de Campos means the ways Chinese ideograms weld the phonic to the graphic plane and semantically magnetize them both. Fenollosa calls this feature "overtone"; de Campos names it "saturation."[27] To Ferdinand de Saussure, however, this is a nightmare.

As we now know, the founding father of modern linguistics spent the twilight years of his life obsessing over anagrams. The two basic principles Saussure had laid down for linguistics state: (1) The bond between the signifier and the signified is arbitrary; (2) The signifier is unfolded linearly in time.[28] In this formulation, Saussure had considered poetic phenomena, such as onomatopoeia and anagram, as mere exceptions, incidental to the system of language. Toward the end of his life, however, Saussure became interested in anagrams, as he discovered among ancient Greek and Latin texts that certain theme words, like a political leader's name PILIPPUM, keep on appearing in different lines in various syllabic combinations. Or, in the *De Rerum Natura* of Lucretius, the name APHRODITE can be detected in various anagrams. "In the text are words whose syllabic composition provides a fresh, running proof that they are not chosen by chance," wrote Saussure in one of the ninety-nine notebooks he had kept while working on what he considered to be the "phantasmagoria" of language. Throughout his notes, Saussure variously used "anagram," "paragram," and "anaphony" to describe words within words, sounds beneath sounds, all elements that seem to undermine both the arbitrary and linear natures of the signifier. Occasionally, he complained and refused to admit to the significance of what he had found: "absolutely incomprehensible if I were not forced to confess that I suffer from a morbid horror of the pen, and that this work is for me an experience of sheer torture, quite out of proportion to its relative unimportance."[29]

To better illustrate what elements in language would give the linguist Saussure a headache, let me quote from a contemporary poem in English, titled "For MIA, Made in America: A Song of Love That Goes Nowhere":

I want to
bask in your basket
toil in your toilet
ski on your skin

nap in your napkin
chat in your chateau
pace in your space

I want to be
the loon in your pantaloon
the brass on your brassiere
and linger on your lingerie

I am big on bigamy
but tiny under scrutiny

I want to be
the flu in your flute
bone in your trombone
pet in your trumpet
no in your piano
bug in your bugle

If there is a lie in the lien
I'll find you a law in the flaw
become a rabbi for your rabbit
bamboo for your bamboozle

I want to be
the ring of your spring
sum of your summer
all of your fall
win of your winter

But would you be
the can of my canto
net of my sonnet
ant in my chant
lad in my ballad
dog in my doggerel

I yearn for your feelings
but flee from my earnings

The "MIA" in the title is a name of a woman, but it is also an acronym of "Made in America." Therefore, what looks like a love poem with overblown sentimentality and unsavory yearning may actually be a satire of the genre of love poetry, a possibility made apparent by the poem's subtitle, "A Song of Love That Goes Nowhere." Perhaps the love goes nowhere; or, more likely, the song itself goes nowhere, due to its repeated use of paragrams, causing the poem to be pulled down by its own weight, stuck in every line, slipping on every semantic slope.

Saussure would have called a poem like this "a Chinese game," as he did when he was poring over hypograms (theme words) prevalent in a Latin poem. It turns out that the poet of "For MIA," a bilingual speaker of English and Chinese, is playing a Chinese game in English.[30] Applying the principles of Chinese ideograms as illustrated by Fenollosa, the poet adopts paragrams in English words as visual rhymes, revealing at once the vividness of icons and the mobility of sounds. Paragram, as Roman Jakobson tells us, is an acoustic image, constituted by the repetition of certain sounds whose combination imitates a given word.[31] The poet is, in essence, writing a Chinese poem in English. Or, Chinese whispers rendered in English. This is not simply a reversal of Weaver's fantasy that "every book written in Chinese is simply a book written in English which was coded into the 'Chinese code,'" but to explore the echo chamber and shadow cave in any language, Chinese, English, or otherwise. A distant cousin to Lin Yutang's Chinglish, the use of paragram here, to paraphrase John Cage, opens up the virtual inside the actual.

In another note, Saussure called these instances of words resounding beneath other words a "Chinese puzzle." Here "Chinese" stands for whatever is inscrutable, quizzical, irrational, or in other words, whatever lies beyond the pale of Western rationality. The earlier Saussure might feel confident about his theory of the arbitrariness and linearity of signs, but the other, later Saussure was no longer so sure, as he confessed:

> When a first anagram appears, it seems like a flash of light. But when one sees that one can add to this a second, third, and even fourth anagram, far from feeling relieved of doubt, one begins to lose confidence in the first discovery. One begins to wonder if one might not find definitive proof of all possible words in any text, and to wonder to what extent those appear without requiring a search are actually surrounded by characteristic guarantees, a query which implies a larger quantity of coincidence than is the case with the first word to appear, or with a word to which we have paid no attention. One is two steps from a reckoning of probabilities, as a final resource, but because this reckoning, spatially, would defy the powers of a mathematician, the ultimate touchstone is the instinct of another person who does not know the probabilities and of that reason is better able to judge them.[32]

Here the linguist begins to speak of probability, doubt, reckoning, and loss of confidence.

"The percolation of language through the paragram," writes the contemporary avant-garde poet Steve McCaffery, "contaminates the notion of an ideal, unitary meaning and thereby counters the supposition that words can 'fix' or stabilize in closure." Conceiving writing as a general economy, McCaffery points out that whether in New Critical hermeneutics or the communication theory of information, meaning is "staged as the telos and destination of the de-materialization of writing.... In light of this one could consider language's materiality as meaning's heterological object, as that area inevitably involved within the semantic apparatus that meaning casts out and rejects." But the appearance of the paragram, or rather, the paragrammatic nature of language, "manufactures a crisis within semantic economy, for whilst engendering meanings, the paragram also turns unitary meaning against itself. If we understand meaning in its classical adequation to truth and knowledge, then paragrammaticized meaning becomes a secretion, an escape or expenditure from semantic's ideal structure into the disseminatory material of the signifier."[33] In other words, meaning regains, or remains inseparable from, its body.

"There is another side to language," to quote again Jean-Jacques Lecercle in his study of the remainder in language. This is the side "that escapes the linguist's attention, not because of his temporary failure or failings, but for necessary reasons. This dark side emerges in nonsensical and poetic texts, in the illuminations of mystics and the delirium of logophiliacs or mental patients."[34] Puns, anagrams, paragrams, paronomasia, nonsense, anaphony—all these are emblems of the remainder, a twilight zone where language consigns itself to chance, excess, anarchy, desire, and insanity. Lecercle rightly compares the work of the remainder to that of the unconscious and joke in Freud's psychoanalytic theory. And Jacques Lacan, critical of Saussurean linguistics, would speak of the "anagrammatic complex" of language, echoing, unknowingly, what Saussure had already secretly scribbled in his notebooks: "Duplication, repetition, and appearance of the same in the form of the other."[35] Dog or god. Melon or lemon. Silent or listen.

Walter Benjamin, perhaps the most visionary theorist of language in the twentieth century, also saw the potential of anagram as the great liberator of language from the repression imposed by instrumental rationalism.

> In anagrams, in onomatopoetic turns, and in many other linguistic virtuoso acts, the word, the syllable, and the sound swagger, emancipated from any connection with meaning, as things that can be allegorically exploited.... Thus language is broken to pieces in order to give over its

> fragments to a transformed and intensified expression.... The shattered language no longer serves mere communication in its pieces, and it establishes its dignity as a newborn object next to the gods, rivers, virtues, and similar forms of nature that oscillated into the allegorical.[36]

In "The Task of the Translator," Benjamin has taken us to the verge of the abyss, the bottomless depth of language where meanings will be lost because of our attention or commitment to the literal. In his musings over anagram, however, we see the light, the possibility that language can finally speak, only not through itself, but through the Other. English speaks through Chinese; Chinese articulates through English. Somewhere José Ortega y Gasset says:

> The stupendous reality that is language cannot be understood unless we begin by observing that speech consists above all in silence. A being who could not renounce saying many things would be incapable of speaking. And each language represents a different equation between manifestations and silences. Each people leaves some things unsaid in order to be able to say others. Because everything would be unsayable. Hence the immense difficulty of translation: translation is a matter of saying in a language precisely what that language tends to pass over in silence.[37]

This is a call for listening across languages, listening for the echoes and whispers of one's own language in the other, seeing the shadows and ghosts of one's own in the other.

* * *

The ultimate, hidden truth of the world is that it is something we make, and could just as easily make differently.

DAVID GRAEBER, *The Utopia of Rules*

In the long history of East-West encounter, we probably cannot find a better instance of interpenetration, seeing one's own reflection in the other and thereby changing perceptions of both the self and the other, than the case to which we now turn: Lin Yutang's Chinese typewriter. In some way Lin's invention makes for a perfect conclusion to this book, for the ingeniously designed machine encapsulates nearly all the issues lying at the heart of what I have tried to articulate as a transpacific poetics: language, meaning, translation, techno-Orientalism, and hybridization of ideas. Especially considering his earlier advocacy of Chinglish as a critique of Basic English and his status as a popular interpreter of the Chinese way of life in the West, Lin's investment in the typewriter, or more precisely, his intervention into the poetics of making, would help us imagine, as David Graeber says in the epigraph above, how we could *make* the world differently.

A machine dealing with language, the typewriter seems destined for the spotlight at the East-West swap meet. In the West, prior to the arrival of the computer, the typewriter was Prince Charming of mechanized writing, an epitome of the technological transformation of the Word. Incidentally, the Graeber quote is from his book on the culture and violence of bureaucratization, whereas the typewriter was once the symbol of bureaucracy, so much so that Martin Heidegger once wondered whether the ontology of a state (that "it *is*") manifests itself in the "fact that the police arrest a suspect, or so-and-so many typewriters are clattering in a government building, taking down the words of ministers and state secretaries." Actually, Heidegger has given us the most influential reflection on the typewriter, although his analysis, especially in light of our study of Lin Yutang's Chinese typewriter, sounds a bit skewed. Understanding technology as the *Gestell*, or enframing—that technological control and direction conceal rather than reveal the essence of our being—Heidegger presents a dim view of the typewriter. Regarding the hand and the word as key distinctions of humanity, he thinks the typewriter tears "writing from the essential realm of the hand, i.e., the realm of the word." Replacing handwriting along with its surrogate sensuality, typographic print "degrades the word to a means of communication." Heidegger deems the typewriter, something "between a tool and a machine," as a continuation of the "increasing destruction of the word.... Therefore, when writing was withdrawn from the origin of its essence, i.e., from the hand, and was transferred to the machine, a transformation occurred in the relation of Being to man."[38]

Following Heidegger, Friedrich A. Kittler also sees the typewriter, a precursor of the computer, as "a new and elegant tautology of technicians," ushering in an age of "discourse network," in which "absolute knowledge will run as an endless loop." Whereas handwriting could store "the fact of its authorization" and "guarantee the perfect securing of traces," in a typed text "paper and body, writing and soul fall apart." Kittler concludes, "Typewriters do not store individuals; their letters do not communicate a beyond that perfectly alphabetized readers can subsequently hallucinate as meaning." Recognizing the shared industrial provenance of Remington typewriters and the machine guns made in the same factories, Kittler goes so far as to call the typewriter a "discourse machine gun."[39]

When we look at the flip side of the story, that is, outside the discursive sphere of the West, we find ourselves unable to fault Kittler for using the seemingly dubious phrase, "perfectly alphabetized readers." It may sound presumptuous for the German scholar to imply, without justification, that the devastating effects of the typewriter, as it were, would apply to alphabetic as well as nonalphabetic languages, but the historical experience of the machine in the nonalphabetic world would actually bear him out—to an extent. Media historians have showed us that the typewriter, originally developed with the Latin alphabet in mind, encountered very few technical roadblocks as the design was extended to non-Latin alphabets and nonalphabetic scripts. Whether it was Siamese, Russian, Arabic, or Hebrew, "a solution was found for each of these puzzles, however, sometimes elegantly and at other times awkwardly: Hebrew became English 'backward,' Arabic became English 'in cursive,' Russian became English 'with different letters,' Siamese became English 'with too many letters,' French became English 'with accents,' and so forth." On this triumphant march of universalism, almost all languages/scripts fell into step in one way or another and each showed its commensurability with the technolinguistic modernity ostensibly represented by the typewriter.[40] In all these cases, it was only a question of "technology transfer." Until, that is, the carnival parade reached the lacquered door of China.

Because the Chinese script is neither alphabetic nor syllabic, designing a typewriter that could accommodate thousands of individual characters on one single platform like the QWERTY keyboard was almost an impossible task. The earlier models dating to the late nineteenth century, though not monstrous machines or colossal concoctions, had never achieved any technological breakthrough to become convenient enough for popular adoption. In his trailblazing study of the Chinese typewriter, Thomas S. Mullaney provides an account of how the technical difficulties of adapting the machine to the Chinese language gave rise to "an unrelenting, multifront character assassination of the Chinese script itself," a rhetorical position conveniently aligned with the long-running Western discourse on the backwardness of the Chinese script. More interestingly, the problem with a Chinese typewriter lent more ammunition to domestic critics of their national language, the usual suspects we have already met in chapter 1. To those vociferous character abolitionists, such as Qian Xuantong, the unfeasibility of a Chinese typewriter was the ultimate validation of their censure of the millennia-old script as a hindrance to the nation's progress.[41] What better proof of the Chinese character's retrogradation than its apparent incompatibility with a modern machine like the typewriter?

And this is where Lin Yutang entered the scene, standing, as he always did, at the crossroads of East and West, clad in a Chinese robe or a Western suit, holding an obligatory pipe. This time he literally put his money where his mouth was: his experiment with the Chinese typewriter, a thirty-year effort, nearly bankrupted him. The significance of his invention, however, has been forgotten until recently.[42]

On May 22, 1947, about two months after Warren Weaver aired his fantasy about the "Chinese code," Lin Yutang unveiled his Chinese typewriter in New York City. In the press release, Lin announced his invention of the first Chinese typewriter that can print ninety thousand Chinese words. Better even, the machine can do in an hour the work of a Chinese copyist in a day and requires no previous training to operate. Emphasizing efficiency, convenience, and progress, Lin claimed that his MingKwai ("Clear and Quick") Typewriter, 明快打字機, would move the clock of progress forward by one or two decades and revolutionize Chinese office life.[43]

In the patent application he had filed a year earlier, Lin detailed the originalities of his invention, ranging from his classification system to the keyboard and the cylindrical drum. While all the other designers of the Chinese typewriters had looked for technology transfer by trying to adapt a machine designed with the Latin alphabet in mind to the Chinese script, Lin began his design by rethinking the linguistic difference between the alphabetic and nonalphabetic languages. "The symbols or characters used in writing the Chinese language consist of one or more components," Lin explained. "Most of these characters consist of a left hand component forming a classifying symbol and a right hand component forming the phonetic of the word. In some of the characters, however, the classifying component is not at the left hand side of the character and the phonetic component is not in the right hand position. Also, many of the components may be used alone. Inasmuch as the components are not always in the same positions in the characters, a simple and logical classification of the characters has never been devised heretofore."[44]

Here Lin was referring to the fact that most Chinese words consist of a pictorial component and a phonetic component, making them 形声字 (*xingshengzi*). The combination of the pictorial and the phonetic, poetic as it might be, creates a roadblock for any typewriter design that relies solely on the principles of the phonetic. Therefore, as Lin explained, "a more definite and concise classification of the characters making up the Chinese language would be required before a satisfactory typewriter or other printing or character-forming device could be produced." Thus came the first step of Lin's technological breakthrough, his system of classification: "I have discovered that all Chinese characters or their components can be classified into smaller groups by referring to the configuration of the strokes at the top of the character and the configuration of the strokes at the bottom of the character. By selecting the characters by their top and bottom configurations, the characters or their components can be divided into relatively small groups from which the desired characters can be selected."[45]

In fact, Lin had first proposed this classification method thirty years earlier, and that proposal was part and parcel of the story of Chinese linguistic modernization. In 1917, Lin published an article titled 创设汉字索引制议 (On Creating the Chinese Index System), introducing his newly developed "first stroke retrieval method." He soon incorporated the ideas into his far more influential essay, 汉字索引制说明 (Notes on the Chinese Index System), published in 新青年 (*La Jeunesse*), the flagship journal of the May Fourth Movement. In both articles, Lin proposed taking the first stroke of a character and then listing the initial strokes of all Chinese characters according to their stroke orders. In his view, the first strokes fall into five categories: horizontal, vertical, left-falling, dot, and hook. "If two characters share the same first stroke, the user would need to check the second stroke by following the same order, which is very similar to aa, ab, ac, ad in the retrieval system in an English dictionary."[46]

Interestingly, Lin's article caught the attention of Cai Yuanpei and Qian Xuantong. The former, an indisputable leader of the New Culture Movement, supplied a preface to Lin's piece, whereas the latter, a major figure in language reform, composed an afterword. In his generous assessment of Lin's work, Cai, chancellor of Peking University, applauded the twenty-two-year-old linguist for having found the equivalence between the Chinese and Western retrieval systems: "The method is as clear and easy as the Western retrieval system, which uses alphabetical order, and the speed is as fast as well." In contrast, Qian's response was predicably lukewarm, for anything short of total alphabetization was not going to impress this diehard abolitionist of Chinese characters.[47]

Despite their difference in opinion, both Cai and Qian recognized the essence of Lin's effort: he was trying to bridge the gap between the alphabetic and Chinese scripts. It was a position not so popular when the debate over the future of the Chinese language was sharply divided between those clamoring for the adoption of a new phonetic system and those wanting to preserve the ancient script. A pragmatist with a vision, Lin, while acknowledging the shortcoming of the Chinese script in comparison to alphabetic systems, fully appreciated the beauty and value of Chinese characters. One day, in *My Country and My People* (1935), the intellectually more mature Lin would give us an unreserved endorsement of Chinese characters as "the visible symbol of China's unity," "a linguistic feat" to achieve cultural homogeneity.[48]

When he unveiled the MingKwai Typewriter in 1947, Lin had perfected his Chinese retrieval system by adding a new element. Improving the earlier first stroke method, his new system of 上下形 (*shang xia xing*) divided Chinese characters into their top left and bottom right components. In this way he organized tens of thousands of characters according to a pseudo-Chinese alphabet, which, unlike a real alphabet, disregarded a character's sound and focused instead on the pictorial of strokes. Describing this unique system, Lin sounded as if he was speaking the language of statistics and probability, the technolingo of the rising Information Age: "In order to answer the need for providing all characters needed in modern communication, I have found that the greater part of characters making up the written Chinese language can be formed from about 70 to 80 left hand components, each forming a classifier, and about 1,300 right hand components, each forming a phonetic. The left hand and right hand components can be combined to print, select or form about 90,000 Chinese characters, some of which actually do not exist, for the same reason that it is possible to spell words in the English language that do not exist."[49] But unlike Shannon, Weaver, and others, who were exploring the alphabet-based digital language by the laws of statistics and probability, Lin drew inspiration from a seemingly unlikely source: the art of calligraphy.

There is no question that calligraphy occupies a unique place in Chinese culture, thanks partly to the Chinese conception of writing as the embodiment of *Dao*, or truth. An art of line and form, calligraphy is tied up with the genesis, or origin stories, of Chinese writing. The *Shuo Wen Jie Zi* (Explaining Writings and Analyzing Characters) by Xu Shen of the Han dynasty describes the myth of Fu Xi designing the Eight Diagrams: "Upwards, watching the celestial phenomena; downwards, learning formulas on the ground."[50] One of the most important classics on calligraphy, *Shu Duan* (Calligraphy Theory), by Zhang Huaiguan of the Tang dynasty, begins with the legend of Cang Jie inventing Chinese words: "[He] watched the various combinations of stars, and studied the veins of turtle shells and the flying traces of birds, from which he learned all kinds of beauties, so that he could invent the characters."[51] The other reason for traditional Chinese literati to cherish calligraphy has to do with the belief in the inseparability between one's brush stroke and personality. As Yang Xiong, a famous Confucian scholar of the Han dynasty, put it, "The lines of calligraphy are the tracks of one's mind."[52] Liu Gongquan, a Tang calligrapher whose technique of writing has been immortalized as the "Liu Style" (*liuti*), said it more bluntly: "A decent man's writing follows formula."[53] To cultivate a good style of calligraphy, then, is a way to nurture one's inner being, an idea Heidegger would have embraced wholeheartedly as he pondered the ills of mechanized writing.

In *My Country and My People*, a book that propelled him to stardom as the interpreter of the Chinese way of life, Lin Yutang not only expressed appreciation of Chinese characters but also emphasized the importance of calligraphy to Chinese culture. As a study of form and rhythm in the abstract, calligraphy has provided the Chinese people with a basic aesthetics. "It is through calligraphy," Lin wrote, "that the Chinese have learned their basic notions of line and form. It is therefore impossible to talk about Chinese art without understanding Chinese calligraphy and its artistic inspiration." In architecture, for instance, whether it be an arcade, pavilion, or temple, there is not one type of Chinese building "whose sense of harmony and form is not directly derived from certain types of Chinese calligraphy." The same with painting; in fact, the Chinese have traditionally regarded calligraphy and painting as sister arts, lumping them together as *shuhua*: "Owing to the use of the brush, which is more subtle and more responsive than the pen, calligraphy has been elevated to the true level of an art on a par with Chinese painting." Quoting the renowned Yuan calligrapher Zhao Mengfu (1254–1322), Lin remarked, "The method of painting lies yet in the 'eight fundamental strokes' of writing." He then went to great lengths to limn the aesthetics of strokes in calligraphy, trying to help his English readers appreciate what he called the "pure witchery of line and beauty of composition": "The Chinese scholar is trained to appreciate, as regards line, qualities like force, suppleness, reserved strength, exquisite tenderness, swiftness, neatness, massiveness, ruggedness, and restraint or freedom; and as regards form, he is taught to appreciate harmony, proportion, contrast, balance, lengthiness, compactness, and sometimes even beauty in slouchiness or irregularity."[54]

Obviously, calligraphy not only holds the key to Chinese art and culture, but also the secret to Lin's success in developing the index system and designing the typewriter. In his patent application, even though Lin adopted such technical terms as "statistical average," the description of his invention, referring to the shape or design of the strokes making up the character, shows a clear affinity to his writings about Chinese calligraphy. "Chinese characters are highly stylized," Lin stated, "and the characters are acceptable only when they are of conventional form. Therefore, it is necessary also to devise type arrangements by means of which acceptable characters can be formed." The font that Lin had chosen for his brainchild was the Song style (*songti*), also called court style, because it had first been adopted by the Song court in important documents and serious affairs. It was known for clarity without the loss of elegance, a good balance between aesthetics and utility. To fit the font to his typewriter, however, Lin needed to make some adjustments.

> I have discovered that in order to achieve the effect of coherence and integration in the characters formed by combination, it is necessary to simulate the overlapping of strokes across the dividing line as actually takes place in the regular printer's types. I have found that, except in the case of two parallel vertical strokes which must not touch each other, it does not hurt, but helps, to have the horizontal and slanting strokes of the two

> parts touch each other. I have found that a composite picture of the seventy odd left hand components shows an empty space at the lower right hand corner. By actual tests, I have found it desirable to design the right hand components so that their horizontal and slanting strokes overlap in a sharply defined and carefully delimited area. Accordingly, in typewriters, printing, or typeforming devices embodying the present invention, the left hand components are arranged to take up approximately two-fifths of the square and the right hand component is arranged to take up approximately three-fifths of the square, and where necessary, to overlap beyond the three-fifths area to tie the two components together.[55]

Lin thus combined his earlier research on the intricacies of strokes for his unique index system with a meticulous, mathematically calculated design of type to produce what might be a machine (fig. 7) but nonetheless a machine saturated in the principles and aesthetics of craftsmanship, not so far removed from the hand, the body.

In addition to the calligraphy-inspired index system and type design, Lin's invention boasted another significant feature: the keyboard (fig. 8). Compared to other designs of the Chinese typewriter, which often had

7. Lin Yutang's Chinese typewriter, early twentieth century. Photograph: Princeton University Library.

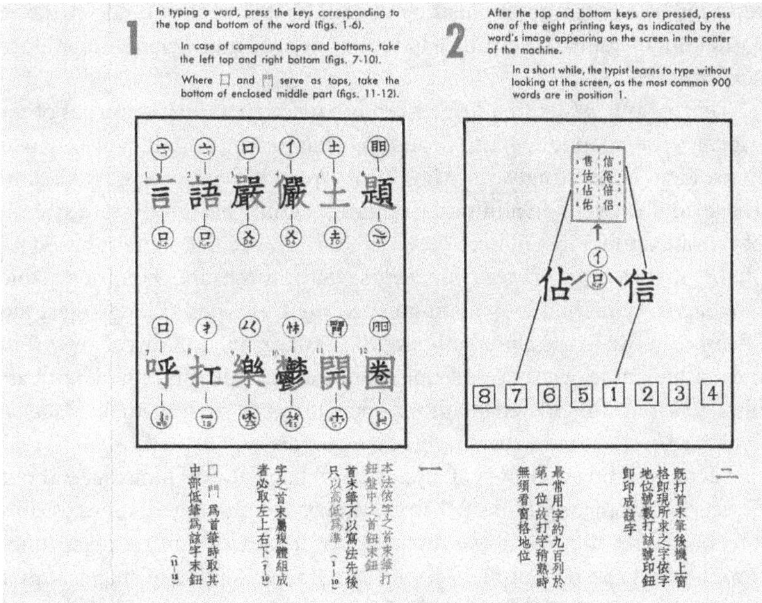

8. Input and search on Lin Yutang's typewriter, early twentieth century. Photograph: Princeton University Library.

hundreds, if not thousands, of keys, MingKwai consisted of only 72 keys: 36 of them correspond to the top configurations of Chinese characters, 28 to bottom configurations, and 8 number keys working as selectors. Moreover, the function of this keyboard is fundamentally different from that of the standard alphabetic, QWERTY keyboard. Pressing a top key and a bottom key will produce eight possible combinations, which appear as qualifying characters in a window called the "magic eye." The typist then presses one of the eight number keys to select from the eight characters in view and the final selection is then printed on the paper. As figure 8 shows, for instance, when the top key 亻 and bottom key 口 are pressed, there will be eight options appearing in the magic eye, 信俗倍侣售估佔佑, with each character assigned a number from 1 to 8. Further pressing the number 1 key will produce 信, whereas doing so with the number 7 key will print 佔.

As Thomas Mullaney points out, "If the fundamental and unspoken assumption of Western-style typewriting was the assumption of correspondence—that the depression of a key would result in the impression of the corresponding symbol upon the typewritten page—MingKwai was something altogether different."[56] The classic what-you-type-is-what-you-get convention, or what Lin called "hunt and peck," was now replaced by a process of input and retrieval.[57] "For the first time," to quote Kittler out of context, "hitting a letter key offered numerous combinatory surprises."[58]

This technical feature of transforming inscription into a process of retrieval, correspondence into searching, has several significant implications. First, interestingly, the MingKwai typewriter can type English, Japanese, and Russian, in addition to Chinese. Using his top-bottom system of classification, Lin had in effect created a new set of ideogram-based alphabet that would work for Chinese, as well as those alphabetic or syllabic languages. What had long distinguished the two types of languages, the false gap between the alphabetic and the nonalphabetic, "dissolves within the double frame of stroke and alphabetic index."[59] In this regard, Lin's arbitrary system anticipated techno-utopian projects, such as Xu Bing's *Book from the Sky* and others, by nearly half a century.

Second, if the advocates of alphabetism have always fantasized about direct graphic inscriptions of abstract thought without mediation,[60] Lin's keyboard with the magic eye, by virtue of its search and retrieval function, leveled the playing field for all languages. Mullaney suggests that MingKwai rescued "Chinese script—or perhaps script itself—from the powerful myth that some writing systems are more immediate than others, and deeper still, that any script is immediate, ever."[61] Haun Saussy has long warned that in the Western view of the ideogram, "the very ways in which the Chinese language was presented as a specimen set it up to fail the term of comparison." Through Lin's typewriter, the conceptual failure of what Saussy dismisses as the "workshop of equivalences" came in plain view.[62]

Third, by combining search and inscription, Lin's invention anticipated "a human-computer interaction now referred to as input, or *shuru* in Chinese."[63] Deep into the digital age, we may have been inured to the simple act of input-output, but we should remember that at the dawn of the cybernetic imagination, when key definitions such as feedback, information, and communication were still subject to negotiation and codification, as we saw in the battle to reify information as a disembodied entity, Lin's design of a feedback loop on a writing machine saturated in the aesthetics of Chinese language and art was not just a stroke of genius, but a profound humanist attempt that resonated with some of the contemporary efforts by fellow writers and artists to engage and counter the paradigm shifts of information technology in which their work was embedded.

"The irony is," said the American poet Charles Olson in a landmark essay composed around the same time as Lin's invention, "from the machine has come one gain not yet sufficiently observed or used, but which leads directly on toward projective verse and its consequences." The machine Olson had in mind was the typewriter. If Heidegger and others conceived the typewriter as a means of withdrawing writing from the body, Olson saw the opposite: the potential of the machine as an enabler of what he called "projective verse," an open form of writing, or "composition by field," as opposed to inherited, traditional forms. Essentially a manifesto of a new American poetics, Olson's essay proclaimed, "Verse now, 1950, if it is to be of essential use, must ... catch up and put into itself certain laws and possibilities of the breath, of the breathing of the man who writes as well as of his listenings." For this kind of kinetic poetry, the typewriter showed its hitherto unrecognized technical advantage. As Olson explained, "Due to its rigidity and its space precisions, it can, for a poet, indicate exactly the breath, the pauses, the suspension even of syllables, the juxtapositions even of parts of phrases, which he intends. For the first time the poet has the stave and the bar a musician has had. For the first time he can, without the convention of rime and meter, record the listening he has done to his own speech and by that one act indicate how he would want any reader, silently or otherwise, to voice his work." Speaking on behalf of his generation of writers, including the Beat guru, Jack Kerouac, whose idiosyncratic typewriting, or "kick-writing," of *On the Road* is now the stuff of legend, Olson declared the typewriter "the personal and instantaneous recorder of the poet's work."[64]

Earlier in his career Olson had worked for the Office of War Information before resigning from the job partly because he was disgusted with the American Cold War machinery of propaganda and misinformation, a geopolitical gambit in which language was turned into bombastic dogmas, jingoistic shibboleths, or cryptic messages. Leery of the top-down, dominative management of information he had experienced at governmental office work, Olson in his call for projective verse was also, as Todd Tietchen puts it in *Technomodern Poetics*, "responding to the foundational theories and emerging technological capabilities that grounded the postwar information society as it assumed its nascent form in Cold War America." By reclaiming the typewriter—a quintessential bureaucratic tool, or at best, something the earlier generation of writers had used mainly to transcribe fair copies of manuscripts—as a "personal and instantaneous recorder," Olson was trying to "humanize the automated information economy."[65]

It is worth remembering, however, that Olson's conception of projective verse, characterized by three P words—"projectile, percussive, prospective"—was grounded in his poetic yearning for "language as the act of the instant," as opposed to "language as the act of thought about the instant."[66] Literary history has showed us that Olson's rendezvous with new American poetics took place in a period when he paid frequent visits to Ezra Pound at St. Elizabeths. Under the influence of the older poet's obsession with Chinese (see chap. 3), Olson composed his own Chinese canto, incorporating the Poundian "make it new" dictum.[67] Moreover, the specter of Fenollosa appeared on the opening pages of *Call Me Ishmael*, Olson's coming-of-age work cementing his place in the subversive genealogy of transpacific America. In his definitive essay, "Projective Verse," Olson quoted Fenollosa again: "What Fenollosa is so right about, in syntax, the sentence as first act of nature, as lightning, as passage of force from subject to object."[68]

In *The Buddha in the Machine*, R. John Williams studies the Western embrace of Eastern aesthetic ideals to counter the fear of the rise of modern technological systems. In this regard he sees Lin Yutang's Chinese typewriter as an instance of the turn to traditional Eastern *technē* as a therapeutic means of living with Western *techno*: "It was as if the relative slowness of Chinese writing in an era of mechanization could be solved by ignoring the temporal elements of the orthography and focusing instead on their spatial aesthetics—a vivid corollary to Lin's turn toward *technê* as a means of appropriating the classic Orientalist denial of coevalness and recasting it as an aesthetic advantage in the search for a way out of (and into) modern technics."[69]

While I agree in sentiment with Williams's thesis and concur with his analysis of the cultural psyche of the West, I believe Lin's invention goes beyond serving merely as a therapeutic alternative. As I have described above, Lin's inspirations for both the index system and the typewriter came from calligraphy, the ancient art of form and line, an aesthetics crystallized in the "pure witchery" of strokes. The technical know-how came from artistic knowledge. This is not a case of being modern by being retrograde, an important thesis often advanced in transnational studies of modernity.[70] Neither is it to resurrect the ghost of Wheelwright Pian in dialogue with Duke Huan. In a famous segment of Zhuangzi, Duke Duan was reading a book in the hall while Wheelwright Pian worked in the courtyard below. Setting down his mallet and chisel, the wheelwright made bold to step up into the hall and asked what the Duke was reading. After being told that the Duke was reading the words of sages who had been dead long before, the wheelwright snickered, "In that case, what you are reading there is nothing but the chaff and dregs of the men of old." The Duke felt insulted and demanded an explanation, to which Wheelwright Pian replied:

> I look at it from the point of view of my own work. When I chisel a wheel, if the blows of the mallet are too gentle, the chisel will slide and won't take hold. But if they're too hard, it will bite and won't budge. Not too gentle, not too hard—you can get it in your hand and feel it in your mind. You can't put it into words, and yet there's a knack to it somehow. I can't teach it to my son, and he can't learn it from me.[71]

This passage has often been interpreted as an allegory for a Daoist appeal to our innate sense of ontological oneness with the world, what Heidegger termed "Dasein-with," as opposed to rational, calculative thinking, which has led to the preponderance of technology. In fact, Heidegger's thinking about modern technology was deeply informed by his familiarity with Zhuangzi and Daoism.[72] In Heidegger's polemic against the typewriter as a machine that tears "writing from the essential realm of the hand," we hear echoes of Wheelwright Pian's words, "you can get it in your hand and feel it in your heart."

In Lin's typewriter, however, there is no false dichotomy between the hand and the machine, the pictorial and the phonetic, or the East and the West. Instead, it is as if Lin were becoming the Wheelwright, the Duke, and the sage all in one body. His Chinese typewriter was no simple technical feat but a poetic enterprise, reimagining technology through the prisms of art, breaking down the fabled wall separating East from West. In his musings over the typewriter and other modern technologies, Heidegger lamented, "There was a time when it was not technology alone that bore the name of *technē*. Once, the revealing that brings forth truth into the splendor of radiant appearance was also called *technē*. Once there was a time when the bringing forth of the true into the beautiful was called *technē*. And the poesis of the fine art was also called *technê*."[73] In Lin Yutang's MingKwai typewriter, clear and quick, equipped with a magic eye, we find the living instance of what Heidegger, dabbling in Orientalism, cherished nostalgically as a thing of the past—the poesis of art, the making of the word and the world.

The Story of Mr. Shi Eating Lions

[CODA]

One important aspect of the translational situation is that language, whether in the form of live speech or in the form of written text, is not apart from the rest of life, but forms a part of life.

CHAO YUEN REN, "Dimensions of Fidelity in Translation with Special Reference to Chinese"

The promotional package for Lin Yutang's Chinese typewriter contains, inter alia, a glowing endorsement by his friend, Chao Yuen Ren. Widely recognized as the founder of Chinese linguistics, Chao gave Lin's brainchild his full-hearted support: "It takes so little learning, whether for Chinese, or for Americans who don't know Chinese characters, to become familiar with the keyboard. I think this is it." A Chinese-language newspaper went even further, predicting, "If Mr. Lin will continue to perfect his invention and apply it to a linotype, his position may be ranked with Gutenberg."[1]

Unfortunately, the MingKwai typewriter never went into commercial production, and Lin's name never became associated with Gutenberg. The information industry moved swiftly from mechanizing word to mechanizing brain—the computer. And the founding of the People's Republic of China in 1949 brought forth a whole new set of technological agendas and strategic priorities, including its own design of a Chinese typewriter. As a result, even though Lin's indexical keyboard inspired other research projects, his invention remained largely a number in the filing system of the US Patent Office.[2] And despite his contribution to the idea of human-computer interface, he was never invited to any of the Macy conferences or had any influence on the future of cybernetics. The unofficial Chinese rep at those meetings was none other than his friend, Chao Yuen Ren.

Like many leading intellectuals of his generation, Chao was born in China, educated in the West, and became a key player in the East-West encounter. A polymath, Chao received a doctoral degree in mathematics from Harvard in 1918, taught physics at Cornell, and eventually settled on linguistics as a career path. A gifted musician with an ear for sound, Chao once served as Bertrand Russell's interpreter during the English philosopher's tour of China in 1920. On their way to Changsha, Chao met a local person and picked up some Hunan dialect from him. Upon the entourage's arrival in the city, Chao used his newly acquired dialect to translate Russell's lecture, and his accent was so nearly perfect that the audience took him to be a native speaker of Hunanese.[3]

Thanks partly to that experience, Chao, as a linguist, devoted himself to the study of phonology and phonetics and did extensive research on regional dialects in China, focusing on the rich tonal variations across the country. In the 1920s, Chao was an active participant in the Chinese language reform movement, championing the initiative of *Gwoyeu Romatzyh* 国语罗马字 (National Language Romanization). Unlike his peers who advocated vernacular writing as the way to modernize Chinese, Chao pursued the same goal in sound, trying to promote a unified system of pronunciation. He believed that tone—Mandarin has four tones, whereas some dialects, such as Hunanese or Cantonese, have more—was one of the most important attributes of Chinese and thus warranted special consideration in language reform. When an opponent questioned his approach, Chao defended himself by insisting that tones were not just sonic stresses, but "a powerful tool for distinguishing meanings." This is an important perception that Chao would try to bring into the dialogue with his cybernetic-minded colleagues in the United States.[4]

When he endorsed Lin Yutang's typewriter in 1947, Chao was about to take up a professorship in linguistics at the University of California, Berkeley, where he would stay until his retirement. That year he had read the manuscript of *Cybernetics* by his friend Norbert Wiener and become interested in the theories of feedback, information, and computation. His personal friendship and intellectual exchange with Wiener and other leaders in the field eventually landed him a ticket to the tenth Macy conference held in April 1953, in Princeton, New Jersey, where Chao delivered a paper, titled "Meaning in Language and How It Is Acquired."

Anticipating a thesis that he would further expound one day in an article on translation,[5] Chao began his Macy presentation by acknowledging the elusive, fluid, and context-dependent nature of meaning, suggesting that an individual mostly "learns the meaning of a word, phrase, sentence, or discourse through certain nonlinguistic contexts, not dictionaries." He then addressed the issue of homeostasis in language, showing his background in structural linguistics by affirming "the rigidity and nonplasticity of language as a system of meaning *en bloc*." As Chen-Pang Yeang points out in his study of Chao's journey in cybernetics, Chao in this presentation played the dual role of a humanist on the one hand and a quasi-quantitative scientist on the other. But ultimately Chao distinguished himself from other linguists and scientists with an emphasis on tones as information carriers. Throughout his career, Chao held the view that "the meaning-carrying features of tones could reduce the average number of syllables needed to represent a word and that tones were more robust against interference than some phonetic units like consonants." In an earlier paper he had shared with Wiener, Chao argued that "oral Chinese was particularly resilient in the face of noise and interference because words used tones to carry information and ended in vowels rather than consonants."[6]

Of course, for Chao to describe the efficacy of oral Chinese as a medium for communication was not to go back to the old language wars, a contest for global dominance in language. Instead, he wanted to draw attention to one aspect of communication that was being ignored by the architects of the cybernetic revolution: sound as an embodied carrier of meaning. Given how invested Claude Shannon and Warren Weaver were, as we saw earlier, in ridding noise and interference in their mathematical model of communication, even a seemingly mundane point raised by Chao, such as "humans recognize correct tones more easily than consonants in a noisy environment," would have had technical, let alone cultural, implications if those cyberneticians had listened. But Chao and his like-minded scholars, such as Gregory Bateson and Margaret Mead, as we saw earlier, were on the losing side of the debate and struggle over the future of information technology. In a host of key issues, positions held by Shannon, Weaver, and Wiener et al. had won the day: Cybernetics is about conceptualizing the mind as a machine rather than the other way around; information is probability without semantics; feedback means the adjustment and refinement of a closed system rather than the participatory openness of a continual process; and a Chinese book is just a book in English coded in Chinese.

As if anticipating that his call for sound to factor into information theory would fall on deaf ears, Chao brought a Chinese "gift" to the Macy conference. It was a poetic tour de force, a piece titled 施氏食獅史 (The Story of Mr. Shi Eating Lions), which Chao had composed himself.

> 石室詩士施氏嗜獅誓食十獅氏時時適市視獅十時氏適
> 市適十碩獅適市是時氏視是十獅恃十石矢勢使是十獅
> 逝世氏拾是十獅屍適石室石室濕氏使侍試拭石室石室
> 拭氏始試食是十獅屍食時始識是十碩獅屍實十碩石獅
> 屍是時氏始識是實事實試釋是事

Stone house poet Mr. Shih was fond of lions and resolved to eat ten lions. The gentleman from time to time went to the market to look for lions.

> When, at ten o'clock, he went to the market, it happened that ten big lions went to the market. Thereupon, the gentleman looked at the ten big lions and, relying on the *momenta* of ten stone arrows, he caused the ten lions to depart from this world. The gentleman picked up the lions' bodies and went to the stone house. The stone house was wet and he made the servant try and wipe the stone house. The stone house having been wiped, the gentleman began to try to eat the ten lions' bodies. When he ate them, he began to realize that those ten big lions' bodies were actually ten big stone lions' bodies. Now he began to understand that this was really the fact of the case. Try and explain this matter.[7]

Despite graphic variations, all the 106 words of the piece are pronounced as /shi/, except in differing tones. Reminiscent of the babbling 100-letter sequence that opens *Finnegans Wake* (bababadalgharaghtakamminarronnkonnbronntonnerronntuonnthunntrovarrhounawnskawntoohoohoordenenthurnuk), which explores the limit of alphabetic languages, Chao's cacophonic story puts Chinese to sort of a stress test, pushing the language to the brink where acoustic truth begins to break away from visual signification. Earlier, Haroldo de Campos suggested via Fenollosa and Pound that individual Chinese characters weld the phonic to the graphic plane to create a poetic intracode or semiotic saturation. Here, in Chao's creative chaos, such a phonic-graphic relationality falls apart in echolalia, the percussive beats of /shi/.

Few of the studies of Chao so far have recognized "The Story of Mr. Shi Eating Lions" as a work of creative genius by a verbal artist, a prose poem that explores and explodes the fraught symbiosis of sound and script. Of course, as Lydia Liu and others have rightly pointed out, Chao composed the improbable story to suggest, in an ironic manner, that "the written character plays an important role in constraining the stochastic occurrences of spoken syllables in Mandarin."[8] He wanted to remind his colleagues at the conference that writing and speech are two different systems: in the case of Chinese, writing "depends heavily on visual differentiation of homophonous characters, which can be incomprehensible if they are pronounced alone, unaccompanied by a text."[9] But a poem, especially one as hilarious as Chao's, is not reducible to a simple message, containable in a thesis statement or, if you will, a fortune cookie. To counter the Shannonian definition of information as what one can say rather than does say, the poet Chao said more than the linguist Chao could say.

As a poem, "The Story" is an ingenious play on the integration and dissolution of writing and speech. On its visual surface, the poem in classical Chinese seems to make perfect sense. Read aloud, however, the piece falls apart, or falls into a kind of Joycean babble. As Steve McCaffery reminds us, a sound poem "can never be reduced to its textual 'equivalent' or notation; it is essentially performative." To McCaffery, who once read aloud as a poem the phonebook of a city where he had been invited to give a reading, sound poetry is "a poetry of complete expenditure in which nothing is recoverable and usable as 'meaning.' Involved is a decomposition of both an operative subject and the historical constraints of a semantic order. Sound poetry shatters meaning at the point where language commits its move to idealization; it sustains the materiality and material effects of the phonematic structures whilst avoiding their traditional semantic purpose."[10] In Chao's piece, the semantic order is maintained by the graphic but shattered by the sonic. Meaning, rather than integrate and accumulate, disintegrates and discharges. If Ezra Pound, as we saw in chapter 3, was interested in exploring the limit of sense/nonsense in Chinese by his "trick line," 閒顯先仙 (all pronounced as /xian/), Chao's 106-syllable sequence of /shi/ took such a Poundian experiment to the extreme.[11]

The sonic subversion of visual stability speaks to Chao's lifetime commitment to the study of tone as a subject of research. It also encapsulates the thrust of his presentation at the conference; that is, sound as a carrier of meaning brings a whole bag of concerns that need to be addressed sufficiently in information theory and technology. In particular, tones pertain to vowels, and vowels are breaths, organs, bodies, and lives. As Charles Olson would proclaim, "The HEAD, by way of the EAR, to the SYLLABLE; the HEART, by way of the BREATH, to the LINE." To Olson, each line is a breath unit, a record of breathing and heartbeat of a living body. Allen Ginsberg, Olson's fellow traveler, once imagined a poem as a "march of vowels."[12] In *Ethnography of Rhythm*, Haun Saussy argues, by way of Marcel Mauss, that rhythm is a technique of the body. English-speaking children, reciting "Ring around the rosy,/pockets full of posy," have internalized with their bodies—hands in the air, feet on the ground, and acoustic memories—the ditty's rhythmic pattern as well as alliteration of phonemes unrecognizable to speakers of some other languages.[13] Like rhythm and phoneme, tone is a Maussian technique of the body. Nothing marks someone as an outsider, the proverbial ain't-from-here, more easily than a slight difference in tone when speaking a local dialect.[14]

There was no recording of the oral presentations of any of the Macy conferences; otherwise, we would have been able to hear Chao, the Chinese translator of *Alice in Wonderland*, reading aloud a piece more riddling, more tongue-twisting than Lewis Carroll's jabberwocky. Nor can we hear any bodily response, a laugh, chuckle, grunt, or murmur, from the cyberneticians in attendance to this perplexing vignette of Chinese whispers, which was arguably the apex of Chinese poetic play:

shí shì shī shì shī shì shì shī shì shí shí shī shì shí shí shì shì shì shī shí shí shì shì shì shì shí shí shī shì shì shì shí shì shì shì shí shī shì shí shí shì shì shǐ shì shí shī shì shì shì shí shì shí shī shī shì shí shì shí shì shī shì shǐ shì shì shì shí shì shí shì shì shì shǐ shì shí shì shí shī shī shí shí shǐ shí shì shí shí shī shī shí shí shí shí shī shī shì shí shì shǐ shí shì shí shì shí shì shì shì shì

Acknowledgments

As befits a study of transpacific poetics, this book owes its existence to countless people on both sides of the Pacific. As I try to compile a mental list of names, I recall what Ralph Waldo Emerson says in "The Poet": "Bare lists of words are found suggestive to an imaginative and excited mind." In my case, this bare list of names, by no means exhaustive, induces in me a great sense of gratitude for the personal friendship and intellectual companionship I have had the good fortune to enjoy over the years: Charles Bernstein, Marjorie Perloff, Hank Lazer, Susan Howe, Rob Wilson, Rita Raley, Candace Waid, Glenn Mott, Bob Weil, Dongfeng Wang, Chunmei Du, Liu Bai, Andrew Sewell, Jianhua Chen, and many others.

I particularly want to thank Nan Da, a visionary thinker and writer, who first saw the potential of this book for her Thinking Literature series and whose unabated enthusiasm sustained me as the manuscript went through various stages of metamorphoses. I am also grateful to Alan Thomas of the University of Chicago Press for his faith in the book, to Randy Petilos for his impeccably professional guidance, and to Anahid Nersessian, coeditor of the series, for her warm support. I want to thank the three anonymous reviewers of the manuscript for their constructive criticism and generous encouragement. Their shrewd assessments have made this a much better book. I am also grateful to Sheila Berg, the final gatekeeper of my writing, for the extraordinary care she took to edit my manuscript.

It is an understatement to say that finishing a book when the world is gripped by the COVID-19 pandemic has not been easy. Borders and walls perennially haunting the dreams of an intellectual migrant like me have suddenly become real roadblocks once again. While quarantines, forbidden entries, canceled flights, and expired visas have defined the past two years of our lives and the day of reunion remains elusive, I wish to express gratitude to my wife, JZ, and our son, Henry, still stuck in China, for the love and strength they send me daily from afar. I am also grateful to Isabelle and Ira, who have always been part of whatever journey I am on.

A shorter version of chapter 1 appeared as an article in *English and Ethnicity*, ed. J. Brutt-Griffler and C. E. Davies (London: Palgrave, 2006). Part of chapter 2 was published as an essay in *Marco Polo and the Encounter of East and West*, ed. Suzanne Akbari and Amilcare Iannucci, with the assistance of John Tulk (Toronto: University of Toronto Press, 2008), 262–79, © University of Toronto Press, 2008, reprinted with permission of the publisher. Part of chapter 3 appeared as an article in *Paideuma* 42 (2015). This book was made possible by a faculty fellowship from the Society for the Humanities at Cornell University and a general research fund from the University Grants Committee in Hong Kong. Grateful acknowledgment is given to Harvard University Archives for providing photographs of the instructional van (figs. 5 and 6) and to Princeton University Library for providing photographs of Lin Yutang's typewriter (figs. 7 and 8).

Notes

Introduction

1. Cary Nelson, *Repression and Recovery: Modern American Poetry and the Politics of Cultural Memory, 1910–1945* (Madison: University of Wisconsin Press, 1989), 35.

2. Bei Dao, *The August Sleepwalker*, trans. Bonnie S. McDougall (New York: New Directions, 1990), 33.

3. Yunte Huang, *Transpacific Displacement: Ethnography, Translation, and Intertextual Travel in Twentieth-Century American Literature* (Berkeley: University of California, 2002), 164–82.

4. Greg Barnhisel, *Cold War Modernists: Art, Literature, and American Cultural Diplomacy* (New York: Columbia University Press, 2015), 1–5.

5. Frances Stonor Saunders, *The Cultural Cold War: The CIA and the World of Arts and Letters* (New York: New Press, 2013), 1. In fact, the title of the British edition of the book is more colorful and direct: *Who Paid the Piper? The CIA and the Cultural Cold War* (London: Granta Books, 1999). For a more recent, panoramic survey of the culture of the Cold War, see Louis Menand, *The Free World: Art and Thought in the Cold War* (New York: Farrar, Straus and Giroux, 2021).

6. Barnhisel, *Cold War Modernists*, 3.

7. Friedrich Nietzsche, *On the Genealogy of Morals*, trans. Walter Kaufman and R. J. Hollingdale (New York: Vintage Books, 1989), 23.

8. Ibid.

9. For an excellent account of this infamous episode of modern Chinese history, see Frank Dikötter, *Mao's Great Famine: The History of China's Most Devastating Catastrophe, 1958–1962* (New York: Walker & Co., 2010).

10. Yunte Huang, ed., *The Big Red Book of Modern Chinese Literature: Writings from the Mainland in the Long Twentieth Century* (New York: Norton, 2016).

11. Perry Link, "If Mao Had Been a Hermit," *New York Review of Books*, April 7, 2016, 2–4.

12. Philip Fisher, *Hard Facts: Setting and Form in the American Novel* (New York: Oxford University Press, 1986), 5.

13. Saunders, *The Cultural Cold War*, 218.

14. Yunte Huang, *Transpacific Imaginations: History, Literature, and Counterpoetics* (Cambridge, MA: Harvard University Press, 2008).

15. John Ashbery, *Chinese Whispers* (New York: Farrar, Straus and Giroux, 2002), 31; Myung Mi Kim, *Dura* (Los Angeles: Sun & Moon Press, 1998), 33.

16. Chao Yuen Ren, "What Is Correct Chinese?," *Journal of the American Oriental Society* 81.3 (1961): 171.

Chapter One

1. Walter Benjamin, "Reflections on Radio," in *Selected Writings*, vol. 2, 1927–1934, trans. Rodney Livingstone et al., ed. Michaels W. Jennings et al. (Cambridge, MA: Harvard University Press, 1999), 544.

2. Eric A. Havelock, *The Muse Learns to Write: Reflections on Orality and Literacy from Antiquity to the Present* (New Haven, CT: Yale University Press, 1986), 32; Friedrich A. Kittler, *Gramophone, Film, Typewriter*, trans. Geoffrey Winthrop-Young and Michael Wutz (Stanford, CA: Stanford University Press, 1999), xi.

3. Richard Jean So, *Transpacific Community: America, China, and the Rise and Fall of a Cultural Network* (New York: Columbia University Press, 2016).

4. Jing Tsu, *Sound and Script in Chinese Diaspora* (Cambridge, MA: Harvard University Press, 2010), 51.

5. Quoted in Rodney Koeneke, *Empires of the Mind: I. A. Richards and Basic English in China, 1929–1979* (Stanford, CA: Stanford University Press, 2003), 76.

6. C. K. Ogden, *Basic English: International Second Language* (New York: Harcourt, Brace & World, 1968), 5–95.

7. John E. Joseph, "Basic English and the Debabelization of China," in *Intercultural Encounters—Studies in English Literatures*, ed. Heinz Antor and Kevin L. Cope (Heidelberg: Universitätsverlag C. Winter, 1999), 52.

8. Ibid., 60.

9. Joseph, "Basic English," 60; John Paul Russo, *I. A. Richards: His Life and Work* (Baltimore, MD: Johns Hopkins University Press, 1989), 110; C. K. Ogden and I. A. Richards, *The Meaning of Meaning: A Study of the Influence of Language upon Thought and of the Science of Symbolism* (New York: Harcourt, Brace & Company, 1923), 208 (hereafter cited in the text as *Meaning*).

10. I. A. Richards, "Beginnings and Transitions" (interview by Reuben Brower), in *I. A. Richards: Essays in His Honor*, ed. Reuben Brower, Helen Vendler, and John Hollander (New York: Oxford University Press, 1973), 34.

11. *Psyche* 9.3 (1929). Available at http://ogden.basic-english.org/psyche35.htm.

12. C. K. Ogden, *Debabelization* (London: Kegan Paul, 1931), 12.

13. Ibid., 13.

14. I. A. Richards, *So Much Nearer: Essays toward a World English* (New York: Harcourt, Brace & World, 1968), 248.

15. C. K. Ogden, "Editorial," *Psyche* 9.1 (1928): 2–3.

16. W. Terrence Gordon, "Undoing Babel: C. K. Ogden's Basic English," *Etc: A Review of General Semantics* 45.4 (1988): 338.

17. C. K. Ogden, *Basic English and Grammatical Reform*, supplement, *Basic News* (July 1937): 10; quoted in Russo, *I. A. Richards*, 768.

18. Michel Foucault, *Discipline and Punish: The Birth of the Prison*, trans. Alan Sheridan (New York: Vintage Books, 1979), 215–16.

19. Foucault, *Discipline and Punish*, 197; I. A. Richards and Christine Gibson, *Techniques in Language Control* (New York: Newbury House Publishers, 1974), 55, 110.

20. Richards, *So Much Nearer*, 242.

21. "Mobile Classroom Aids Language Teaching," *New York Times*, April 30, 1961, E9. See also the four-page typescript, "Memorandum for the New York Times," now in the I. A. Richards collection at Harvard University Archives, HUGB R461.10, Box 2.

22. Mary Peter Mack, ed., *A Bentham Reader* (London: Pegasus, 1969), 189.

23. I. A. Richards, *Practical Criticism: A Study of Literary Judgment* (New York: Harcourt, Brace & Company, 1929), 3.

24. Richards, *So Much Nearer*, 175.

25. Ibid., 49.

26. Ibid., 242.

27. Marjorie Perloff, *The Poetics of Indeterminacy: Rimbaud to Cage* (Princeton, NJ: Princeton University Press, 1981; reprint, Evanston, IL: Northwestern University Press, 1999); Peter Quartermain, *Disjunctive Poetics: Gertrude Stein and Louis Zukofsky to Susan Howe* (New York: Cambridge University Press, 1992).

28. Perloff, *Poetics of Indeterminacy*, back cover.

29. Susan Sontag, *Against Interpretation and Other Essays* (New York: Farrar, Straus and Giroux, 1966), 6.

30. Vaugh Anderson, "'Revision of the Golden Rule': John Cage, Latin America, and the Poetics of Non-Intervention," *Journal of Modern Literature* 41.1 (2017): 65.

31. Ezra Pound, "Debabelization and Ogden," *New English Weekly*, February 28, 1935, 410.

32. Ibid., 411. See also Ezra Pound, *Selected Letters: 1907–1941*, ed. D. D. Paige (London: Faber and Faber, 1950), 267; Ezra Pound, *Literary Essays of Ezra Pound*, ed. T. S. Eliot (London: Faber and Faber, 1954), 3.

33. Ezra Pound, *ABC of Reading* (New York: New Directions, 1951), 34.

34. Ezra Pound, *The Cantos* (New York: New Directions, 1970), 815.

35. Richards and Gibson, *Techniques in Language Control*, 6–7.

36. Pound, "Debabelization and Ogden," 410.

37. Pound, *Selected Letters*, 266.

38. Ernest Fenollosa and Ezra Pound, *The Chinese Written Character as a Medium for Poetry*, ed. Haun Saussy, Jonathan Stalling, and Lucas Klein (New York: Fordham University Press, 2008), 7.

39. Haroldo de Campos, *Novas: Selected Writings*, ed. Antonio Sergio Bessa and Odile Cisneros (Evanston, IL: Northwestern University Press, 2007), 229, 230. See also Marjorie Perloff, "'Raising the Referential Temperature': Poundian Reverberation in Brazilian Concrete Poetry," *Paideuma* 42 (2015): 5–38.

40. John Bishop, Introduction to James Joyce, *Finnegans Wake* (New York: Penguin Books, 1999), vii–iii; subsequent quotations from *Finnegans Wake* are from this edition.

41. Marshall McLuhan, *The Gutenberg Galaxy: The Making of Typographic Man* (Toronto: University of Toronto Press, 1962), 75.

42. C. K. Ogden, "James Joyce's Anna Livia Plurabelle (in Basic English)," *transition* 21 (1932): 259.

43. Ibid., 215–62.

44. Pound, "Debabelization and Ogden," 411.

45. Louis Zukofsky, "Basic," in *Prepositions +: The Collected Critical Essays*, foreword Charles Bernstein (Hanover, NH: University Press of New England, 2000), 163

46. Quartermain, *Disjunctive Poetics*, 13–14.

47. Barret Watten, "New Meaning and Poetic Vocabulary: From Coleridge to Jackson Mac Low," *Poetics Today* 18.2 (Summer 1997): 147–86.

48. Zukofsky, "Basic," 163; emphasis original.

49. Ibid., 156–57; emphasis original.

50. Qian Xuantong, "Zhongguo jinhouzhi wenzi wenti," quoted in Q. S. Tong, "The Bathos of a Universalism: I. A. Richards and His Basic English," in *Tokens of Exchange: The Problem of Translation in Global Circulations*, ed. Lydia H. Liu (Durham, NC: Duke University Press, 1999), 339.

51. Lu Xun, "Reply to an Interview from My Sickbed," in *Complete Works of Lu Xun*, vol. 6 (Beijing: Renmin wenxue chubanshe, 1981), 160.

52. Richards, *So Much Nearer*, 223–24; emphasis original.

53. Ibid., 224–25.

54. Quoted in Koeneke, *Empires of the Mind*, 109–10.

55. See my discussion of Lin Yutang's criticism of Basic and defense of pidgin in Huang, *Transpacific Displacement*, 126–33.

56. Lin Yutang, *The Little Critic: Essays, Satires and Sketches on China (Second Series: 1933–1935)* (Westport, CT: Hyperion Press, 1983), 50.

57. Ibid., 52–53.

58. Ibid., 59.

59. Michel Foucault, *The Order of Things: An Archaeology of the Human Sciences* (London: Tavistock Publications, 1970), x; emphasis original.

60. It's worth pointing out that in the case of Edward Sapir, his notion of linguistic relativism is closely associated with the concept of poetic indeterminacy; that is, his relativity hypothesis does not refer to language as such but to poetic language: "the poetic potential of language—not logic or basic reference—most massively determines the imagination." See Edgar Garcia, *Signs of the Americas: A Poetics of Pictography, Hieroglyphs, and Khipu* (Chicago: University of Chicago Press, 2020), 9–10.

61. Lin, *The Little Critic*, 54–57.

62. T. F. Chu, "This Easy Chinese Language," *China Critic* 6.35 (1933): 856.

63. Otto Jespersen, *Progress in Language* (London: Swan Sonnenschein, 1894), 127.

64. Lin, *The Little Critic*, 55.

65. Ibid., 48.

66. Chu, "This Easy Chinese Language," 856.

67. For an excellent, most up-to-date account of the Chinese script reform, see Yurou Zhong, *Chinese Grammatology: Script Revolution and Literary Modernity, 1916–1958* (New York: Columbia University Press, 2019).

68. Charles Bernstein, *My Way: Speeches and Poems* (Chicago: University of Chicago Press, 1999), 113–37.

69. For a most representative Asian American critique of Lin Yutang, see Elaine H. Kim, *Asian American Literature: An Introduction to the Writings and Their Social Context* (Philadelphia, PA: Temple University Press, 1982), 28.

70. Bernstein, *My Way*, 134.

71. Richards, *Practical Criticism*, 319.

72. I. A. Richards, *Basic English and Its Uses* (London: Kegan Paul, 1943), 5.

73. Suzanne Romaine, *Pidgin and Creole Languages* (New York: Longman, 1988), 24.

74. F. R. Leavis, *Mass Civilization and Minority Culture* (Cambridge: Minority Press, 1930), 29–30.

75. Henry James, *The Question of Our Speech* (Boston: Houghton Mifflin, 1905), 42–43.

76. Milton Murayama, *All I Asking for Is My Body* (Honolulu: University of Hawaii Press, 1988), 28.

77. Lois-Ann Yamanaka, *Saturday Night at the Pahala Theatre* (Honolulu: Bamboo Ridge Press, 1993), 35.

78. Doris Sommer, *Bilingual Aesthetics: A New Sentimental Education* (Durham, NC: Duke University Press, 2004), 35, xii, xix.

79. Gertrude Stein, *Tender Buttons* (Los Angeles: Sun & Moon Press, 1990), 11.

80. Sommer, *Bilingual Aesthetics*, 43.

81. Dennis Tedlock, "Towards a Poetics of Polyphony and Translatability," in *Close Listening: Poetry and the Performed Word*, ed. Charles Bernstein (New York: Oxford University Press, 1998), 186–87, 179, 189.

82. Sommer, *Bilingual Aesthetics*, 14, 18.

83. Marcel Proust, *Remembrance of Things Past*, trans. C. K. Scott Moncrieff et al. (New York: Vintage Books, 1982), vol. 3, 111–14.

Chapter Two

1. Peter Szendy, *All Ears: The Aesthetics of Espionage*, trans. Roland Vegso (New York: Fordham University Press, 2017), 9.

2. Jean-Luc Nancy, *Listening*, trans. Charlotte Madell (New York: Fordham University Press, 2007), 4.

3. David Hendy, *Noise: A Human History of Sound and Listening* (London: Profile Books, 2013), 5. For a fascinating exploration of the mythopoetics of prehistoric cave paintings, see Clayton Eshleman, *Juniper Fuse: Upper Paleolithic Imagination and the Construction of the Underworld* (Hanover, NH: Wesleyan University Press, 2003).

4. Frances Wood, *Did Marco Polo Go to China?* (Boulder, CO: Westview Press, 1996), 63. See also John W. Haeger, "Marco Polo in China? Problems with Internal Evidence," *Bulletin of Sung and Yuan Studies* 14 (1979): 22–30; and Craig Clunas, "The Explorer's Tracks," *Times Literary Supplement*, April 14, 1982.

5. Marco Polo, *The Travels of Marco Polo: The Complete Yule-Cordier Edition*, 2 vols. (New York: Dover, 1993; hereafter cited in the text as *Polo*), vol. 1, 1; emphasis mine.

6. Italo Calvino, *Invisible Cities*, trans. William Weaver (New York: Harcourt, Brace & Company, 1974), 62.

7. Marshall McLuhan and Bruce Powers, *The Global Village: Transformations in World Life and Media in the 21st Century* (New York: Oxford University Press, 1989), 8, 39.

8. Foucault, *Discipline and Punish*, 202.

9. Szendy, *All Ears*, 20.

10. Foucault, *Discipline and Punish*, 317.

11. Szendy, *All Ears*, 50.

12. Calvino, *Invisible Cities*, 5, 43, 69.

13. Calvino, *Invisible Cities*, 135.

14. While not a focus of my reading of Marco Polo, there is certainly a way to see

the narrative, especially his envy of the Khan's unsurpassable power of wealth creation, as a prequel to what we now call techno-Orientalism, defined as "the phenomenon of imagining Asia and Asians in hypo- or hypertechnological terms in cultural productions and political discourse" (David S. Roh et al., eds., *Techno-Orientalism: Imagining Asia in Speculative Fiction, History, and Media* [New Brunswick, NJ: Rutgers University Press, 2015], 2).

15. Pound, *The Cantos*, 190.

16. Charles Goldfinger, "Intangible Economy and Electronic Money," in *The Future of Money* (Paris: Organisation for Economic Co-operation and Development [OECD], 2002), 93.

17. Luciano Floridi, *Information: A Very Short Introduction* (New York: Oxford University Press, 2010), 4–5.

18. Christian Marazzi, *Capital and Affects: The Politics of the Language Economy*, trans. Giuseppina Mecchia (Los Angeles: Semiotext(e), 2011), 23.

19. Goldfinger, "Intangible Economy and Electronic Money," 98.

20. George Soros, *The Crisis of Global Capitalism: Open Society Endangered* (New York: Public Affairs, 1998), 14–15, xxiii.

21. McLuhan and Powers, *The Global Village*, 35.

22. Elinor Harris Solomon, *Virtual Money: Understanding the Power and Risks of Money's High-Speed Journey into Electronic Space* (New York: Oxford University Press, 1997), ix.

23. Stephen W. Hawking, *A Brief History of Time: From the Big Bang to Black Holes* (New York: Bantam Books, 1988), 187.

24. Goldfinger, "Intangible Economy and Electronic Money," 92–93.

25. Lien-sheng Yang, *Money and Credit in China: A Short History* (Cambridge, MA: Harvard University Press, 1952), 51–52.

26. Solomon, *Virtual Money*, 205.

27. Samuel Taylor Coleridge, *The Complete Poems*, ed. William Keach (New York: Penguin, 1997), 249.

28. The lines from Samuel Purchas, *Purchas his Pilgrimage* (1613), read, "In Xamdu did Cublai Can build a stately Palace, encompassing sixteene miles of plaine ground with a wall, wherein are fertile Meddowes, pleasant Springs, delightful Streams, and all sorts of beasts of chase and game, and in the middest thereof a sumptuous house of pleasure, which may be removed from place to place" (quoted in Coleridge, *Complete Poems*, 526).

29. For an insightful discussion of duplication as a literate, visual preference, see Vanessa Smith, *Literary Culture and the Pacific: Nineteenth-Century Textual Encounter* (Cambridge: Cambridge University Press, 1998).

30. Samuel Taylor Coleridge, *Biographia Literaria; or, Biographical Sketches of My Literary Life and Opinions*, ed. George Watson (New York: Everyman's Library, 1956), 167.

31. M. H. Abrams, *The Mirror and the Lamp: Romantic Theory and the Critical Tradition* (London: Oxford University Press, 1953), 47.

32. Marazzi, *Capital and Affects*, 44.

33. Quoted in Abrams, *The Mirror and the Lamp*, 48.

34. Coleridge, *Complete Poems*, 439.

35. Goldfinger, "Intangible Economy and Electronic Money," 110.

36. Calvino, *Invisible Cities*, 69, 22.

37. Ibid., 29, 22–23.

38. Jacques Attali, *Noise: The Political Economy of Music*, trans. Brian Massumi (Minneapolis: University of Minnesota Press, 1995), 25.

39. Michael Hardt and Antonio Negri, *Empire* (Cambridge, MA: Harvard University Press, 2000), 182, 190.

40. Francis Woodman Cleaves, "A Chinese Source Bearing on Marco Polo's Departure from China and a Persian Source of His Arrival in Persia," *Harvard Journal of Asiatic Studies* 36 (1976): 186–87, 195–96.

41. Eugene O'Neill, *Marco Millions: A Play* (New York: Boni and Liveright, 1927), v.

42. Marcel Duchamp, *The Writings of Marcel Duchamp*, ed. Michel Sanouillet and Elmer Peterson (New York: Da Capo Press, 1973), 23.

43. Sheldon Pollock, "Cosmopolitanism and Vernacular in History," in *Cosmopolitanism*, ed. Carol A. Breckenridge et al. (Durham, NC: Duke University Press, 2002), 28–29, 24.

44. Ibid., 29.

45. Martha Nussbaum, *For the Love of Country: Debating the Limits of Patriotism*, ed. Joshua Cohen (Boston: Beacon Press, 1996), 9.

46. Walter Mignolo, "The Many Faces of Cosmo-polis: Border Thinking and Critical Cosmopolitanism," in Breckinridge, *Cosmopolitanism*, 158.

47. Homie Bhabha and John Comaroff, "Speaking of Postcoloniality, in the Continuous Present: A Conversation," in *Relocating Postcolonialism*, ed. D. T. Goldberg and A. Quayson (Oxford: Blackwell, 2002), 25; Homi Bhabha, "Unsatisfied Notes on Vernacular Cosmopolitanism," in *Text and Narration: Cross-Disciplinary Essays on Cultural and National Identities*, ed. L Garcia-Moreno and P. C. Pfeiffer (Columbia, SC: Camden House, 1996), 29.

48. Paul Gilroy, *After Empire: Melancholia or Convivial Culture?* (New York: Routledge, 2006), 75.

49. Peter Nyers, "Abject Cosmopolitanism: The Politics of Protection in the Anti-Deportation Movement," *Third World Quarterly* 24.6 (2003): 1089.

50. Stuart Hall, "Political Belonging in a World of Multiple Identities," in *Conceiving Cosmopolitanism: Theory, Context, and Practice*, ed. S. Vertovec and R. Cohen (Oxford: Oxford University Press, 2002), 30.

51. Elaine Scarry, "The Difficulty of Imagining Other People," in Nussbaum, *For Love of Country?*, 103, 105, 106.

52. Ibid., 100.

53. Marc Shell, *The Economy of Literature* (Baltimore, MD: Johns Hopkins University Press, 1978), 69.

54. Coleridge, *Complete Poems*, 525.

55. Lydia H. Liu, *The Clash of Empire: The Invention of China in Modern World Making* (Cambridge, MA: Harvard University Press, 2004), 234.

56. About the province of Sukchur, which he would later confuse with the city of Suju, Polo says, "Over all the mountains of this province rhubarb is found in great abundance, and thither merchants come to buy it, and carry it thence all over the world" (*Polo*, vol. 1, 217).

57. Liu, *Clash of Empires*, 234.

58. Joseph W. Prueher, "The Ambassador's Letter," www.pbs.org/newshour/bb/asia/china/plane/letter_4-11.html.

59. See also Huang, *Transpacific Imaginations*, 157.

Chapter Three

1. Zhaoming Qian, ed., *Ezra Pound and China* (Ann Arbor: University of Michigan Press, 2003), 49.

2. Fenollosa and Pound, *Chinese Written Character*, 41.

3. Yang Lian and John Cayley, "hallucination and Coherence," *Positions* 10.3 (2002): 773.

4. Marjorie Perloff, *Unoriginal Genius: Poetry by Other Means in the New Century* (Chicago: University of Chicago Press, 2010), 16.

5. De Campos, *Novas*, 310.

6. Emily Apter, *Against World Literature: On the Politics of Untranslatability* (New York: Verso, 2013); David Damrosch, *What Is World Literature?* (Princeton, NJ: Princeton University Press, 2003); Yunte Huang, "Was Ezra Pound a New Historicist?: Poetry and Poetics in the Age of Globalization," *Foreign Literature Studies* 28.6 (2006): 28–44.

7. See also Yunte Huang, "Translating Pound Translating Translating," *River City* 17.2 (1997): 118–22.

8. Hugh Kenner, *The Pound Era* (Berkeley: University of California Press, 1971), 474.

9. Ibid.

10. Pound, *The Cantos*, 457.

11. James Legge, *The Four Books* (Shanghai: Commercial Press, 1923), 138.

12. Huang, "Translating Pound," 120.

13. Susan Howe, *The Midnight* (New York: New Directions, 2003), 58.

14. Angela Palandri, "Homage to a Confucian Poet," *Paideuma* 3.3 (1974): 305.

15. Zhaoming Qian, ed., *Ezra Pound's Chinese Friends: Stories in Letters* (New York: Oxford University Press, 2008), 52.

16. Ibid., 58.

17. Ibid.

18. Quoted in de Campos, *Novas*, 295.

19. Walter Benjamin, "The Task of the Translator," in *Selected Writings*, vol. 1, ed. Marcus Bullock and Michael W. Jennings (Cambridge, MA: Harvard University Press, 1996), 70.

20. Warren Weaver, "Translation," in *Machine Translation of Languages*, ed. William N. Lock and Andrew Donald Booth (Cambridge, MA: Technology Press of the Massachusetts Institute of Technology, 1955), 22.

21. Erwin Reifler, "MT," *Studies in Mechanical Translation* 1 (January 1950); and "General Mechanical Translation and Universal Grammar" (Paper presented at the conference on Mechanical Translation, June 1952, Massachusetts Institute of Technology), both available at www.mt-archive.info; Tsu, *Sound and Script in Chinese Diaspora*, 76.

22. Margaret Magnus, *Gods of the Word: Archetypes in the Consonants* (Kirksville, MS: Thomas Jefferson University Press, 1999), 3–13.

23. Roman Jakobson, *Language in Literature*, ed. Krystyna Pomorska and Stephen Rudy (Cambridge, MA: Harvard University Press, 1987), 423.

24. Walter Benjamin, "The Doctrine of the Similar," in *Selected Writings*, vol. 2, 697.

25. Qian, *Ezra Pound's Chinese Friends*, 207. The following quotations from Qian are cited by page number in the text.

26. De Campos, *Novas*, 297–301. For a very insightful study of Pound's influence on Haroldo de Campos and his fellow Brazilian poets in the 1950s on, see Marjorie Perloff, "'Raising the Referential Temperature': Poundian Reverberations in Brazilian Concrete Poetry." *Paideuma* 42 (2015): 5-38.

27. Jean-Jacques Lecercle, *The Violence of Language* (London: Routledge, 1990), 61.

28. Ibid., 6.

29. Jean Starobinski, *Words upon Words: The Anagrams of Ferdinand de Saussure*, trans. Olivia Emmet (New Haven, CT: Yale University Press, 1979), 9.

30. Lecercle, *The Violence of Language*, 60.

31. Jerome Kavka, "The Dreams of Ezra Pound," *Paideuma* 39 (2013): 156.

32. Qian, *Ezra Pound's Chinese Friends*, 75.

33. Palandri, "Homage to a Confucian Poet," 303.

34. Qian, *Ezra Pound's Chinese Friends*, 75–76.

35. Ibid., 93.

36. Ludwig Wittgenstein, *Philosophical Investigations*, trans. G. E. M. Anscombe (New York: Blackwell, 2001), 117.

37. Lecercle, *The Violence of Language*, 25.

38. Pound, *ABC of Reading*, 28.

39. Pound, *The Cantos*, 449.

40. Benjamin, "Task of the Translator," 262.

41. Pound, *ABC of Reading*, 34.

42. Pound, "Debabelization and Ogden," 410.

43. Ezra Pound, *Guide to Kulchur* (New York: New Directions, 1970), 323.

Chapter Four

1. Charles Bernstein, "Poetry Bailout Will Restore Confidence of Readers," *Harper's Magazine* (October 2008).

2. In the next sections of the chapter, I quote one of the thirteen stanzas/panels of "Thirteen Ways of Looking at a Blackbird" as both an epigraph and a lead text for interpretation. Wallace Stevens, *Collected Poetry and Prose*, ed. Frank Kermode and Joan Richardson (New York: Library Classics of the United States, 1997), 74–76; hereafter cited in the text as *CPP*.

3. Helen Vendler, *On Extended Wings: Wallace Stevens' Longer Poems* (Cambridge, MA: Harvard University Press, 1969), 75.

4. Susan Howe, *The Quarry* (New York: New Directions, 2015), 3; Marjorie Perloff, *Infrathin: An Experiment in Micropoetics* (Chicago: University of Chicago Press, 2021), 125.

5. Kenneth Lincoln, *Sing with the Heart of a Bear: Fusions of Native and American Poetry, 1890–1999* (Berkeley: University of California Press, 2000), 21.

6. Ian Hacking, *The Taming of Chance* (Cambridge: Cambridge University Press, 1990), 1, 11–15.

7. Ibid., 6.

8. Jason Puskar, "Insurance," in *Wallace Stevens in Context*, ed. Glen G. MacLeod (Cambridge: Cambridge University Press, 2017), 306.

9. Michael Szalay, *New Deal Modernism: American Literature and the Invention of the Welfare State* (Durham, NC: Duke University Press, 2000), 156–57.

10. It might be worth noting that like Wallace Stevens, the famous American composer Charles Ives worked all his life in the insurance industry. Ives even founded his own insurance company. Ives was credited with introducing the now very popular asset management product called estate planning.

11. Peter Brazeau, *Parts of a World: Wallace Stevens Remembered: An Oral Biography* (New York: Random House, 1985), 172, 38.

12. Lewis Nichols, "Talk with Mr. Stevens," *New York Times Book Review*, October 3, 1954, 3.

13. Zhaoming Qian, *The Modernist Response to Chinese Art: Pound, Moore, Stevens* (Charlottesville: University of Virginia Press, 2003), 90.

14. Robert Frost, "The Figure a Poem Makes," in *The Norton Anthology of American Literature*, vol. D, ed. Robert Levine (New York: Norton, 2016), 239.

15. Ibid., 230.

16. Stein, *Tender Buttons*, 1.

17. Levine, *The Norton Anthology*, 238.

18. Jakobson, *Language in Literature*, 256.

19. Levine, *The Norton Anthology*, 238.

20. Edgar Allan Poe, *Selected Writings of Edgar Allan Poe*, ed. David Galloway (New York: Penguin Books, 1967), 78.

21. Ibid., 482.

22. Aristotle, *Aristotle's Poetics: A Translation and Commentary for Students of Literature*, trans. Leon Golden (Englewood Cliffs, NJ: Prentice-Hall, 1968), 16–17.

23. Poe, *Selected Writings*, 490.

24. Marjorie Perloff, "Beyond 'Adagia': Eccentric Design in Stevens's Poetry," *Wallace Stevens Journal* 35.1 (2011): 24.

25. Hacking, *The Taming of Chance*, 36.

26. Helen Vendler, *The Music of What Happens: Poems, Poets, Critics* (Cambridge, MA: Harvard University Press, 1988), 75; Joseph Harrington, "Wallace Stevens and the Poetics of National Insurance," *American Literature* 67.1 (March 1995): 107; Mark Halliday, *Stevens and the Interpersonal* (Princeton, NJ: Princeton University Press, 1991), 94; Edward Ragg, *Wallace Stevens and the Aesthetics of Abstraction* (Cambridge: Cambridge University Press, 2010), 8.

27. Szalay, *New Deal Modernism*, 127.

28. Hacking, *The Taming of Chance*, 38.

29. François Ewald, "Insurance and Risk," in *The Foucault Effect: Studies in Governmentality*, ed. Colin Gordon et al. (London: Wheatsheaf, 1991), 202–3.

30. Szalay, *New Deal Modernism*, 127.

31. Randall Jarrell, "Very Graceful Are the Uses of Culture," *Harper's Maagazine* 209 (1954): 100.

32. Quoted in Richard Alan Schwartz, "A Textual History of Wallace Stevens' 'Three Travelers Watch a Sunrise,'" *Studies in Bibliography* 39 (1986): 271.

33. William Bevis, *Mind of Winter: Wallace Stevens, Meditation, and Nature* (Pittsburgh, PA: University of Pittsburgh Press, 1988), 210–11.

34. Schwartz, "A Textual History," 273.

35. Ibid., 271–72.

36. Puskar, "Insurance," 311.

37. Jason Puskar, *Accident Society: Fiction, Collectivity, and the Production of Chance* (Stanford, CA: Stanford University Press, 2012), 20.

38. www.stakeholdermap.com/risk/risk-definition.html.

39. Ulrich Beck, *Risk Society: Towards a New Modernity*, trans. Marl Ritter (London: Sage, 1992), 21, 13, 22.

40. Harrington, "Wallace Stevens and the Poetics of National Insurance, 99.

41. Puskar, "Insurance," 307.

42. Deborah Lupton, *Risk* (New York: Routledge, 2013), 55–57.

43. Ralph Waldo Emerson, *Essays: First and Second Series* (New York: Library of America, 1990), 173.

44. Simon Critchley, *Things Merely Are: Philosophy in the Poetry of Wallace Stevens* (New York: Routledge, 2005), 6; emphasis original.

45. Qian, *Modernist Response*, 93.

46. Nassim Taleb, *The Black Swan: The Impact of the Highly Improbable* (New York: Random House, 2007), xvii–xviii. As I write these words, in the depth of winter in 2020, the novel coronavirus, dubbed COVID-19, is raging in China, causing a global health emergency. Having recently traveled to the Mainland, I am now in the midst of a self-imposed fourteen-day quarantine at home in Hong Kong, and I just saw a Moody's analyst commenting on the Bloomberg news channel that the ongoing epidemic is a "black swan."

47. Klein and Friedman, quoted in Christopher Nealon, *The Matter of Capital: Poetry and Crisis in the American Century* (Cambridge, MA: Harvard University Press, 2011), 140–46.

48. Nicholas Rescher, *Risk: A Philosophical Introduction to the Theory of Risk Evaluation and Management* (Washington, DC: University Press of America, 1983), 7.

49. Richard Kostelanetz, ed., *John Cage: An Anthology* (New York: Da Capo Press, 1991), 117–18.

50. Carl G. Jung, *Synchronicity: An Acausal Connecting Principle*, in *Collected Works of C. G. Jung*, vol. 8 (Princeton, NJ: Princeton University Press, 1960), 19; Carl G. Jung, foreword to *The I Ching; or, Book of Changes*, trans. Richard Wilhelm, rendered in English by Cary F. Baynes (Princeton, NJ: Princeton University Press, 1967), xxvi.

51. Jung, *Synchronicity*, 22.

52. Jung, "Foreword," xxiv.

53. Ibid., xxiii, xxiv–xxv.

54. In 1950, John Cage was presented a copy of the English translation of the *I Ching*, which contains a foreword by Carl Jung. It became the source of Jung's concept "synchronicity" for Cage, who later would recommend the book and the essay to the poet Joan Retallack (see John Cage, *Musicage: Cage Muses on Words Art Music*, ed. Joan Retallack [Hanover, NH: Wesleyan University Press, 1996], xviii).

55. John Cage, *Silence* (Hanover, NH: Wesleyan University Press, 1961), 15, 8.

56. Emerson, *Essays*, 227.

57. Fenollosa and Pound, *Chinese Written Character*, 46.

58. John Cage, *X: Writings '79–'82* (Hanover, NH: Wesleyan University Press, 1983), 159.

59. Benjamin Piekut, "Chance and Certainty: John Cage's Poetics of Nature," *Cultural Critique* 84 (2013): 141–42.

60. John Cage, *Roaratorio: An Irish Circus on Finnegans Wake*, Sound and Text, ed. Klaus Schoening (Koeningstein: Atheneum Verlag, 1982), 173.

61. Marjorie Perloff, *Radical Artifice: Writing Poetry in the Age of Media* (Chicago: University of Chicago Press, 1991), 139–40.

62. Bruno Latour, *We Have Never Been Modern*, trans. Catherine Porter (Cambridge, MA: Harvard University Press, 1993), 4–5.

63. Graham Harman, *Prince of Networks: Bruno Latour and Metaphysics* (Melbourne: Re Press, 2009), 58.

64. John Cage, *M: Writings '67–'72* (Hanover, NH: Wesleyan University Press, 1973), 212.

65. Peter Jaeger, *John Cage and Buddhist Ecopoetics* (New York: Bloomsbury, 2013), 29–30.

66. Cage, *Roaratorio*, 85. See also Perloff, *Radical Artifice*, 155.

67. Cage, *X*, 109.

68. Perloff, *Radical Artifice*, 150.

69. Cage, *X*, iv.

Chapter Five

1. Ashbery, *Chinese Whispers*, 31.

2. Weaver, "Translation," 22.

3. Another notable instance of the entanglement of Orientalism and technology may be found in John Searle's trope of the "Chinese room." Searle used the example of an imaginary "Chinese room" to challenge the notion that machines can think. Suppose, Searle said, that a person who knows not a word of Chinese is stuck inside a room. Texts written in Chinese are slid through a slot in the door, and the room is equipped with baskets of Chinese characters and a rulebook correlating the symbols written on the texts with other symbols in the basket. Using the rulebook, he assembles strings of characters and pushes them out the door. Although his Chinese interlocutors outside the room consider these strings clever responses to their inquiries, the prisoner actually has no idea of the meaning of the texts he has produced. The scenario proves, Searle argued, that machines cannot think, just as the prisoner does not know the meaning of the Chinese texts. See John Searle, "Minds, Brains, and Programs," *Behavioral and Brain Sciences* 3.3 (1980): 417–57.

4. Claude Shannon first published the article in 1947, and in 1949, with the help of Warren Weaver, it was republished as a book. Unless otherwise noted, I quote from the book version of the text, Claude E. Shannon and Warren Weaver, *The Mathematical Theory of Communication* (Chicago: University of Illinois Press, 1998).

5. Ibid, 1; emphasis original.

6. Norbert Wiener, *Cybernetics or Control and Communication in the Animal and the Machine* (Cambridge, MA: MIT Press, 1961), 41.

7. N. Katherine Hayles, *How We Became Posthuman: Virtual Bodies in Cybernetics, Literature, and Informatics* (Chicago: University of Chicago Press, 1999), 50.

8. Gregory Bateson, *Mind and Nature: A Necessary Unity* (New York: E. P. Dutton, 1979), 104; Daniel Belgrad, "Democracy, Decentralization, and Feedback," in *American Literature and Culture in an Age of Cold War*, ed. Steven Belletto and Daniel Grausam (Iowa City: University of Iowa Press, 2012), 59. See also Jean-Pierre Dupuy, *On the Or-*

igins of Cognitive Science: The Mechanization of the Mind, trans. M. B. DeBevoise (Cambridge, MA: MIT Press, 2009).

9. Hayles, *How We Became Posthuman*, 63, 53.

10. Shannon and Weaver, *Mathematical Theory of Communication*, 7–8.

11. Floridi, *Information*, 42–43.

12. Shannon and Weaver, *Mathematical Theory of Communication*, 13.

13. Floridi, *Information*, 43.

14. Shannon and Weaver, *Mathematical Theory of Communication*, 56.

15. Gilles Deleuze, *The Logic of Sense*, trans. Mark Lester (New York: Columbia University Press, 1990), 47.

16. Jean-François Lyotard, *Driftworks*, ed. Roger McKeon (New York: Semiotext(e), 1984), quoted in *Imagining Language: An Anthology*, ed. Jed Rasula and Steve McCaffery (Cambridge, MA: MIT Press, 1998), 536.

17. Tsu, *Sound and Script in Chinese Diaspora*, 76–77.

18. Ogden and Richards, *The Meaning of Meaning*, 9–10.

19. Ibid., 205–6.

20. Floridi, *Information*, 44.

21. Robert von Hallberg, *American Poetry and Culture, 1945–1980* (Cambridge, MA: Harvard University Press, 1985), 38.

22. Dupuy, *On the Origins of Cognitive Science*, x.

23. Hayles, *How We Became Posthuman*, 57.

24. Fenollosa and Pound, *Chinese Written Character*, 44–60.

25. Sergei Eisenstein, "The Cinematographic Principle and the Ideogram," in *Film Form: Essays in Film Theory*, trans. Jay Leyda (New York: Harcourt, 1949), 90–103.

26. Fenollosa and Pound, *Chinese Written Character*, 45.

27. Ibid., 60; de Campos, *Novas*, 310.

28. Ferdinand de Saussure, *Course in General Linguistics*, trans. Wade Baskin, ed. Perry Meisel and Haun Saussy (New York: Columbia University Press, 2011), 67–70.

29. Starobinski, *Words upon Words*, 3–9; Steve McCaffery, *North of Intention: Critical Writings, 1973–1986* (New York: Roof Books, 1986), 208–9. See also John E. Joseph, *Saussure* (New York: Oxford University Press, 2012), 483–89, 555–58.

30. In the spirit of this book, which deals with Chinese whispers, gossip, hearsay, and unreliability versus rationalist verifiability and accurate information, the poet of "For MIA" shall remain anonymous.

31. Quoted in de Campos, *Novas*, 279.

32. Starobinski, *Words upon Words*, 100.

33. McCaffery, *North of Intention*, 204–6.

34. Lecercle, *The Violence of Language*, 6.

35. Starobinski, *Words upon Words*, 150.

36. Walter Benjamin, *The Origin of German Tragic Drama*, trans. John Osborne (New York: Verso, 2009), 207.

37. José Ortega y Gasset, *Man and People* (New York: Norton, 1963), 246.

38. Martin Heidegger, *Parmenides* (Bloomington: Indiana University Press, 1992), 84–85.

39. Friedrich A. Kittler, *Gramophone, Film, Typewriter*, trans. Geoffrey Winthrop-Young and Michael Wutz (Stanford, CA: Stanford University Press, 1999), 7–18.

40. Thomas S. Mullaney, *The Chinese Typewriter: A History* (Cambridge, MA: MIT Press, 2017), 64.

41. Ibid., 65, 190–91.

42. For recent studies of Lin Yutang's Chinese typewriter, see So, *Transpacific Community*; R. John Williams, *The Buddha in the Machine: Art, Technology, and the Meeting of East and West* (New Haven, CT: Yale University Press, 2014); Tsu, *Sound and Script in Chinese Diaspora*; Mullaney, *The Chinese Typewriter*.

43. Lin Yutang, "MingKwai Typewriter" (Press Release, August 21, 1947), Archives of the John Day Company, Princeton University, box 144, folder 6, no. C0123.

44. Lin Yutang, "A Chinese Typewriter: Part of a Patent Filed by Lin Yutang," *The Indexer* 27.3 (2009): 108.

45. Ibid.

46. Lin Yutang, "Notes on the Chinese Index System" 汉字索引制说明, in Lin Yutang, *Yuyanxue Luncong* 语言学论丛 (Shenyang: Northeastern Normal University Press, 1994), 254–56. See also Peng Chunling, "Lin Yutang and the National Language Movement in Modern China," in *The Cross-Cultural Legacy of Lin Yutang: Critical Perspectives*, ed. Qian Suoqiao (Berkeley: Institute of East Asian Studies, 2015), 71–74.

47. Lin, *Yuyanxue Luncong*, 257–60.

48. Lin Yutang, *My Country and My People* (New York: John Day Company, 1935), 17–18.

49. Lin, "A Chinese Typewriter," 108–9.

50. Xu Shen, *Shuo Wen Jie Zi* (Beijing: Zhonghua Press, 1963), 12.

51. Zhu Guangtian, ed., *History of Chinese Calligraphy*, vol. 4 (Nanjing: Jiangsu Educational Press, 2002), 120.

52. Yang Xiong, *Fa Yan* (Chengdu: Sichuan University Press, 2001), 254.

53. Liu Heng, ed. *History of Chinese Calligraphy*, vol. 7 (Nanjing: Jiangsu Educational Press, 1999), 56.

54. Lin, *My Country and My People*, 291–92.

55. Lin, "A Chinese Typewriter," 109.

56. Mullaney, *The Chinese Typewriter*, 245.

57. Lin Taiyi, *A Biography of Lin Yutang* (Taipei: Lianjing Press, 1989), 235.

58. Kittler, *Gramophone, Film, Typewriter*, 251.

59. Tsu, *Sound and Script in Chinese Diaspora*, 69.

60. Lydia H. Liu, "Postphonetic Writing and New Media," *Writing Technologies* 1.1 (2014): 2.

61. Mullaney, *The Chinese Typewriter*, 316.

62. Haun Saussy, *Great Walls of Discourse and Other Adventures in Cultural China* (Cambridge, MA: Harvard University Press, 2001), 75–90, 32.

63. Mullaney, *The Chinese Typewriter*, 247.

64. Charles Olson, *Collected Prose*, ed. Donald Allen and Benjamin Friedlander (Berkeley: University of California Press, 1997), 239, 245–46. For a more detailed study of how American avant-garde poets reacted to the ascendant information technology in the postwar era, see Todd F. Tietchen, *Technomodern Poetics: The American Literary Avant-Garde at the Start of the Information Age* (Iowa City: University of Iowa Press, 2018). Tietchen suggests, for instance, "The *On the Road* scroll might be read as a particularly verbose, meandering, and nonutilitarian reaction to [Claude] Shannon's arguments on behalf of eliminating ambiguity and uncertainty—or what he had deemed

'noise'—from technical communication, thereby ensuring the more efficient circulation of information through teletype networks and other media formats" (10).

65. Tietchen, *Technomodern Poetics*, 5, 10.

66. Olson, *Collected Prose*, 239, 156.

67. Charles Olson, *Charles Olson and Ezra Pound: An Encounter at St. Elizabeths*, ed. Catherine Seelye (New York: Grossman Publishers, 1975), 69, 128.

68. Olson, *Collected Prose*, 19, 244.

69. Williams, *The Buddha in the Machine*, 135–36.

70. See T. J. Jackson Lears, *No Place of Grace: Antimodernism and the Transformation of American Culture, 1880–1920* (Chicago: University of Chicago Press, 1981).

71. Burton Watson, trans. *The Complete Works of Zhuangzi* (New York: Columbia University Press, 2013), 106–7.

72. Eric S. Nelson, "Technology and the Way: Buber, Heidegger, and Lao-Zhuang 'Daoism,'" *Journal of Chinese Philosophy* 41.3-4 (2014): 307–27; David Chai, "Thinking through Words: The Existential Hermeneutics of Zhuangzi and Heidegger," in *Relational Hermeneutics: Essays in Comparative Philosophy*, ed. Paul Fairfield and Saulius Geniusas (London: Bloomsbury Academic, 2018), 205–19.

73. Martin Heidegger, *The Question Concerning Technology, and Other Essays*, trans. William Lovitt (New York: Harper & Row, 1977), 34.

Coda

1. *Chinese Nationalist Daily*, May 26, 1947.

2. For information on the development of the Chinese typewriter in the People's Republic of China, see Mullaney, *The Chinese Typewriter*, 283–313. For information on how Lin Yutang's invention inspired other research projects in the field of Chinese-language computation and machine translation, see Tsu, *Sound and Script in Chinese Diaspora*, 72–79.

3. Chao Yuen Ren, *Aspects of Chinese Sociolinguistics: Essays by Yuen Ren Chao*, selected and introduced by Anwar Dil (Stanford, CA: Stanford University Press, 1976), 13.

4. Chen-Pang Yeang, "From Modernizing the Chinese Language to Information Science: Chao Yuen Ren's Route to Cybernetics," *Isis* 108.3 (2017): 559–66.

5. See Chao Yuen Ren, "Dimensions of Fidelity in Translation with Special Reference to Chinese," *Harvard Journal of Asiatic Studies* 29 (1969): 109–30.

6. Chao Yuen Ren, "Meaning in Language and How It Is Acquired," in *Cybernetics, Circular Causal and Feedback Mechanisms in Biological and Social Systems: Transactions of the Tenth Conference*, ed. Heinz von Foerster (New York: Josiah Macy Jr. Foundation, 1953), 49–67; Chao Yuen Ren, "The Efficiency of the Chinese Language as a Symbolic System," in *Reflections on Our Age: Lectures Delivered at the Opening Session of UNESCO at the Sorbonne University Paris* (New York: Columbia University Press, 1949), 317–26. See also Yeang, *From Modernizing the Chinese Language*, 562, 570.

7. Chao, "Meaning in Language," 65–66.

8. Liu, *The Freudian Robot*, 111.

9. Yeang, *From Modernizing the Chinese Language*, 572.

10. McCaffery, *North of Intention*, 214–15.

11. Steeped in the aesthetics of classical literature, Chao must be familiar with the long tradition of wordplay and other poetic trickery in China. For instance, a trick dis-

tich 对联 is found at a temple in my hometown, Wenzhou, which runs: 雲朝朝朝朝朝朝朝朝散/潮長長長長長長長長消. Unlike Chao's play on homophony, or words that look different but sound almost the same, this distich, attributed to the local poet Wang Shipeng (1112–71) of the Song dynasty, plays on homograph, words that look the same but sound different. Whereas in Chao's case acoustic gibberish subverts visual coherence, in this couplet sound provides a subterranean coherence of meaning beneath the visual portmanteau, when it is vocalized as 雲朝潮朝朝潮朝潮朝散/潮常漲常常漲常漲常消.

12. Olson, *Collected Prose*, 243.

13. Haun Saussy, *The Ethnography of Rhythm: Orality and Its Technologies* (New York: Fordham University Press, 2016), 157–58.

14. I once served on a grant committee that provided funding for research projects related to the Pacific Rim. Among the many applications I had to review there was one that really caught my eye. It proposes to redesign hearing aids for Chinese speakers. As the PI points out, the cochlear implants designed in the United States are not usable in China because they are "tone-deaf."

Bibliography

Abrams, M. H. *The Mirror and the Lamp: Romantic Theory and the Critical Tradition*. London: Oxford University Press, 1953.

Anderson, Vaugh. "'Revision of the Golden Rule': John Cage, Latin America, and the Poetics of Non-Intervention." *Journal of Modern Literature* 41.1 (2017): 58–80.

Apter, Emily. *Against World Literature: On the Politics of Translatability*. New York: Verso, 2013.

Aristotle. *Aristotle's Poetics: A Translation and Commentary for Students of Literature*. Trans. Leon Golden. Englewood Cliffs, NJ: Prentice-Hall, 1968.

Ashbery, John. *Chinese Whispers*. New York: Farrar, Straus and Giroux, 2002.

Attali, Jacques. *Noise: The Political Economy of Music*. Trans. Brian Massumi. Minneapolis: University of Minnesota Press, 1995.

Barnhisel, Greg. *Cold War Modernists: Art, Literature, and American Cultural Diplomacy*. New York: Columbia University Press, 2015.

Bateson, Gregory. *Mind and Nature: A Necessary Unity*. New York: E. P. Dutton, 1979.

Beck, Ulrich. *Risk Society: Towards a New Modernity*. Trans. Marl Ritter. London: Sage, 1992.

Bei Dao. *The August Sleepwalker*. Trans. Bonnie S. McDougall. New York: New Directions, 1990.

Belgrad, Daniel. "Democracy, Decentralization, and Feedback." In *American Literature and Culture in an Age of Cold War*, ed. Steven Belletto and Daniel Grausam, 59–83. Iowa City: University of Iowa Press, 2012.

Benjamin, Walter. "The Doctrine of the Similar." In *Selected Writings*, vol. 2, 1927–1934, trans. Rodney Livingstone et al., ed. Michael W. Jennings et al., 694–98. Cambridge, MA: Harvard University Press, 1999.

———. *The Origin of German Tragic Drama*. Trans. John Osborne. New York: Verso, 2009.

———. "Reflections on Radio." In *Selected Writings*, vol. 2, 1927–1934, trans. Rodney Livingstone et al., ed. Michael W. Jennings et al., 543–44. Cambridge, MA: Harvard University Press, 1999.

———. "The Task of the Translator." In *Selected Writings*, vol. 1, ed. Marcus Bullock and Michael W. Jennings, 253–63. Cambridge, MA: Harvard University Press, 1996.

Bernstein, Charles. *My Way: Speeches and Poems*. Chicago: University of Chicago Press, 1999.

———. "Poetry Bailout Will Restore Confidence of Readers." *Harper's Magazine* (October 2008). https://harpers.org/2008/09/poetry-bailout-will-restore-confidence-of-readers/.

Bevis, William. *Mind of Winter: Wallace Stevens, Meditation, and Nature*. Pittsburgh, PA: University of Pittsburgh Press, 1988.

Bhabha, Homi. "Unsatisfied Notes on Vernacular Cosmopolitanism." In *Text and Narration: Cross-Disciplinary Essays on Cultural and National Identities*, ed. L. Garcia-Moreno and P. C. Pfeiffer, 191–207. Columbia, SC: Camden House, 1996.

Bhabha, Homi, and John Comaroff. "Speaking of Postcoloniality, in the Continuous Present: A Conversation." In *Relocating Postcolonialism*, ed. D. T. Goldberg and A. Quayson, 15–46. Oxford: Blackwell, 2002.

Bishop, John. Introduction to James Joyce, *Finnegans Wake*. New York: Penguin Books, 1999.

Brazeau, Peter. *Parts of a World: Wallace Stevens Remembered: An Oral Biography*. New York: Random House, 1985.

Cage, John. *Musicage: Cage Muses on Words Art Music*. Ed. Joan Retellack. Hanover, NH: Wesleyan University Press, 1996.

———. *M: Writings '67–'72*. Hanover, NH: Wesleyan University Press, 1973.

———. *Roaratorio: An Irish Circus on Finnegans Wake*. Sound and Text. Ed. Klaus Schoening. Koeningstein: Atheneum Verlag, 1982.

———. *Silence*. Hanover, NH: Wesleyan University Press, 1961.

———. *X: Writings '79–'82*. Hanover, NH: Wesleyan University Press, 1983.

Calvino, Italo. *Invisible Cities*. Trans. William Weaver. New York: Harcourt Brace & Company, 1974.

Chai, David. "Thinking through Words: The Existential Hermeneutics of Zhuangzi and Heidegger." In *Relational Hermeneutics: Essays in Comparative Philosophy*, ed. Paul Fairfield and Saulius Geniusas, 205–19. London: Bloomsbury Academic, 2018.

Chao, Yuen Ren. *Aspects of Chinese Sociolinguistics: Essays by Yuen Ren Chao*. Selected and introd. Anwar Dil. Stanford, CA: Stanford University Press, 1976.

———. "Dimensions of Fidelity in Translation with Special Reference to Chinese." *Harvard Journal of Asiatic Studies* 29 (1969): 109–30.

———. "The Efficiency of the Chinese Language as a Symbolic System." In *Reflections on Our Age: Lectures Delivered at the Opening Session of UNESCO at the Sorbonne University Paris*, 317–26. New York: Columbia University Press, 1949.

———. "Meaning in Language and How It Is Acquired." In *Cybernetics, Circular Causal and Feedback Mechanisms in Biological and Social Systems: Transactions of the Tenth Conference*, ed. Heinz von Foerster, 49–67. New York: Josiah Macy Jr. Foundation, 1953.

———. "What Is Correct Chinese?" *Journal of the American Oriental Society* 81.3 (1961): 171–77.

Chu, T. F. "This Easy Chinese Language." *China Critic* 6.35 (1933): 855–56.

Cleaves, Francis Woodman. "A Chinese Source Bearing on Marco Polo's Departure from China and a Persian Source of His Arrival in Persia." *Harvard Journal of Asiatic Studies* 36 (1976): 181–203.

Clunas, Craig. "The Explorer's Tracks." *Times Literary Supplement*, April 14, 1982.

Coleridge, Samuel Taylor. *Biographia Literaria; or, Biographical Sketches of My Literary Life and Opinions*. Ed. George Watson. New York: Everyman's Library, 1956.

——. *The Complete Poems*. Ed. William Keach. New York: Penguin, 1997.

Critchley, Simon. *Things Merely Are: Philosophy in the Poetry of Wallace Stevens*. New York: Routledge, 2005.

Damrosch, David. *What Is World Literature?* Princeton, NJ: Princeton University Press, 2003.

De Campos, Haroldo. *Novas: Selected Writings*. Ed. Antonio Sergio Bessa and Odile Cisneros. Evanston, IL: Northwestern University Press, 2007.

Deleuze, Gilles. *The Logic of Sense*. Trans. Mark Lester. New York: Columbia University Press, 1990.

Dikötter, Frank. *Mao's Great Famine: The History of China's Most Devastating Catastrophe, 1958–1962*. New York: Walker & Co., 2010.

Duchamp, Marcel. *The Writings of Marcel Duchamp*. Ed. Michel Sanouillet and Elmer Peterson. New York: Da Capo Press, 1973.

Dupuy, Jean-Pierre. *On the Origins of Cognitive Science: The Mechanization of the Mind*. Trans. M. B.

DeBevoise. Cambridge, MA: MIT Press, 2009.

Eisenstein, Sergei. "The Cinematographic Principle and the Ideogram." In *Film Form: Essays in Film Theory*, trans. Jay Leyda, 28–43. New York: Harcourt, 1949.

Emerson, Ralph Waldo. *Essays: First and Second Series*. New York: Library of America, 1990.

Eshleman, Clayton. *Juniper Fuse: Upper Paleolithic Imagination and the Construction of the Underworld*. Hanover, NH: Wesleyan University Press, 2003.

Ewald, François. "Insurance and Risk." In *The Foucault Effect: Studies in Governmentality*, ed. Colin Gordon et al., 197–210. London: Wheatsheaf, 1991.

Fenollosa, Ernest, and Ezra Pound. *The Chinese Written Character as a Medium for Poetry*. Ed. Haun Saussy, Jonathan Stalling, and Lucas Klein. New York: Fordham University Press, 2008.

Fisher, Philip. *Hard Facts: Setting and Form in the American Novel*. New York: Oxford University Press, 1986.

Floridi, Luciano. *Information: A Very Short Introduction*. New York: Oxford University Press, 2010.

Foucault, Michel. *Discipline and Punish: The Birth of the Prison*. Trans. Alan Sheridan. New York: Vintage Books, 1979.

——. *The Order of Things: An Archaeology of the Human Sciences*. London: Tavistock Publications, 1970.

Frost, Robert. "The Figure a Poem Makes" and "The Road Not Taken." In *The Norton Anthology of American Literature*, vol. D, ed. Robert Levine, 230, 238–39. New York: Norton, 2016.

Garcia, Edgar. *Signs of the Americas: A Poetics of Pictography, Hieroglyphs, and Khipu*. Chicago: University of Chicago Press, 2020.

Gilroy, Paul. *After Empire: Melancholia or Convivial Culture?* New York: Routledge, 2006.

Goldfinger, Charles. "Intangible Economy and Electronic Money." In *The Future of Money*, 87–122. Paris: Organisation for Economic Co-operation and Development (OECD), 2002.

Gordon, W. Terrence. "Undoing Babel: C. K. Ogden's Basic English." *Etc: A Review of General Semantics* 45.4 (1988): 337–40.

Graeber, David. *The Utopia of Rules: On Technology, Stupidity, and the Secret Joys of Bureaucracy*. New York: Melville House, 2016.

Grimm, Jacob, and Wilhelm. "Cinderella." www.pitt.edu/~dash/grimm021.html.

Hacking, Ian. *The Taming of Chance*. Cambridge: Cambridge University Press, 1990.

Haeger, John W. "Marco Polo in China? Problems with Internal Evidence." *Bulletin of Sung and Yuan Studies* 14 (1979): 22–30.

Hall, Stuart. "Political Belonging in a World of Multiple Identities." In *Conceiving Cosmopolitanism: Theory, Context, and Practice*, ed. S. Vertovec and R. Cohen, 25–31. Oxford: Oxford University Press, 2002.

Hallberg, Robert von. *American Poetry and Culture, 1945–1980*. Cambridge, MA: Harvard University Press, 1985.

Halliday, Mark. *Stevens and the Interpersonal*. Princeton, NJ: Princeton University Press, 1991.

Hardt, Michael, and Antonio Negri. *Empire*. Cambridge, MA: Harvard University Press, 2000.

Harman, Graham. *Prince of Networks: Bruno Latour and Metaphysics*. Melbourne: Re Press, 2009.

Harrington, Joseph. "Wallace Stevens and the Poetics of National Insurance." *American Literature* 67.1 (March 1995): 95–114.

Havelock, Eric A. *The Muse Learns to Write: Reflections on Orality and Literacy from Antiquity to the Present*. New Haven, CT: Yale University Press, 1986.

Hayles, N. Katherine. *How We Became Posthuman: Virtual Bodies in Cybernetics, Literature, and Informatics*. Chicago: University of Chicago Press, 1999.

Hawking, Stephen W. *A Brief History of Time: From the Big Bang to Black Holes*. New York: Bantam Books, 1988.

Heidegger, Martin. *The Question Concerning Technology, and Other Essays*. Trans. William Lovitt. New York: Harper & Row, 1977.

———. *Parmenides*. Bloomington: Indiana University Press, 1992.

Hendy, David. *Noise: A Human History of Sound and Listening*. London: Profile Books, 2013.

Howe, Susan. *The Midnight*. New York: New Directions, 2003.

———. *The Quarry*. New York: New Directions, 2015.

Huang, Yunte, ed. *The Big Red Book of Modern Chinese Literature: Writings from the Mainland in the Long Twentieth Century*. New York: Norton, 2016.

———. *CRIBS*. Honolulu: Tinfish Press, 2005.

———. "Translating Pound Translating Translating." *River City* 17.2 (1997): 118–22.

———. *Transpacific Displacement: Ethnography, Translation, and Intertextual Travel in Twentieth-Century American Literature*. Berkeley: University of California Press, 2002.

———. *Transpacific Imaginations: History, Literature, and Counterpoetics*. Cambridge, MA: Harvard University Press, 2008.

——. "Was Ezra Pound a New Historicist?" *Foreign Literature Studies* 28.6 (2006): 28–44.

Jaeger, Peter. *John Cage and Buddhist Ecopoetics*. New York: Bloomsbury, 2013.

Jakobson, Roman. *Language in Literature*. Ed. Krystyna Pomorska and Stephen Rudy. Cambridge, MA: Harvard University Press, 1987.

James, Henry. *The Question of Our Speech*. Boston: Houghton Mifflin, 1905.

Jarrell, Randall. "Very Graceful Are the Uses of Culture." *Harper's Magazine* 209 (1954): 100.

Jespersen, Otto. *Progress in Language*. London: Swan Sonnenschein, 1894.

Joseph, John E. "Basic English and the Debabelization of China." In *Intercultural Encounters—Studies in English Literatures*, ed. Heinz Antor and Kevin L. Cope, 51–71. Heidelberg: Universitätsverlag C. Winter, 1999.

——. *Saussure*. New York: Oxford University Press, 2012.

Joyce, James. *Finnegans Wake*. New York: Penguin Books, 1999.

Jung, Carl G. Foreword to *The I Ching; or, Book of Changes*. Trans. Richard Wilhelm, rendered into English by Cary F. Baynes, xxi–xxxix. Princeton, NJ: Princeton University Press, 1967.

——. *Synchronicity: An Acausal Connecting Principle*. In *Collected Works of C. G. Jung*, vol. 8, 417–519. Princeton, NJ: Princeton University Press, 1960.

Kavka, Jerome. "The Dreams of Ezra Pound." *Paideuma* 39 (2012): 147–61.

Kenner, Hugh. *The Pound Era*. Berkeley: University of California Press, 1971.

Kim, Elaine H. *Asian American Literature: An Introduction to the Writings and Their Social Context*. Philadelphia, PA: Temple University Press, 1982.

Kim, Myung Mi. *Dura*. Los Angeles: Sun & Moon Press, 1998.

Kittler, Friedrich A. *Gramophone, Film, Typewriter*. Trans. Geoffrey Winthrop-Young and Michael Wutz. Stanford, CA: Stanford University Press, 1999.

Koeneke, Rodney. *Empires of the Mind: I. A. Richards and Basic English in China, 1929–1979*. Stanford, CA: Stanford University Press, 2003.

Kostelanetz, Richard, ed. *John Cage: An Anthology*. New York: Da Capo Press, 1991.

Latour, Bruno. *We Have Never Been Modern*. Trans. Catherine Porter. Cambridge, MA: Harvard University Press, 1993.

Lears, T. J. Jackson. *No Place of Grace: Antimodernism and the Transformation of American Culture, 1880–1920*. Chicago: University of Chicago Press, 1981.

Leavis, F. R. *Mass Civilization and Minority Culture*. Cambridge: Minority Press, 1930.

Lecercle, Jean-Jacques. *The Violence of Language*. New York: Routledge, 1990.

Legge, James. *The Four Books*. Shanghai: Commercial Press, 1923.

Levine, Robert. ed. *The Norton Anthology of American Literature*, vol. D. New York: Norton, 2016.

Lincoln, Kenneth. *Sing with the Heart of a Bear: Fusions of Native and American Poetry, 1890–1999*. Berkeley: University of California Press, 2000.

Link, Perry. "If Mao Had Been a Hermit." *New York Review of Books*, April 7, 2016, 1–9.

Lin, Taiyi. *A Biography of Lin Yutang*. Taipei: Lianjing Press, 1989.

Lin, Yutang. "A Chinese Typewriter: Part of a Patent Filed by Lin Yutang." *The Indexer* 27.3 (2009): 107–10.

——. *The Little Critic: Essays, Satires and Sketches on China (Second Series: 1933–1935)*. Westport, CT: Hyperion Press, 1983.

———. *My Country and My People*. New York: John Day Company, 1935.
———. *Yuyanxue Luncong* 语言学论丛. Shenyang: Northeastern Normal University Press, 1994.
Liu, Heng, ed. *History of Chinese Calligraphy*, vol. 7. Nanjing: Jiangsu Educational Press, 1999.
Liu, Lydia H. *The Clash of Empires: The Invention of China in Modern World Making*. Cambridge, MA: Harvard University Press, 2004.
———. *The Freudian Robot: Digital Media and the Future of the Unconscious*. Chicago: University of Chicago Press, 2010.
———. "Postphonetic Writing and New Media." *Writing Technologies* 1.1 (2014): 1–3.
———, ed. *Tokens of Exchange: The Problem of Translation in Global Circulations*. Durham, NC: Duke University Press, 1999.
Lupton, Deborah. *Risk*. New York: Routledge, 2013.
Lu Xun. "Reply to an Interview from My Sickbed." In *Complete Works of Lu Xun*, vol. 6, 160. Beijing: Renmin wenxue chubanshe, 1981.
Lyotard, Jean-François. *Driftworks*. Ed. Roger McKeon. New York: Semiotext(e), 1984.
Mack, Mary Peter, ed. *A Bentham Reader*. London: Pegasus, 1969.
Magnus, Margaret. *Gods of the Word: Archetypes in the Consonants*. Kirksville, MS: Thomas Jefferson University, 1999.
Manovich, Lev. *The Language of New Media*. Cambridge, MA: MIT Press, 2001.
Marazzi, Christian. *Capital and Affects: The Politics of the Language Economy*. Trans. Giuseppina Mecchia. Los Angeles: Semiotext(e), 2011.
McCaffery, Steve. *North of Intention: Critical Writings, 1973–1986*. New York: Roof Books, 1986.
McLuhan, Marshall, and Bruce R. Powers. *The Global Village: Transformations in World Life and Media in the 21st Century*. New York: Oxford University Press, 1989.
———. *The Gutenberg Galaxy: The Making of Typographic Man*. Toronto: University of Toronto Press, 1962.
Menand, Louis. *The Free World: Art and Thought in the Cold War*. New York: Farrar, Straus and Giroux, 2021.
Mignolo, Walter. "The Many Faces of Cosmo-polis: Border Thinking and Critical Cosmopolitanism." In *Cosmopolitanism*, ed. Carol Breckenridge et al., 157–88. Durham, NC: Duke University Press, 2002.
Mullaney, Thomas S. *The Chinese Typewriter: A History*. Cambridge, MA: MIT Press, 2017.
Murayama, Milton. *All I Asking for Is My Body*. Honolulu: University of Hawaii Press, 1988.
Nagele, Rainer. *Echoes of Translation*. Baltimore, MD: Johns Hopkins University Press, 1997.
Nancy, Jean-Luc. *Listening*. Trans. Charlotte Madell. New York: Fordham University Press, 2007.
Nealon, Christopher. *The Matter of Capital: Poetry and Crisis in the American Century*. Cambridge, MA: Harvard University Press, 2011.
Nelson, Cary. *Repression and Recovery: Modern American Poetry and the Politics of Cultural Memory, 1910–1945*. Madison: University of Wisconsin Press, 1989.

Nelson, Eric S. "Technology and the Way: Buber, Heidegger, and Lao-Zhuang 'Daoism.'" *Journal of Chinese Philosophy* 41.3–4 (2014): 307–27.

Nichols, Lewis. "Talk with Mr. Stevens." *New York Times Book Review*, October 3, 1954.

Nietzsche, Friedrich. *On the Genealogy of Morals*. Trans. Walter Kaufman and R. J. Hollingdale. New York: Vintage Books, 1989.

Nussbaum, Martha. *For the Love of Country? Debating the Limits of Patriotism*. Ed. Joshua Cohen. Boston: Beacon Press, 1996.

Nyers, Peter. "Abject Cosmopolitanism: The Politics of Protection in the Anti-Deportation Movement." *Third World Quarterly* 24.6 (2003): 1069–93.

Ogden, C. K. *Basic English and Grammatical Reform*. Supplement, *Basic News* (July 1937).

———. *Basic English: International Second Language*. New York: Harcourt, Brace & World, 1968.

———. *Debabelization*. London: Kegan Paul, 1931.

———. "Editorial." *Psyche* 9.1 (1928): 2–3.

———. "James Joyce's Anna Livia Plurabelle (in Basic English)." *transition* 21 (1932).

Ogden, C. K., and I. A. Richards. *The Meaning of Meaning: A Study of the Influence of Language upon Thought and the Science of Symbolism*. First published 1923. London: Routledge and Kegan Paul, 1972.

Olson, Charles. *Charles Olson and Ezra Pound: An Encounter at St. Elizabeths*. Ed. Catherine Seelye. New York: Grossman Publishers, 1975.

———. *Collected Prose*. Ed. Donald Allen and Benjamin Friedlander. Berkeley: University of California Press, 1997.

O'Neill, Eugene. *Marco Millions: A Play*. New York: Boni & Liveright, 1927.

Ortega y Gasset, José. *Man and People*. New York: Norton, 1957.

Palandri, Angela. "Homage to a Confucian Poet." *Paideuma* 3.3 (1974): 301–11.

Peng Chunling. "Lin Yutang and the National Language Movement in Modern China." In *The Cross-Cultural Legacy of Lin Yutang: Critical Perspectives*, ed. Qian Suoqiao, 67–94. Berkeley: Institute of East Asian Studies, 2015.

Perloff, Marjorie. "Beyond 'Adagia': Eccentric Design in Stevens' Poetry." *Wallace Stevens Journal* 35.1 (2011): 16–32.

———. *Infrathin: An Experiment in Micropoetics*. Chicago: University of Chicago Press, 2021.

———. *The Poetics of Indeterminacy: Rimbaud to Cage*. Princeton, NJ: Princeton University Press, 1981; reprint, Northwestern University Press, 1999.

———. *Radical Artifice: Writing Poetry in the Age of Media*. Chicago: University of Chicago Press, 1991.

———. "'Raising the Referential Temperature': Poundian Reverberation in Brazilian Concrete Poetry." *Paideuma* 42 (2015): 5–38.

———. *Unoriginal Genius: Poetry by Other Means in the New Century*. Chicago: University of Chicago Press, 2010.

Piekut, Benjamin. "Chance and Certainty: John Cage's Poetics of Nature." *Cultural Critique* 84 (2013): 134–63.

Plato. "Cratylus." In *Plato, the Collected Dialogues*. Ed. Edith Hamilton and Huntington Cairns. Princeton, NJ: Princeton University Press, 1961.

Poe, Edgar Allan. *Selected Writings of Edgar Allan Poe*. Ed. David Galloway. New York: Penguin Books, 1967.

Pollock, Sheldon. "Cosmopolitan and Vernacular in History." In *Cosmopolitanism*, ed. Carol A. Breckenridge et al., 15–53. Durham, NC: Duke University Press, 2002.

Polo, Marco. *The Travels of Marco Polo: The Complete Yule-Cordier Edition*. Vols. 1 and 2. New York: Dover, 1993.

Pound, Ezra. *ABC of Reading*. New York: New Directions, 1951.

———. *The Cantos*. New York: New Directions, 1970.

———. "Debabelization and Ogden." *New English Weekly*, February 28, 1935.

———. *Guide to Kulchur*. New York: New Directions, 1970.

———. *Literary Essays of Ezra Pound*. Ed. T. S. Eliot. London: Faber and Faber, 1954.

———. *Selected Letters: 1907–1941*. Ed. D. D. Paige. London: Faber and Faber, 1950.

Proust, Marcel. *Remembrance of Things Past*. Trans. C. K. Scott Moncrieff et al. New York: Vintage Books, 1982.

Prueher, Joseph W. "The Ambassador's Letter." www.pbs.org/newshour/bb/asia/china/plane/letter_4-11.html.

Puskar, Jason. *Accident Society: Fiction, Collectivity, and the Production of Chance*. Stanford, CA: Stanford University Press, 2012.

———. "Insurance." In *Wallace Stevens in Context*, ed. Glen G. MacLeod, 306–15. Cambridge: Cambridge University Press, 2017.

Qian, Zhaoming, ed. *Ezra Pound and China*. Ann Arbor: University of Michigan Press, 2003.

———, ed. *Ezra Pound's Chinese Friends: Stories in Letters*. New York: Oxford University Press, 2008.

———. *The Modernist Response to Chinese Art: Pound, Moore, Stevens*. Charlottesville: University of Virginia Press, 2003.

Quartermain, Peter. *Disjunctive Poetics: Gertrude Stein and Louis Zukofsky to Susan Howe*. New York: Cambridge University Press, 1992.

Ragg, Edward. *Wallace Stevens and the Aesthetics of Abstraction*. Cambridge: Cambridge University Press, 2010.

Rasula, Jed, and Steve McCaffery, eds. *Imagining Language: An Anthology*. Cambridge, MA: MIT Press, 1998.

Reifler, Erwin. "General Mechanical Translation and Universal Grammar." Paper presented at the conference on Mechanical Translation, June 1952, Massachusetts Institute of Technology. www.mt-archive.info.

———. "MT." *Studies in Mechanical Translation* 1 (January 1950). Paper presented at the conference on Mechanical Translation, June 1952, Massachusetts Institute of Technology. www.mt-archive.info.

Rescher, Nicholas. *Risk: A Philosophical Introduction to the Theory of Risk Evaluation and Management*. Washington, DC: University Press of America, 1983.

Richards, I. A. *Basic English and Its Uses*. London: Kegan Paul, 1943.

———. "Beginnings and Transitions" (interview by Reuben Brower). In *I. A. Richards: Essays in His Honor*, ed. Reuben Brower, Helen Vendler, and John Hollander, 15–30. New York: Oxford University Press, 1973.

———. *Practical Criticism: A Study of Literary Judgment*. New York: Harcourt, Brace & Company, 1929.

——. *So Much Nearer: Essays toward a World English*. New York: Harcourt, Brace & World, 1968.

Richards, I. A., and Christine Gibson, *Techniques in Language Control*. New York: Newbury House, 1974.

Roh, David S., et al., eds. *Techno-Orientalism: Imagining Asia in Speculative Fiction, History, and Media*. New Brunswick, NJ: Rutgers University Press, 2015.

Romaine, Suzanne. *Pidgin and Creole Languages*. New York: Longman, 1988.

Russo, John Paul. *I. A. Richards: His Life and Work*. Baltimore, MD: Johns Hopkins University Press, 1989.

Saunders, Frances Stonor. *The Cultural Cold War: The CIA and the World of Arts and Letters*. New York: New Press, 2013.

Saussure, Ferdinand de. *Course in General Linguistics*. Trans. Wade Baskin, ed. Perry Meisel and Haun Saussy. New York: Columbia University Press, 2011.

Saussy, Haun. *The Ethnography of Rhythm: Orality and Its Technologies*. New York: Fordham University Press, 2016.

——. *Great Walls of Discourse and Other Adventures in Cultural China*. Cambridge, MA: Harvard University Press, 2001.

Scarry, Elaine. "The Difficulty of Imagining Other People." In Martha Nussbaum, *For Love of Country? Debating the Limits of Patriotism*, ed. Joshua Cohen, 98–110. Boston: Beacon Press, 1996.

Schwartz, Richard Alan. "A Textual History of Wallace Stevens' 'Three Travelers Watch a Sunrise.'" *Studies in Bibliography* 39 (1986): 269–76.

Searle, John. "Minds, Brains, and Programs." *Behavioral and Brain Sciences* 3.3 (1980): 417–57.

Shannon, Claude E., and Warren Weaver. *The Mathematical Theory of Communication*. Chicago: University of Illinois Press, 1998.

Shell, Marc. *The Economy of Literature*. Baltimore, MD: Johns Hopkins University Press, 1978.

Smith, Vanessa. *Literary Culture and the Pacific: Nineteenth-Century Textual Encounter*. Cambridge: Cambridge University Press, 1998.

So, Richard Jean. *Transpacific Community: America, China, and the Rise and Fall of a Cultural Network*. New York: Columbia University Press, 2016.

Solomon, Elinor Harris. *Virtual Money: Understanding the Power and Risks of Money's High-Speed Journey into Electronic Space*. New York: Oxford University Press, 1997.

Sommer, Doris. *Bilingual Aesthetics: A New Sentimental Education*. Durham, NC: Duke University Press, 2004.

Sontag, Susan. *Against Interpretation and Other Essays*. New York: Farrar, Straus and Giroux, 1966.

Soros, George. *The Crisis of Global Capitalism: Open Society Endangered*. New York: Public Affairs, 1998.

Starobinski, Jean. *Words upon Words: The Anagrams of Ferdinand de Saussure*. Trans. Olivia Emmet. New Haven, CT: Yale University Press, 1979.

Stein, Gertrude. *Tender Buttons*. Los Angeles: Sun & Moon Press, 1990.

Stevens, Wallace. *Collected Poetry and Prose*. Ed. Frank Kermode and Joan Richardson. New York: Library Classics of the United States, 1997.

——. "Three Travelers Watch a Sunrise." *Poetry* 8.4 (July 1916): 163–79.

Szalay, Michael. *New Deal Modernism: American Literature and the Invention of the Welfare State*. Durham, NC: Duke University Press, 2000.

Szendy, Peter. *All Ears: The Aesthetics of Espionage*. Trans. Roland Vegso. New York: Fordham University Press, 2017.

Taleb, Nassim. *The Black Swan: The Impact of the Highly Improbable*. New York: Random House, 2007.

Tedlock, Dennis. "Towards a Poetics of Polyphony and Translatability." In *Close Listening: Poetry and the Performed Word*, ed. Charles Bernstein, 178–99. New York: Oxford University Press, 1998.

Tietchen, Todd F. *Technomodern Poetics: The American Literary Avant-Garde at the Start of the Information Age*. Iowa City: University of Iowa Press, 2018.

Tong, Q. S. "The Bathos of a Universalism: I. A. Richards and His Basic English." In *Tokens of Exchange: The Problem of Translation in Global Circulations*, ed. Lydia H. Liu, 331–54. Durham, NC: Duke University Press, 1999.

Tsu, Jing. *Sound and Script in Chinese Diaspora*. Cambridge, MA: Harvard University Press, 2010.

Tsur, Reuven. *What Makes Sound Patterns Expressive? The Poetic Mode of Speech Perception*. Durham, NC: Duke University Press, 1992.

Vendler, Helen. *The Music of What Happens: Poems, Poets, Critics*. Cambridge, MA: Harvard University Press, 1988.

———. *On Extended Wings: Wallace Stevens' Longer Poems*. Cambridge, MA: Harvard University Press, 1969.

Watson, Burton, trans. *The Complete Works of Zhuangzi*. New York: Columbia University Press, 2013.

Watten, Barret. "New Meaning and Poetic Vocabulary: From Coleridge to Jackson Mac Low." *Poetics Today* 18.2 (Summer 1997): 147–86.

Weaver, Warren. "Translation." In *Machine Translation of Languages*, ed. William N. Lock and Andrew Donald Booth, 15–23. Cambridge, MA: Technology Press of the Massachusetts Institute of Technology, 1955.

Wiener, Norbert. *Cybernetics or Control and Communication in the Animal and the Machine*. Cambridge, MA: MIT Press, 1961.

Williams, R. John. *The Buddha in the Machine: Art, Technology, and the Meeting of East and West*. New Haven, CT: Yale University Press, 2014.

Wittgenstein, Ludwig. *Philosophical Investigations*. Trans. G. E. M. Anscombe. New York: Blackwell, 2001.

Wood, Frances. *Did Marco Polo Go to China?* Boulder, CO: Westview Press, 1996.

Xu, Shen. *Shuo Wen Jie Zi*. Beijing: Zhonghua Press, 1963.

Yamanaka, Lois-Ann. *Saturday Night at the Pahala Theatre*. Honolulu: Bamboo Ridge Press, 1993.

Yang, Lian, and John Cayley. "Hallucination and Coherence." *Positions* 10.3 (2002): 773–84.

Yang, Lien-sheng. *Money and Credit in China: A Short History*. Cambridge, MA: Harvard University Press, 1952.

Yang, Xiong. *Fa Yan*. Chengdu: Sichuan University Press, 2001.

Yang, Zhijiu. "A Passage in Chinese Concerning Marco Polo's Departure from China (revised)." In *Zhongxi wenhua jiaoliu xianqu—Marco Polo*, ed. Lu Guojun et al., 17–25. Beijing: Commercial Press, 1995.

Yeang, Chen-Pang. "From Modernizing the Chinese Language to Information Science: Chao Yuen Ren's Route to Cybernetics." *Isis* 108.3 (2017): 553–80.

Yule, Henry. "Marco Polo and His Book: Introductory Notices." In Marco Polo, *The Travels of Marco Polo: The Complete Yule-Cordier Edition*, vol. 1, 1–144. New York: Dover, 1993.

Zhong, Yurou. *Chinese Grammatology: Script Revolution and Literary Modernity, 1916–1958*. New York: Columbia University Press, 2019.

Zhu, Guangtian, ed., *History of Chinese Calligraphy*, vol. 4. Nanjing: Jiangsu Educational Press, 2002.

Zukofsky, Louis. "Basic." In *Prepositions +: The Collected Critical Essays*. Foreword Charles Bernstein. Hanover, NH: University Press of New England, 2000.

Index

Page numbers in italics refer to figures.